Loving Without Giving In

Christian Responses to Terrorism & Tyranny

Published in association with George Fox University.

Loving Without Giving In

Christian Responses to Terrorism & Tyranny

Ron Mock

Foreword by Mark Hatfield

Cascadia

Publishing House
the new name of Pandora Press U.S.
Telford, Pennsylvania

copublished with
Herald Press
Scottdale, Pennsylvania

Cascadia Publishing House orders, information, reprint permissions:
contact@CascadiaPublishingHouse.com
1-215-723-9125
126 Klingerman Road, Telford PA 18969
www.CascadiaPublishingHouse.com

Loving Without Giving In
Copyright © 2004 by Cascadia Publishing House.
Telford, PA 18969
Copublished with Herald Press, Scottdale, PA
Library of Congress Catalog Number: 2004015583
ISBN: 1-931038-24-4
Book design by Cascadia Publishing House.
Cover design by Merrill R. Miller

The paper used in this publication is recycled and meets the
minimum requirements of American National Standard for Information Sciences—Permanence of Paper for Printed Library Materi-
als, ANSI Z39.48-1984.1984

Library of Congress Cataloguing-in-Publication Data
Mock, Ron.
Loving without giving in : Christian responses to terrorism and
tyranny /
Ron Mock.
p. cm.
Includes bibliographical references and index.
ISBN 1-931038-24-4 (alk. paper)
1. Terrorism--Religious aspects--Christianity. 2. Despotism--Re-
ligious
aspects--Christianity. 3. Peace--Religious aspects--Christianity.
4. Spiritual
life--Christianity.   I. Title.
BT736.15.M55 2004
261.7--dc22

2004015583

12 11 10 09 08 07 06 05   10 9 8 7 6 5 4 3 2

To Melanie

Contents

Connection and Reconciliation: The Heart of the Gospel?

Foreword

Since September 11, 2001, we have faced a terrible dilemma and have not yet discovered an effective a response to it. When a small group of men destroyed the World Trade Center and hit the Pentagon, most of us were stunned by the ferocity and destructiveness of the attack. As a result, our nation was politically unprepared to answer the question, "What do we do now?"

In the confusion following September 11, American policy makers were under pressure to act quickly. With little time to imagine or plan for new approaches, our leaders turned quickly to familiar ideas and methods. The situation was defined as "war" and military modes of thinking took the fore. The United States engineered the Fall of the Afghani Taliban regime using military might. But the world's leading terrorists eluded our grasp. Civilians suffered, and children died. We failed to stamp out the existing terrorist network.

When the United States focused its attention on Iraq, the "War on Terror" became even more complex. Allegations that the Hussein regime had helped Al-Qaida, and concerns that Iraq had stockpiled weapons of mass destruction which could be given to terrorists, have not been supported by the evidence as of this writing. But the brutality of the Hussein regime, never in doubt, was even more graphically confirmed after the regime had been toppled. Hussein was a terrorist to his own people, and fostered terrorism in Israel and other places. Leaders in the United States and Britain linked terrorism and Iraqi tyranny but had trouble convincing the public of the connection. So, three years after the September 11 attack, our national leaders are still struggling to find an effective response. Terrorists and would-be tyrants still ply their trades around the globe.

We need some new ideas, new approaches to combating terror and tyranny. We cannot surrender, but neither can we fight over the long term using our current methods. Endless warfare will in the long run erode our way of life and undermine our democratic institutions, giving the terrorists and the tyrants the victory they seek.

In my half-century in politics, I learned that God never leaves us without a way forward. So when governmental leaders ran out of good ideas, I found that the most promising new thinking could be found somewhere else. It took private citizens acting boldly to lead our country out of its decades of paralysis on civil rights. Private citizens led the way to new ideas for how to be good stewards of our environment. In Eastern Europe, brave citizens acted on a new vision and ended the Cold War that had stymied policy makers for two generations. In cases like these, crucial leadership was provided by thoughtful Christians seeking ways to apply the gospel to new problems.

We have arrived at a similar point in the history of our response to terror and tyranny. So, in a way, I have been expecting a book like *Loving Without Giving In* to appear. Ron Mock does here what his predecessors have done in other times of crisis: He draws on sources typically ignored by policymakers to suggest some new responses that offer genuine hope for a long-term winning strategy against terror and tyranny.

This book reminds me of John Howard Yoder's *Politics of Jesus*, which helped Christians sort through their responses to the war in Vietnam. It also reminds me of Ron Sider's groundbreaking *Nuclear Holocaust and Christian Hope*, which did so much to help believers find a prophetic voice and help me work in the U.S. Senate for an end to the nuclear arms race. And it reminds me of Walter Wink's *Violence and Nonviolence in South Africa*, which proved so prophetic itself in suggesting from a Christian basis a nonviolent path out of the seemingly hopeless conflict in apartheid-era South Africa.

Like those works, the direct effect of this book will be on prayerful Christian peacemakers. But I have hope that, once again, God will use their faithful responses as one of his tools to create a victory over terror and tyranny that seems so elusive to us now.

—*Mark O. Hatfield*
  U.S. Senator—Oregon, Retired

Author's Preface

The other day a student dropped by to see me about his graduation requirements. He is an intelligent young man, personable, full of vigor. Of all my current advisees, he is one of the most delightful, and not only because he has such a wry sense of humor. His life story is fascinating, mirroring so many of the issues our world faces.

I will never forget the first time I heard part of his story, in September 1999. Four newly arrived students from Kosovo, including my student, stood in front of a standing-room only crowd on the George Fox University campus. Just months earlier, they and their families fled their homes in Kosovo, escaping Serbian terrorists trying to cleanse that province of the majority of its population. A string of improbabilities brought these four to George Fox University, and we asked them to tell their stories.

They did so, in harrowing detail, made all the more powerful by their matter-of-fact tone: relatives killed, houses burned, hiding from bands of Serbian killers, escaping across a border with streams of other refugees. We sat, stunned and shaken, listening to what these four had suffered.

Toward the end of the long meeting, my colleague Ralph Beebe asked a simple question. "Can you ever forgive these people, your neighbors? Can you ever live with them in peace?"

My student, speaking on behalf of the group, gave an even simpler answer.

"Never."

Not after all that pain, violence, malice, injustice—these young people who had lost so much could see no way to live with their former neighbors. I couldn't blame them, but it was still an infinitely sad moment. I asked myself, *What can I say to these students to help them find a path to reconciliation in their country?*

As the director of the Center for Peace Learning at George Fox University, this was not just an idle question. Essentially, my job description was to help people find ways to change "Never" to "Someday, and we are on the way." But I didn't know how to do that part of my job for our Kosovar students. I began to wonder if I was in the right line of work.

For two years my restlessness grew. So it was that September 11 reverberated with me as loudly as any terrorist could hope. Like millions of others around the world, I was transfixed by the television and Internet images of falling buildings and the mostly off-camera sufferings of thousands. I spent every spare minute for days trying to absorb the shock to the world and my view of it.

Almost immediately I was called on to help others do what I had not yet done for myself: digest what had happened and decide what we should do about it. Some of these requests came from the public and the media, but my notoriety has always been mercifully small, so I was not overwhelmed on that front. This was good, because I needed to give my attention elsewhere, especially to students.

The kernel out of which this book grew was my e-mail correspondence with students (and colleagues) at George Fox. For the next few days after September 11, I partook in a running electronic and face-to-face conversation on campus about the meaning of the attacks and how we might respond as Americans and Christians. That campus-wide conversation was the crucible in which this book was born.

When I urged students to resist appeals to vengeful retaliation, some challenged me. The attack demanded a response, they said. We can't allow people to get away with terrorism. Terrorists deserve punishment, and those who would attack us again need to be stopped. How, they asked, would my pacific response prevent another, even worse attack from happening?

These questions needed answers, especially since among the George Fox student body were several who were likely to be called to active military duty in a war on terror. They were not academic questions. Lives could turn on the answers. How was it possible to love our enemies without giving in to their evil?

So I wrote, including some all-night sessions in which sleep was an impossible alternative. I wrote e-mails to campus discussion groups, and to individuals, and pondered their replies. Those e-mails became the first draft of about one-third of this volume, including extensive sections of chapter 1 defining terrorism, and chapters 6 through 9 describing how we can respond to terror's spiritual and political causes.

The pace of writing cooled, but by Christmas 2001 it was clear I had on my hands a book. Over the next eighteen months, I wrote to fill out the pieces I had sent to students, connecting them into chapters, making them coherent as a whole. Chapter 2 emerged early in 2002 as I dug deeper into the essential nature of terrorism. Chapters 4 and 5 came into shape during the spring, as I stepped back to reflect on what we might learn from the main Christian schools of thought about war and from the latest thinking among peace scholars. Those chapters in turn dictated the organization of Chapters 6-9 and suggested much of their contents. By fall 2002, I thought I had just about finished a helpful book on terrorism. I began searching in earnest for a publisher.

Apart from the time it can take to locate the right publisher, the book was still hung up at three points. First, I had no chapter 10, no way of tying together the thematic threads. There were almost a hundred practical ideas in it for responding to terrorism, but they didn't yet amount to a coherent picture of loving without giving in.

Second, I spent summer 2002 (and much of my time since then) working with thirteen other Quakers from around the world on an International Quaker Working Party on Israel and Palestine, trying to sketch a vision for justice and reconciliation in that intractable conflict. With suicide bombing, targeted assassination, and wall-building so prominently disfiguring the Holy Land, including while our group was making its fact-finding trip to the area, some aspects of terror that I had only imagined became much more concrete—even literally. I saw

---

world-class corrosive grievance at work, on both sides of the 1967 borders, and learned much anew about dehumanizing hatred and the myth of effective violence.

As I worked to revise this book during the 2002-2003 academic year, world attention moved on to the buildup toward the war in Iraq, and I realized that terrorism wasn't the only scourge to which Christians needed to respond. So in summer 2003, I rewrote major portions of the book, adding a section (chapter 3) on political misery, especially tyranny, and revising other chapters.

I had promised Cascadia Publishing House the manuscript at the end of summer 2003. I guess we had an unusually long summer here in Oregon. Chapter 10 did not fight its way into final form until Thanksgiving 2003.

The picture of world events reflected in this book ends at about early 2004, not long after the capture of Saddam Hussein However, since neither terror nor tyranny is about to depart the world stage, we still need to discover how we can love our enemies without giving in. So one might expect that this volume will not be soon out of date.

My hopes lie in another direction. This book is a thought experiment. Other than my visit to the Middle East in 2002, the book was written almost entirely from northwest Oregon, in the region of the planet perhaps the most remote from direct experience of either terror or tyranny. There is, I hope, something to be gained by delegating to someone as sheltered as I am some of the task of envisioning practical responses.

But mine has been the easy part of the job. There are people right now doing the hard part of the work that lies before all of us. I think of people I know working with Christian Peacemaker Teams in Baghdad, Hebron, and Colombia. I think of the non-violent Peace Force at work in Sri Lanka. I think of democracy activists in Zimbabwe, Myanmar, and Hong Kong. I think of development and aid workers in Iraq, Jerusalem, Afghanistan, and elsewhere. I think of pastors and teachers I know trying to bring reconciliation in Burundi and Rwanda.

Some of these people are native to their lands, others are foreigners. They are all working on the scenes, implementing (and inspiring) some of the ideas in this book, and no doubt others that should be here. They are the ones right now writing the definitive work on loving without giving in, writing it in the lives and hearts of those they serve.

Hopefully someday soon someone will write these stories on paper for all of us to read, and begin the inevitable process of relegating this book to the dusty dim corners of the library. To that day let us hasten.

We need haste, brothers and sisters. In 1999, when I heard my student flatly reject the possibility of reconciliation in his homeland, I wondered how it would be possible to live with such a bitter grievance. *What if the whole world were that way?* I asked myself that evening.

Since then, the whole world has moved much closer to being that way—stuck in its pain, unable to move beyond to a place of reconciliation and justice. The young man who said "Never" is about to leave our sheltered campus and go on to make his way in the world. He will not be alone in his causes for bitterness. We all need a reason for hope and a practical vocation for healing our world.

Such as it is, here is my small vision for transforming the tide of outrageous violence. May you find in it reasons for hope, and hear through it a Voice calling you to act.

—Ron Mock
  Dundee, Oregon

Loving Without Giving In

Christian Responses to Terrorism & Tyranny

Chapter 1

....

What is Terrorism?

Ambiguity about Terrorism

Some say we are in a "war on terrorism," although this war is unusual: on one side the world's only superpower and many allies, varying widely in commitment to the cause and capacity to be of any help; on the other side, hidden networks of groups and individuals, with an unknown number of connections to governments and other openly operating organizations.

If this is a war, it's an odd one. But even if it doesn't fit the classic definition of a war, the struggle to limit and eliminate terrorism is as urgent as a war, and it will require of its warriors variations on the stamina, courage, discipline, and incisive skill required in traditional war. Soldiers will take risks and deal out destruction much as they would in any war. Governmental structures will change and the legal environment will flex in response to threats, in efforts to strengthen security from attack while minimizing costs to human and civil rights. Economic activity may be affected, with more effort focused on war preparations and more human resources absorbed in various kinds of security forces.

These measures will create distortions in the "normal" peacetime economy, which (if the war ever ends) will cause hardship for many while the economy regains its postwar footing. Fighting wars is costly, and this one will be no exception, especially since it promises to be a long one.

The war on terrorism, if it is going to be sustainable over the long run necessary for success, has to deal with a fault line running right through its heart: We are not always clear who is the enemy. People around the world have different ideas of what constitutes terrorism and of who is guilty of carrying it out. "One person's terrorist is another person's freedom fighter," or so they say.

When President George W. Bush first issued his worldwide challenge to join America in fighting terrorism, an impressive number of countries jumped on the bandwagon. But before long it became clear that what America meant by terrorism, and what some of the rest of the world meant, might not be exactly the same thing. This is not just a result of cultural or religious differences. Even within one culture, or one faith, people disagree regarding how to define the enemy in a war on terrorism.

We have experienced this debate from practically the day after September 11, 2001. Almost immediately, debates flared, as some objected while others branded various groups with the label *terrorist*. The debate raged especially hot over whether, for example, Palestinians resisting Israeli occupation were terrorists or liberators.

Another excellent—and harrowing—example of how hard it is to be clear about terrorism emerged after a shadowy group engineered an attack on India's Parliament in December 2001. Several people were killed, and Indian public opinion flared into outrage. Indian leaders pinned blame for the attack on Islamic Kashmiri separatists supported from Pakistan. Backed by massive troop movements to the Pakistani border, India loudly demanded of Pakistan, the United States, and the world in general that the fight to stop terrorism include targeting Kashmiri terrorists, too.

Indian rage thrust Pakistani leaders into a political tangle. With large parts of its military committed to trying to stop Taliban and Al-Qaida fighters from crossing the northern border with Afghanistan, Pakistan was hard-pressed to match India's buildup on the eastern border. But Indian demands for action against Kashmiri militants were not easy to satisfy.

Among other things, Pakistanis do not agree that Kashmiri militants are necessarily terrorists. To Pakistani eyes, Kashmir should never have been allowed to fall under Indian control.

Most Kashmiri residents are Moslem. According to Pakistanis, after the Indian subcontinent was given its independence from Great Britain in 1947, the decision was made to divide the subcontinent into a predominantly Hindu India and a predominantly Islamic Pakistan. But India claimed Moslem Kashmir for itself. This seemed to Pakistani eyes to be an injustice the Kashmiri militants were heroically trying to remedy.

Thus Pakistan has long supported the Kashmiri rebels. Pakistan acknowledged giving political and rhetorical help. India accused Pakistan of also helping with weapons, money, training, and operational bases. Some of that help, according to India, resulted in the attack on the Indian Parliament.

So how do we categorize groups like the Kashmiri militants? Are they worthy of inclusion as targets in a worldwide war on terrorism? Or are they freedom fighters, trying to liberate their lands from illegitimate Indian occupation?

The Essentials of Terrorism

Defining terrorism is, apparently, a tricky business, given the wide variations among terrorism "experts" who have made the attempt.[1] As early as 1988 there had already been at least 109 different definitions in the literature, involving at least twenty-two different factors.[2]

Most of these definitions resist the easy, sloppy folk wisdom that says "one person's terrorist is another person's freedom fighter." We will resist that relativist quagmire, too. Working from an overall impression of how terrorism is described in the media, and some of these more scholarly definitions, we will try to distill the essence of what it means to be a terrorist.

Identifying terrorists seems to rest on five basic features that distinguish terrorism from other human activity: violence, lawlessness, political motivation, civilians as targets, and intent to have its influence primarily through fear.

Violent

First, terrorists are *violent*. This is probably the easiest point of agreement about terrorists—they engage in dramatic, even graphic violence.

However, we may need to be more precise about the kinds of violence that would meet this criterion. Is lethality required for an action to be labeled terroristic? Must people be killed directly? There are other forms of violence, too. Groups labeled as "eco-terrorists" in the United States have burnt buildings, usually avoiding human fatalities. Do they still qualify as terrorists even if they never deliberately target humans, and thus direct their violence primarily against property?

When it reaches certain levels, violence against property becomes, in effect, violence against people. Since we all depend on things for our livelihood—farms, offices, factories, power plants, and so forth—destroying enough things will inevitably lead to deaths. If you create food shortages that push prices beyond the reach of economically marginal people, or destroy roads or power lines and thereby disrupt health care, or interrupt research and delay the discovery of cures to illness, you are killing people almost as directly as if you left a bomb at a bus stop. The victims will be just as random, not individuals you have singled out, but they will be just as dead, and possibly even more painfully.

So unjustified destruction of property is violent if it results in increased human vulnerability to death or misery. The same can be said for the destruction of human institutions, cultural patterns, and social structures. If such an act fits the remaining criteria, it is terrorism.

Lawless

Second, terrorists pursue their violence *lawlessly*. As a pacifist, I am inclined to think of all violence as illegitimate and lawless, at least in terms of God's law. But I recognize that my pacifist position places me among a small minority. Most people accept some violence as legitimate. For example, most political philosophers, as well as most Christian theologians, argue that the state, marked by its monopoly on the legitimate use of coercion, has the right to do violence in some situations—say, to apprehend a fleeing dangerous criminal, or to prevent an invasion by a foreign power. I assume this is a valid position for the purposes of this book, although I insert from time to time notes on how pacifists view matters.

When governments use violence, victims suffer. But if the government metes outs its violence appropriately, the people suffering will generally have done or threatened to do something that could be even worse. Perhaps a criminal is planning to murder people. Lives will be saved even if at the cost of the criminal's, if police can kill him before he kills others. Even more lives will be saved—at least in theory—as other would-be murderers abandon their projects when they take into account the risk of being discovered and held accountable.

Probably the ultimate risk posed by lawless violence is the potential for a society to spiral downward into complete anarchy. If one private citizen claims the right to choose whether a fellow citizen dies, then others have every right to do the same. Thomas Hobbes described the result: a "war of every man against every man" requiring all of us to be on constant vigilance to protect ourselves, our families, and our economic investments (crops in the ground, ideas in print, and so forth). The result would be a world in which "the life of man [is] solitary, poor, nasty, brutish, and short."[3]

To avoid such a lawless hell, governments have been accorded the right to do violence when necessary to maintain law and order. But this only works if the delegation is complete. If members of the populace act as if they personally retain the right to decide when to do violence, our Hobbesian bargain breaks down. If I can be judge, jury, and executioner some of the time in cases I encounter, and mete out my own private justice, sooner or later a case will arise in which my judgment about who needs some violent justice will not be the same as your judgment. In fact, since I am most likely to feel intensely about situations in which I am personally involved, I will always be tempted to act as a one-man vigilante when I am a party to the situation. But most of the time there is inherently going to be at least one other citizen with an opposing view as to whom is due a little corrective violence. Thus when I enact my own justice, you are likely to feel equally justified in punishing me for the violence I so wrongly (in your eyes) levied against "innocents."

The only remedy for this kind of melee-ridden society is to confine all rights of violence in one agency (with the possible exception of cases of emergency self-defense). In the modern nation-state system, national governments (and, in federal systems, specific subdivisions such as American states or Swiss cantons) hold that monopoly. Terrorists threaten the foundations of this world-order-preserving system when they take upon themselves, as private groups, the right to decide when people shall die.

If Al Qaida can decide that New York office workers deserve to die, then I suppose my Quaker Sunday school class could issue fatwas against whomever we think is complicit in evil: Al Qaida operatives, perhaps, or maybe culture-corrupting sitcom writers, or possibly people who drive while using cell phones, or Baptists, or Yankees fans. And if we picked Al Qaida as our first target, its members would have no cause to complain about the justification for our actions, since we have as much right as they to enforce our private religious and moral codes even to the point of death.

But some might argue that revolutionary violence, aimed at establishing local independence, is not terrorism. And Americans must listen to this claim and consider it carefully. After all, we celebrate our founding fathers as moral models for the entire world. They took up arms against an established government, the British monarchy, at a time when Britain was one of the most progressive countries on earth in terms of democratization and respect for human rights. Yet we claim the Minutemen at Lexington as heroes, exemplars of liberty and democracy.

What is the difference between a Kashmiri bomber in Delhi and a Massachusetts farmer on the road to Lexington? Thomas Jefferson tried to lay out the American rebels' case in the Declaration of Independence, in which he listed allegations against the British king. The Americans believed that the king lost his legitimate right to use violent coercion because he committed so many injustices against Americans that his rule here no longer was even arguably for the good of Americans.

Instead, the king was oppressing Americans and favoring his subjects on the British Isles to such a degree that the whole arrangement had become little more than a means for exploiting one people for the benefit of another. Thus, the underlying justification for letting the king have the monopoly on legitimate coercion—that it was necessary to benefit society and prevent lawless anarchy—had broken down.

The Declaration of Independence argues, then, that the king, by exploiting Americans for the benefit of Britons, left the Americans not much better off than if they had lived under anarchy. Thus Britain abandoned its right to rule America, and

America had the right—even the moral duty—to set up its own government so as to have (among other things) a more just and reliable place to locate the right to use violence.

This elaborate argument underlies American claims to have used force legitimately in its own revolution. By this standard, Kashmiri separatists would have to make the case that Indian rule of Kashmir was such an injustice that the local residents were not much better off than if they lived in anarchy. And they would also have to claim that they represented another agency with popular support ready to assume the role of a legitimate government in Kashmir, becoming the sole public authority there in a moral and political position to exercise the legitimate monopoly on coercion.

Note that whether a revolutionary is a terrorist depends, in part, on the justice of his cause. If the government he or she wants to remove is oppressive, to the degree that citizens are not being given the basic benefits of government, then the cause may be just. But justice is not the only criterion. Pursuing revolution in such a way as to leave the society under violent anarchy replaces one evil with another. Running up a toll of human life has to be justified, if at all, by some greater good being accomplished. Replacing oppression with anarchy is unlikely to be a greater good.

So the just cause has to be linked to an alternative government-in-waiting. That government-in-waiting has to be ready to assume, on taking power, the legitimate monopoly of coercive power. Killers enlisted in its cause must, then, be under its discipline. Private vigilante revolution is not justifiable; not only does it undermine the legitimacy of the government-in-waiting, but it also sets a social precedent. If vigilante violence is accepted in society before the revolution succeeds, what will prevent it from continuing after the revolution? Will a society which has accepted the principle of vigilante violence ever be able to achieve stability? As soon as some group disagrees with the direction of the new government, it will be justified under that society's accepted standards if it takes up arms again.

American history provides little comfort here. Vigilante violence in western Massachusetts alarmed American leaders when it broke out soon after peace was concluded with Great Britain. Talk of secession plagued the new nation, until three

generations later when the South actually seceded. The resulting Civil War, was many times more deadly and destructive
than the Revolution had been—still the most costly war in terms
of American casualties in the history of the country. Violent secession was politically possible because it was following the
precedent set by the Union in securing its own independence.

Only by subjecting revolutionary fervor to the authority
and control of a government-in-waiting can the revolution be
conducted with political legitimacy. Any other form of revolutionary violence may be terrorism, if the other criteria are satis-
fied.

But here is another tough question: is government itself terrorist if it uses violence in ways or for ends inconsistent with its
fundamental purposes? For example, if an American state police force was used to carry out the governor's personal vendettas, could this be terrorism? Or what if an American governor,
frustrated by the slow pace of modern American criminal procedure, ordered the police to execute his state's ten most wanted
suspects wherever they might be found (even outside the state
boundaries), without bothering with the technicalities of arrest
and trial? Would this constitute state-sponsored terrorism?

If we are serious about treating all lawless violence as possible terrorism, then we have to pay careful attention to the limits
on government's legitimacy in using violence to protect public
order or national security. Where the government exceeds those
limits, it is lawless. Where rebel governments-in-waiting cannot
make a case for the illegitimacy of the current regime, or for
their own readiness to assume the role of sole legitimate authority, then their violence is lawless.

And we will need to consider extending the label *lawless* to
actions, even in wartime, that exceed rightful limitations on the
conduct of war. Thus a My Lai massacre would be lawless and a
candidate for terrorism, as would Nazi death camps, and arguably the kind of "illegal combat" the U.S. accused the Taliban
of practicing in Afghanistan (the use of plainclothes soldiers
who melt in among civilian populations, and so forth). Whenever an act of violence embodies a principle that, if extended to
others in like situations, would lead to anarchic violent society,
the act is lawless and a candidate for the terrorist label.

Politically motivated

Third, terrorists use violence for a *political motive*. Not all lawless violence is terrorism. Killing the 7-Eleven clerk in the commission of a robbery isn't what we mean by terrorism. The motive in such a killing is venal, for one's own financial benefit. Killing in rage or passion would also fall outside the scope of terrorism, since the motive does not extend beyond the immediate situation or the private relationships at stake.

Terrorists act to affect political outcomes. While their tactical target is the facility or the people directly injured or killed, terrorists' strategic aim is broader. They want to engineer the resolution of a political question in directions favorable to them or the cause they represent. Random or selfish violence is not terrorism. Terrorism is always purposeful, intended to change policy or power structures, or at least the terms of debate.

Kashmiri rebels score highly on this test of terror. Their motives in attacking the Indian legislative buildings were clearly political, intending to change the pressure dynamics on the Indian government and make it move toward relinquishing Kashmir.

Mobsters killing other mobsters is a tougher case. The direct intent seems to be to incapacitate a rival, or even to punish someone who has challenged the mob's authority in some way. But the leaders of an organized crime family may also have in mind the "need" to send a message to others who might challenge the organization's place. Mob violence as a way of carrying on a private struggle among rival gangs is not terrorism. But some mob violence is targeted at key public officials—judges, prosecutors, police chiefs, and so forth

We can see the effects of this kind of intimidation of public officials in countries like Colombia, where chronic corruption and vivid intimidation by drug lords have combined to push that nation toward the brink of civil anarchy. The Ku Klux Klan used violent intimidation of public officials to create space for its racist vigilantes, who managed to make the lives of African-Americans hang on the whims of hateful mobs.

So we will include in our definition of terrorism acts against public officials and citizens designed to impact public policy or the enforcement of justice. In either case, the terrorist is trying to override the process of deciding matters on their merits, hoping to pave the way for the imposition of their own will, no matter what.

Civilians are intended targets

Fourth, terrorists *target civilians* with their violence.

We are familiar with the term *civilian* in the case of military law: Civilians are those who are not part of any military service. Or, to get at the essence of the matter, civilians are noncombatants—they are not part of the groups trained and equipped by the government to apply lethal force to a chosen target.

Civilians may morally support the war effort and may be of practical help as well, by paying taxes, producing military equipment or supplies, or even encouraging their sons and daughters to join the armed forces. But the rules of war, such as they are, emphasize a critical distinction between civilians and combatants. Part of the ethical justification for such a distinction is the moral imbalance between a civilian, who is not personally threatening anyone's life, and a soldier, who is. Soldiers declare their readiness to kill by wearing a uniform, displaying insignia of their rank, and submitting to the discipline of their duly constituted superiors. They are readily identifiable as dangerous, as people who in wartime will kill.

Civilians, on the other hand, have not joined the specialized group of killers. They pose no lethal threat. They may manufacture weapons as their day job, but they aren't threatening to take one from the assembly line and use it on an enemy. If they were going to do that, they would first join the armed forces who would train them in the use of the weapon *and* in submission to the discipline of the legitimate government as represented by commanding officers. As part of this process, they would acquire the trappings of a soldier, the uniform and insignia, which serve to put others on notice of their specialized status.

Civilians, then, are those not part of the recognized armed forces subject to control, command, and discipline by a legitimate government or government-in-waiting. But the concept is broader than that. In a gang war, the civilians would be those not involved in gangs. In a snowball fight in the church parking lot, civilians are the middle-aged adults too staid to be caught participating in the battle and the toddlers who wish they could but can't pack a coherent snowball.

So also, in the war on terrorism, "civilians" are "people who have not joined the game the terrorists are playing." Gangs cannot inflict terrorism on one another. Sure, their violence is lawless, and is sometimes for a political end, but as long as the violence is directed only at the members of the rival gang, it is hard to call it terrorism.

This is because rival gangs are in rough moral reciprocity toward each other. They are playing the same game, they have already consented to its rules. If I am ready and willing to shoot you while driving by, I cannot complain too much if you hit me first in a drive-by shooting. Or at least I can't complain how unfair you are. You are just better at the game than I am.

The most outrageous thing about September 11 is that so many people died in a game they never chose. The people in the World Trade Center were playing the nonviolent game of international commerce. This may not have always been a fair game, at least in the eyes of those who get left out in international trade, but it was not a moral system that included killing your rivals. However, without warning these people's lives were demanded of them. They had no opportunity to protect themselves, nor even to leave the scene of battle. There was no moral reciprocity between them and the terrorists.

Thus a bus bomb in Jerusalem is a terrorist act partly because the targets are not members of the military forces occupying the West Bank and Gaza. Eco-saboteurs qualify as terrorists because they are playing a violent game—property destruction under conditions that could cause human fatalities—that their victims are not playing against them.[4]

On the other hand, a gangland attack on police verges on being outside the moral boundaries marking terrorism. In a sense, the police are participating in the mobster's game, at least to the extent that police are willing to use force, sometimes lethal, against suspected racketeers. However, take careful note: the police officer and the gangster are not really playing the same game, even though some of their methods may overlap and both sides can die. First, the police are the commissioned agents of a government, and thus exercising delegated authority from the agency with a monopoly on legitimate lethal force. But more important to the current point, the police are playing a restrained game, governed by rules, the ultimate intent of which is to capture suspected outlaws and subject their fate to a decision on the merits of their case, in a court of law. Mobsters, on the other hand, are playing a game to avoid having their choices subjected to judgment on their merits. Mobsters are trying to enact lawlessness, while the police are agents of the law.

Thus the police and the gangster are not in a state of rough moral equivalence. The risks they impose on each other, while similar, are not for morally equivalent ends. Were the criminal to submit to the police officer, his fate would be decided at a trial. Were the police to submit to the criminal, our fate would be a lawless society ruled by the gun. Criminals are acting on their own behalf, for their own personal gain, while police officers act on behalf of the public under a legitimate delegation of authority from the state.

Civilians are people who are not in moral equivalence with the killer because they have not joined his game. The terrorist seeks out these people as his targets. In mob warfare, police are civilians, and violence against them for political ends would be terrorism.

Having dressed the police in the white hats, let me note an important caveat: When the police operate outside the restraints of law, then they cease to be the agents of the people through their government for the resolutions of issues on their merits. A police officer who plants evidence out of racist motives is as much a terrorist as the eco-saboteur who plants tree spikes out of non-democratic motives. They become private vigilantes, and thus have joined a game that is morally equivalent to the game the gangsters are playing: the unrestrained effort to prevail by force rather than by submitting to the merits of one's claim as determined by a duly constituted deliberative process.

John Keegan worries that even in outright warfare among competing militaries, the contest is getting to be so one-sided that it is hard to use the ancient terminology of "battle." If things get too one-sided, if the most successful killer is so isolated from his targets as to be taking negligible risks while imposing devastating ones, is it really fair to think of the two sides as morally equivalent participants in the same game? Keegan wrote, in the 1970s, that we had arrived at the time when the moral and tactical environment of battle had so shifted that our ethical evaluation of warfare needs to be reconsidered.[5] And this was before America's one-sided imposition of death reached its current pinnacle, represented in the Gulf War, Kosovo, Afghanistan, and Iraq.

I am not ready to go so far as to portray one-sided warfare as terrorism. In each of the last four cases cited, the most lopsided risks were connected to American aerial bombardment, in which Americans might inflict hundreds or thousands of deaths over several weeks while suffering only a handful—or none—themselves. In most of these cases targets of American aerial bombardment had already chosen warfare as their modus operandi. The Americans made them pay dearly, without accepting anything like equal risks, but the game was still the one the Iraqis, Serbians, and Taliban/Al Qaida had originally chosen: warfare. Insofar as America targeted military assets and personnel, it was within the boundaries of what most of the world would consider legitimate in a time of war.[6] Having chosen to wage war, it is hard to complain when it turns out that one of your foes is a lot better at it than you are, or has a bigger brother than you do. This is one of the things decision-makers have to take into account while assessing whether starting a war is justified, as we shall see in a later chapter.

The 2003 war in Iraq is a slightly tougher case, since surviving members of the old Iraqi regime will tell you they did not choose the war. It may be true that they did not choose to start hostilities in this round of fighting, as they did in 1990. But it is also true that the Iraqi government had spent enormous resources assembling and preparing a vast and multi-layered military organization, ready to conduct war. It is also true that they chose to defend themselves militarily. Unless the U.S. and Great Britain had no legitimate grounds to initiate combat,[7] then Iraqi military personnel who found themselves targets of American or British attacks cannot complain that they did not choose to participate in the game of war.

Operate through fear

Fifth, terrorists design their violence to have much, or even most, of its effect by *instilling fear* in others.

Immanuel Kant summarized the basics of human ethics as treating other people as ends, never only as means. That is, people are of immeasurable value. Each person is so valuable that no goal we might pursue, however vast or glorious, is worth enough to allow us to treat a fellow human as nothing more than a stepping stone to that goal. We may well need others to reach our goals, but our actions always have to reflect our recognition that the other person is more than a cog in our machinery. Even in my brief interactions with people who perform routine tasks for me with minimal human contact—say, a toll booth attendant, or a fast food server—I should remember their humanity and thus their surpassing worth.[8]

The terrorist operates with almost the opposite view of his victims. The terrorist treats his victims as mere means to an end; in fact, terror may be the ultimate in reducing humans to means only, and not ends. The ones who suffer are not the ultimate targets of his actions. He is not trying to reach his goals by eliminating people directly. Osama bin Laden did not consider the World Trade Center attack a victory because it represented 3,000 deaths on the way to eliminating all North Americans. The real goal of a terrorist is to change the minds of those who observe the attack, not of those who suffer it. Bin Laden celebrated September 11 because of the message it sent. The terrorist needs his victims to suffer, because suffering is his tool to reach other people who are watching.

The terrorist's perversion of normal ethics opens enormous vistas of evil. First, the terrorist needs victims to suffer and, preferably, die, but he needs them to do so publicly, where the maximum number of people can see. A terrorist would thus consider it a disaster if people died in one of his attacks and no one ever knew about it. Not that the deaths would be so bad, but the suffering would go unnoticed, and (especially galling) no one would connect the deaths to his cause.

This gives terrorists every incentive to spread death as spectacularly as possible, under conditions which generate the most human pathos. And as people get used to death at one level, or in faraway places, terrorists must escalate both the spectacle and the scope of the death they wreak, to continue to grab headlines and reduce to a minimum the number of places where people can feel safe. Since visible, searing suffering is the medium for his message, and visceral impact on observers is his goal, human individuals steadily decrease in value even as means—

until lives are nothing and capacity to suffer while dying is the only thing terrorists value in potential victims.

Wantonness becomes a cardinal virtue in the terrorist's moral economy. Killing people who stray into the terrorist's neighborhood might have a certain value for the cause, but observers can detach themselves from such geographically limited terror by resolving not to visit those areas. Killing people who work for the military, or work as journalists in war zones, or otherwise have put themselves in harm's way will have some effect, but observers can distance themselves from those deaths by ascribing them to the dangerous work the victims did.

But when terrorists strike where people live, far from the terrorists' homeland, the impact of victims' suffering is multiplied many times over. If Osama can take down the World Trade Center, people learn to fear that he can reach into their own communities. The more unpredictable the terrorist's reach, the better. If people can no longer flee to a place, or a lifestyle, or a community of safety, the terrorist has maximized his impact. Leaders who might have an effect on the fate of his cause can no longer afford to ignore him. The terrorist buys worldwide influence by spreading worldwide suffering, and maximum impact by striking in the most unpredictable places possible.

In its fullest forms, terrorism is a modern phenomenon, and democracy has accelerated its spread. There is not much point being a terrorist if all the important political decisions are made by a heartless autocrat. Could someone have terrorized Rome under Nero? Perhaps, but to achieve his goals, the first-century terrorist would have had to compete for public attention with Nero's own terrors. And since Nero hardly listened to public opinion anyway, getting the public's attention would not have been worth much. Even if he was ready to value his victims only for their capacity to suffer vividly and publicly, the first-century Roman terrorist would have had little incentive to go to the bother of terrorizing. Terrorism would not have flourished in such circumstances.

But in countries where political leaders are sensitive to public opinion, terrorism has tremendous allure. If political leaders cannot afford to ignore the sufferings of their people, or the fears of bystanders—on the scene, or via the media—the terrorist can get mileage out of spectacles of suffering.

Not too long after the September 11 attack, I listened as a woman stood in a public meeting and opposed building a gas station across the street from her children's school in my hometown, tiny Dundee, Oregon. One of her worries was that a terrorist might blow up a gasoline delivery truck as it passed in front of the school. Terrorists dream of days like this one, when parents fear to send their children three blocks to school because of terrorists hiding in caves eight thousand miles away. Terrorists only have the incentive to achieve this dream when those parents can make their fears count in the councils of their political leaders.

Terror is a monstrous evil. Its monstrosity comes into the sharpest focus when we grasp that the terrorist thinks of people as crops, valuable only for the visceral suffering he can reap from them. The rights of victims count for nothing to a terrorist, so their suffering has no downside. Suffering is nearly pure gold then, a currency with which the terrorist hopes to buy a political result. The more wanton, far-reaching, spectacular, and horrifying the deed, the more valuable it is to the terrorist.

A Working Definition for Terrorism

We are working toward a definition of terrorism that runs something like this: *Terrorism is lawless violence directed at noncombatants to spread fear as a means to a political goal.*

Some grave evils fall outside this definition of terrorism. Most crime, no matter how heinous, is excluded, because its motives are not political. Much warfare is also excluded, because it is either lawful or aimed at military combatants. Political revolutions, even when pursued by guerrilla tactics, can avoid the terrorist label as long as civilians are not targeted.

On the other hand, important features of terrorism lurk in the definition but are not made explicit by it. For example, terrorism requires extreme devaluation of the human beings who are targeted for the most vivid and heartrending destruction possible. It rewards wantonness and the ability to reach people in surprising places, so as to eliminate, if possible, any sense of safety among the target population.

Consider how many victims there are in every terrorist attack and what they suffer. The direct victims lose their lives, or perhaps "only" their limbs, or their sight, or months or years in rehabilitation. Their families lose loved ones, and they also lose what every trauma survivor loses: a sense of well-being, the ability to sleep or concentrate or enjoy life to its fullest.

But any terrorist who caused only this kind of suffering would consider himself a failure. His goal is to cause this kind of direct misery in such a way that it will reverberate through an entire nation. He succeeds all too often. Fear spreads. People are deterred from doing many things that would be productive for them and their communities. Expenditures grow for non-productive security, and intrusions on liberty and privacy proliferate. It becomes more expensive to live, both financially and psychologically. We all suffer at least a little every time a terrorist attacks. Probably the worst of this reverberating pain concentrates in the lives of those on the margins of the workforce, or on the brink of poverty, since their lives are more precarious, their jobs are the first to go when productivity falls, and they have fewer personal surpluses with which to absorb losses.

One of the most destructive aspects of terrorism is its threat to force resolution of issues on something other than their merits. Terrorism short-circuits discussion and reflection, impatient with the weight such processes give to opinions other than the terrorists'. If the terrorists succeed, they substitute their opinion for the results of democracy or the rule of law. One-sided decision-making results in poor decisions, which lead to poor public policy and ineffective public services. Almost everyone is impoverished at least a little when decisions get made for reasons other than the merits of the case.

Yet the list of casualties is not yet exhausted. Think what has to die in a person to bring him to the point where he values others only for the pain they can feel. Some of this internal death is the cause, rather than the result, of his participation in terrorism, as we shall see later in this book. But some of it surely happens during the course of his decision to terrorize and his planning and execution of the act itself.

Then, of course, there is the suffering of the terrorists who die in the course of their attacks, as many do, and of their survivors. But think also for a moment of what life must be like for those terrorists who send their colleagues to die in their steads, and thus live beyond the attack. These surviving conspirators do not suffer physically. But what is left of their souls?

Yet perhaps no more needs to be made of this point. Extending our empathy to the terrorists, victims of their own attacks, may be a difficult task for most of us. And it may be largely a fruitless one, since the suffering of their victims is motive enough to address terrorism. Still, I believe it is important to keep in mind as much of this picture of suffering as we can while we turn our attention to some of the "theoretical" questions that accompany terrorism, and later to the practical questions concerning our responses to it.

Chapter 2

....

Tough Questions About Terrorism

We have distilled a working definition of terrorism but have also encountered some troubling issues to consider before bringing the topic into sharpest focus. In this chapter we will investigate them:

- Does the justice of the cause matter?
- Can governments be terrorists?
- What about collateral casualties?

Does the Justice of the Cause Matter?

It is easy to label someone a terrorist when we are appalled by her goals as much as her methods. But sometimes people choose methods we do not approve to pursue goals we might favor. These are the cases that put our ethics to the test. Is our opposition to terrorist methods principled, or only a matter of our own personal convenience? Do we rage against American deaths precisely because they are American deaths? Would we experience the same outrage if others died in a similar attack carried out by people fighting, say, for democracy against tyrants?

We have said that terrorism occurs whenever someone uses unlawful violence to seek a political goal by trading upon the suffering of civilian victims. We might like to amend the definition to include a proviso: "except where the end is one we like."

Or perhaps we can be fairer, and reframe our proviso this way: "except where the end is worth so much that it will create more good than the harm done by the terrorist." This invites us to think about terrorism from a utilitarian perspective: Would terrorism be acceptable (and thus not terrorism) if it resulted in more good than harm, taking everything into account?

There is a nasty little problem with this approach which threatens to make further inquiry about means and ends pointless. The utilitarian wants to know about results, not intentions. If we focus on results—finding a violent act against civilians morally acceptable as long as more good is done than harm— we have put potential attackers in a nearly impossible position. They must decide to act before they know the consequences of their actions. None of the rest of us has to live up to this kind of standard. In a few minutes I will be getting in my car and driving to my office at George Fox University. Must I wait to decide whether to drive until I know whether I will be in an accident along the way? I am unlikely to make it to my appointments on campus today, if that is the rule.

But if we excuse the violent one from having to be sure of all the consequences of her actions, and let her decide what to do based on her intentions, we introduce other problems. Perhaps her intention in blowing herself up in a crowded public place is to topple an oppressive regime and win freedom for her people, which she believes will in the long run result in a net reduction in human suffering. Instead, however, let's imagine that her suicide bombing only results in dozens of deaths and scores of others suffering intensely and fails to bring about the regime change she is seeking. Is she to be held accountable for her intent, which was possibly defensible on utilitarian grounds? Or is she accountable for her results, which brought no recognizable gains to compensate for all the suffering she caused?

The law deals with this kind of problem constantly. In some cases it punishes for the results regardless of the intent—pollution violations, for example, or some torts such as defamation (where any kind of action to intentionally publish an untruth is wrongful no matter whether the defendant meant to harm the plaintiff's reputation). In other cases, intent is a crucial factor, and if I meant no harm, no foul is called. In still other cases the law scales responsibility to what a reasonable person in the defendant's shoes would have foreseen to be a possible consequence, were she to act with a reasonable person's care.

A terrorist is morally responsible for the suffering she should reasonably have foreseen and for failing to reach her goals in ways she should have foreseen as being possible. Her incompetence, her willful blindness, or her starry-eyed cluelessness cause people to suffer without purpose, and are inexcusable.

So we can already narrow our question about intent considerably. If the terrorist intends more harm than good, we have no trouble calling him a terrorist. For example, if he is acting in pursuit of a genuine good (say, a reduction in the price of banana-strawberry smoothies) but he goes about it by causing more harm than the good could possibly be worth (by kidnapping members of a yogurt company executive's family), he is clearly a terrorist. And if he has no reasonable prospect of causing more good than harm, even when he has deluded himself into thinking otherwise, we have no trouble holding him morally accountable for a grave evil like terrorism. Causing useless suffering is wrong.

Now we return to the main question—is lawless violence against civilians for political purposes justified (and thus not terrorism) when the attacker has a reasonable basis for believing that his attack will cause more good than harm in the long run?

Uncertainty crops up again here: How can the attacker have any idea whether the payoff is going to be worth the pain? The consequences of an action so dramatic as a lethal attack on civilians will be practically infinite, rippling out into the future far beyond the limits of anyone's ability to clearly trace them. Of course this problem besets all human activity. We would be paralyzed were we required to be certain of all the effects of our actions. But most human activity does not start with anything like the obvious and unmistakable negative consequences of a terrorist attack. So it would seem fair to require someone trying to justify lawless violence against civilians to demonstrate that it is even possible for the consequences to be a net gain.

I am ready to acknowledge the weight and depth of the vision that might motivate a person to become, at least in his own mind, a "freedom fighter." To liberate one's people from oppression, to help them achieve self-determination so they can be free to pursue whatever ends in life loom large to them—these are some of the most basic of human aspirations. Achieving them is one of the greatest legacies any generation can leave to its successors.

But dreaming about these goals, then acting upon them, does not guarantee a causal connection. The actions have to be tailored to the need and have a realistic chance of bringing about the dream. Can one build freedom on an infrastructure of violence against civilians?

Actually, I wouldn't be surprised if most people believe the answer is "yes." It is true that civilian-targeted violence practically forces a ruling regime to change its practices. But the attacker cannot be sure these changes will be in a direction that favors his cause. From a superficial glance at history, it would seem that attacking civilians is as likely to stimulate additional repression as to stimulate liberation. From a game-theory perspective, such a result would hardly be surprising. A policymaker considering whether to acquiesce to terrorist demands has to take into account secondary effects of such actions, including at least this crucial one: Giving in to one attacker communicates to others that attacks on civilians will get political results.

I want to say more in a later chapter about effects of giving in to terrorists. For now, it's enough to point out that an attack on civilians intended to secure concessions in favor of liberation has a high probability of securing nothing, or even enhancing repression. Those in power are also likely to be rational about their response to an attack and will probably try to think through the probable secondary consequences of any concession—including the consequences likely to flow if people learn they can win concessions by making attacks.

But even in the (by now) obviously rare case in which an attack against civilians might result in achieving the overthrow of a hated regime or abandonment of an oppressive government policy, the attacker is not home free on utilitarian grounds. Something as dramatic as a suicide bombing, or its various rough equivalents from the terrorist manual, cannot have only one effect.

Imagine that the Kashmiri separatists who bombed the Indian parliament building end up succeeding. Imagine they win

Kashmir's independence. Now consider other probable results of a "successful" campaign conducted through spreading fear by violence. Who will rule in Kashmir? At the outset, the people with the most power in an independent Kashmir are likely to be those who won its independence—in this case the terrorists.

How can we expect terrorists to conduct the affairs of an independent Kashmir? What do they know of power and influence? It would not be wise to be a dissident in the new Kashmir, not with a ruling class that has learned little in revolution but how to influence people by spreading fear. Is Kashmir under the heel of successful terrorists likely to be better off than Kashmir under a Hindu-led government? Revolutions, when they succeed, boost the new nation's first leaders into prominence and authority. Even if we assume that an independent Kashmir would be a good thing in the abstract, we have to pay attention to what kind of Kashmir the method of independence brings.

And even if a terrorist group could make a successful transition into a nonviolent, public-spirited, democratic government, the new Kashmir's problems would not be over. Sooner or later in every nation dissent arises. In Kashmir, the dissent would be built in, with a sizable Hindu population that would begin immediately to chafe under a more Islamic government. But with a terrorist-led revolution, the national story of Kashmir has at its very core a powerful myth: Change can occur via terror, and successful terrorists become national leaders, not to mention national heroes. Thus few will be able to complain, and many can be expected to applaud, when Kashmir discovers it has its own bands of terrorists attempting to follow in the footsteps of the men who secured their country's independence.

The myth of effective violence will get more attention later. But for now, let me just point out how a successful terrorist-led revolution would make an impression far beyond Kashmir's borders. Those who bombed the parliament in Delhi might inspire others on Mindanao in the Philippines, or in Northern Ireland, or possibly even Tutsis eyeing Hutus in Burundi. Any revolution is a powerful story, and powerful stories teach. The terrorist has to consider what he is teaching those who watch and what those pupils will do with their lessons. Some of the blood copycats spill is on his hand too and must be taken into account in computing profit and loss from a terrorist attack.

Terrorists do not extend the Golden Rule to their attacks, obviously. No attacker would be likely to conclude that he would want someone to kill him or his loved ones to pursue a political goal. The terrorist does not do unto his victims what he would have them do unto him.

But the Golden Rule also works in reverse: "You cannot complain if others do unto you as you have done unto them." In fact, Jesus took the principle even further. "He who lives by the sword shall die by the sword" is just a particular way of illustrating the inescapable law: Our actions create the world we live in. Terrorists engender terrorism. The fruits of their labors can as easily be snatched from them by someone else who has watched and learned their craft. Anything bought with the coin of lawless violence directed at civilians for political aims helps build the kind of politics where, to get things done, people resort to the expedience of lawless violence against civilians.

I am describing this in the abstract, but history has coughed up enough examples to demonstrate my claims to anyone's grim satisfaction. Consider Israel, born (in part) out of Irgun bombings at hotels, and maintained (in part) by the force of arms against invasions and occupied populations. The Palestinians who suffered the brunt of these attacks are not stupid. They learned. They were front row "A" students of the Israelis and bought wholesale the Israeli myth that violence skillfully wielded can lead to results. The Palestinians faced a daunting task against a determined and skillful foe, but recently they have outdone their teachers.

Consider Israel again, from another direction. Did Israel invent violent suppression of restive populations? Not at all. History is full of examples of what happens when people wield violence against each other. Bulldozing homes and "targeted" assassinations are mere variations on the themes Israelis ancestors heard playing against them in periodic European pogroms against Jewish populations. It is easy to understand why Israel is resolved, as a nation, never to go back to a situation where its citizens are outgunned by hostile neighbors.

And consider Palestine again. Yasser Arafat rose to the top of the Palestinian movement on the backs of hijackers and other (now quaintly outdated) terrorists. The Palestinian Authority is authoritative only because it has been successfully (to some degree) violent. But as of this writing Arafat has more than one sword pointed at him. The Israelis wave one in his face and may yet use it to finish him off. But if they don't, other Palestinians may, if not directly against his person, then indirectly by engaging in their own violence against Israelis even when Arafat wants them to stop. He has moved the Palestinians beyond Israeli control largely by violence. Now other violent Palestinians have moved beyond his control, using the same general tactics he perfected in the Palestinian cause.

We make the world we live in by living in it. Kant warned us to act only in such a way that the principle of our action could be extended to everyone. What he meant is that we run the risk of having the principles of our actions extended to everyone. If that is not a happy prospect, we need to change the principles of our actions.

No world can survive if anyone with a cause can decide to kill people at random in pursuit of that cause. Once one person arrogates to herself the right to conduct such violence, she grants to everyone else the same right. That way lies anarchy, and what Hobbes described as "the war of all against all" leading to lives that are "solitary, poor, nasty, brutish, and short." In other words, life in a world of terrorists is much worse than life under almost any regime, even oppressive ones.

So we come to the answer to our question. Is lawless violence against civilians for political purposes justified (and thus not terrorism) when the attacker has a reasonable basis for believing that his attack will cause more good than harm in the long run? The question poses an impossibility. Terrorism embodies a principle that, when extended universally, leads to a world worse than practically any oppression. And terrorism will beget more terrorism, if it succeeds, as the myth spreads that it provides a way of achieving political objectives that would be frustrated otherwise. Terrorism can never do more good than harm in the long run, if all its effects are taken into account.

But note that the problem with the terrorism is not that it stands up to oppression. Its goals are not the problem. The problem lies with its methods. Later in this book we will be exploring in depth what people can do to fight terrorism without using violence. Every one of the suggestions I make in those chapters is adaptable to resisting oppression. History suggests that nonviolence is at least as effective in overturning tyrants as is violence, and that it tends to result in regimes better suited to democracy.

So here is the tragedy of terrorism. It can't work, if by "work" we mean for it to result in a better world, because terrorism spreads the seeds of a world much worse than any we live in right now. And it isn't even the best method available for achieving the short-term goals of ending oppressions. No cause, regardless of its justice, can justify such dual enormity.

Can Governments be Terrorist?

The question about justice is whether the terrorist's goals matter. But there are also tough issues involving the cases on the borderlines between terrorism and other human endeavors. We have said that terrorists pursue unlawful violence. What does "unlawful" mean? Is this just another way of sneaking in our own cultural standards and labeling those who disagree with them "unlawful"?

For example, under American law, suspects cannot be executed for petty crimes, or without first having exhaustive opportunity for appeals. Would an execution in a country without such laws, if done to intimidate a population into obedience, be terrorism? Or what about the American death penalty, which its advocates consistently defend as a means of deterring future crime (i.e., striking fear into others for a political end), and which most Western countries think of as barbaric? Is this terrorism, because it would not be lawful in England or Germany? Or is the American death penalty terrorism if applied to Europeans charged in America with capital crimes, but not terrorism if applied to Americans charged with the same crimes?

Actually, I don't mean by "unlawful" the same thing we might mean by "illegal" or "criminal." The question is not so much whether the act violates a legal code, which would propel us into a discussion of whose legal code should govern and the morality of various legal codes. Rather, defining terrorism as "unlawful" equates with defining it as "not sanctioned by a legitimate government operating within its jurisdiction." That is, to avoid being terrorism, a violent act against civilians to achieve a political end must be the action of a government operating within the scope of its legitimate authority.

This is a very controversial notion, amounting to something like "governments cannot be terrorists, even when they act violently toward civilians for political ends." I have some important qualifications to make in relation to this idea, and I hope readers will bear with me until I can make them. But first, let me explain why the distinction between governmental violence and civilian violence is important, then defend its implications.

As we have already noted, one of the worst aspects of terrorism is its lack of a limiting principle. If I can set off a bomb in a shopping mall in pursuit of a political goal and claim my action is justified by the importance of my political objective, then so can you. And we do not have to agree about our respective political objectives. All we need is sincere conviction. If I am sincerely convicted about the rightness of my views, and you are sincerely convicted about yours, then we stand in identical moral positions when we begin to plan our terrorism.

If after thinking about it as carefully as we can we both further conclude that we have a reasonable chance of succeeding, then we still stand in identical moral positions when we begin to carry out our terrorism. And if we both take similar measures to make sure that the suffering of our victims is not "wasted"— that is, we both make sure that the spectacle we create attracts as much attention to our cause as possible—then we stand in identical moral positions when we complete our terrorist act.

I can't complain about your actions without undermining my own moral claim to have acted rightly. Nor can you. It won't do for me to insist "But I was pursuing justice and you were not," because I have no better credentials for declaring what is just than you do. In fact, acting as a private citizen, or even on behalf of a group of private citizens, I stand in an equivalent position to every individual and/or group in the entire society. If I may kill civilians in pursuit of my aims, so may anyone.

An established government is different. It is, by definition, the one agency in society with a legitimate monopoly on coercive force. This is the most basic function of government, the one which led Thomas Hobbes to practically conclude that might makes right—or at least that whoever was able to secure a monopoly on coercive power had the right to demand our obedience, so as to avoid sending society back out into a hellish state of anarchy.[9]

So if a government embarks on a campaign of violence against civilians, it may be evil and worthy of opposition. However, this is still morally different than nongovernmental terrorism, because it does not set a precedent for a pandemic of violent attacks coming from all angles.

But this stark contrast (between the acts of government and of private terrorists) is not the final picture, once we readjust our focus a bit. First of all, a government can lose its claim to legitimacy, and one of the fastest ways to do so is to kill civilians. A regime does not lose its legitimacy the first time it kills a bystander to make a larger point. All human agencies do evil. If each case of injustice brought down a government, order would be impossible.

Discerning when governments cross the line and lose legitimacy is a tricky proposition, one worthy of at least a book of its own. The clearest cases arise when a government habitually violates its own internal rules for deciding matters on their merits. Corruption and nepotism eat away at the government's ability to act for the welfare of its people. Arbitrariness and usurpation detach decisions from their merits, too. Adherence to a government's internal rules—one of the key aspects of what we call the "rule of law"—carries immense moral import. The alternative to a rule of law is arbitrary rule, which would rapidly corrode a government's legitimacy. On the other hand, when a government follows its own rules, it earns political legitimacy and avoids the worst depths of moral illegitimacy. Even if the decision to kill is evil, if it is taken in accord with the government's internal rules, it avoids setting a precedent for non-governmental killing. The decision rule built into the structure of the government is one line of protection against pandemic killing.

I am not saying that whatever a government does in accordance with its own internal rules is morally justifiable. Governments have done many evil things. Furthermore, rulers who establish a pattern of doing evil can lose their legitimacy, even when their decisions follow proper procedure. Care must be taken here—do we really want to say that no government which enforced slavery was ever legitimate?

On the other hand, we can identify governments which seem to have gone so bad that their citizens had every right to remove them. This is what the Americans claimed in 1776, although probably with less justification than the Eastern Europeans had in 1989, or the Germans would have had during the Nazi era. In all these examples, the government acted as if it was bound by no law, reducing itself to a band of thugs whose only claim to legitimacy was raw power. But power alone wouldn't even satisfy Hobbes, since the purpose for the power is to secure order for the benefit of citizens.

Wherever a government succeeds in maintaining the rule of law—that is, where disputes are settled on their merits, in accord with its own principles, and order is maintained against criminals and usurpers—an isolated episode of killing civilians is distinguishable from terrorism on one key variable. It might still be heinous, and the officials responsible might still merit trial and imprisonment. But one episode will not obliterate the legitimacy of the regime and thus will not provide a precedent for pandemic violence initiated by private parties.

What about two episodes of violence against civilians? Or four? Or twenty? When evil is rare, a regime can claim to be working for justice, order, and the good of its citizens. But at some point, when a government establishes a pattern of abuse, the essence of its rule changes. At that point, when it loses its basis for legitimacy, acts of killing take on the character of a gang intimidating its neighbors to make them docile for the gang's own ends. The government loses its legitimacy and its killings are no more than terrorism.

Furthermore, even a government with legitimate authority to act in its own territory does not have a blanket right to act outside it. Unless we adopt pacifism as a rule of international relations, governments can defend their territory from external threats. Governments, according to prevailing assumptions of international conduct, can even strike with violence outside their borders when it is necessary to pre-empt a real and impending threat against targets inside the borders. As long as we allow for military operations in defense of the homeland, we have to accept as a corollary a wide enough range of tactical and strategic options to allow the government to succeed in its task.

So killing people outside one's own border is among the options for a legitimate government in military self-defense. But note the inherent limiting principle here: The killing has to be related to self-defense. And even defense has its limits. Perhaps the ultimate in pre-empting attack from abroad would be the extermination of all foreign populations. But no one would claim that any nation had the right to undertake this "perfect" defense. So where is the line beyond which a government killing outside its borders is a terrorist?

This is a hard question to answer. Nations relate to one another in almost a state of nature. No clear authority exists to which nations are subject, since international law is unsettled and without reliable means of enactment or enforcement. Perhaps our best approach is a minimal one: discerning what would be the logical consequences if all nations adopted the principles behind a particular behavior. If the principle of a behavior would result in worldwide calamity were it adopted by every country, then the behavior would not be within the rights of a government and might constitute terrorism.

What, then, might be examples of terrorism as conducted by national governments outside their borders? Killing soldiers who are preparing to attack may be justified, since the threat to national security is obvious, and the targets have already joined the killing "game" by their own military preparations. Just as clearly, any killing that has no real bearing on national defense would be problematic.

We cannot have a principle that allows one government to kill citizens of another willy nilly. Such a principle would operate very much like the one embodied in standard nongovernmental terror: Any government can kill anyone anywhere, regardless of national borders. Any government that acted with a pattern of such arrogant impunity might be considered to have abandoned its privileged role of monopolizing coercion to keep order, having shown willingness to apply deadly force toward ends having no connection to order. Such a regime would be more like a gang of bandits than a government, and would no longer enjoy the distinction of having a legitimate monopoly on coercion.

Consider the case of the Israeli response to suicide bombers in 2001 and 2002. Suicide bombers are terrorists. They attack civilian targets with the aim of killing civilians, apparently without regard to age, gender, or other distinctions that might be thought to matter. The attacks are initiated by private groups, over whom the Palestinian Authority claims it has no control.

Their attacks are clearly designed for some larger political purposes—to force Israel to withdraw from the occupied territories, if not from Israel itself. The suicide bombers and their "pimps"—those who recruit and delude them into self-destructive behavior for the profit of the recruiters—are acting on the terrorist's principle: private citizens can decide that others should die as fodder for a political campaign.

What about the Israeli responses? Let's examine for the moment two aspects of Israeli response: targeted assassination, and retaliatory destruction against civilians in the occupied territories.

Targeted assassination is deadly violence carried out partly for political effect. Israel accuses its targets of being de facto military commanders, and perhaps that would be an appropriate label—if, in fact, they were agents of a legitimate government or government-in-waiting pending a legitimate rebellion against an oppressor. But Israel denies that the Palestinian Authority is a legitimate government-in-waiting, because it denies that the occupation of the West Bank and Gaza is oppressive. If the suicide bombers and their pimps are not representatives of a government or a government in waiting, they are civilians.

They are also criminals. And members of police forces can legitimately act to preempt a crime that is about to be committed, in defense of public order and safety. But killing people on general suspicion of a crime is not consistent with the rule of law. The proper approach to a criminal suspect at large, who is not at that moment in the process of immediately endangering others' lives, is to apprehend the suspect and put him on trial for his crimes. Targeted assassination short-circuits that process. Should district attorneys in the U.S. begin a practice of assassinating suspected gang members?

The Israeli policy of targeted assassination embodies a principle something like this: "People who hold positions in legitimate governments can order the execution of others on mere suspicion of their complicity in crimes." Such a principle risks abolishing the rule of law and thus negating the government's claim to a legitimate monopoly on coercion. All its violent acts against civilians risk becoming terrorism.

But is the Israeli policy of targeted assassination really analogous to a renegade American sheriff executing suspects? Israelis might argue that the moral landscape changes when the suspects are part of a political revolution, rather than everyday criminals. Isn't there a big difference between law enforcement actions against individuals or groups working for their private illicit gain, and national defense against those whose aims include the overthrow or obliteration of a political system? The Israelis are fighting to preserve the existence of their state, of their chosen legitimate monopoly on coercive force. The police fighting a crime syndicate are not in such a contest.

In wartime, one does not bother with apprehending and trying one's enemies. To do so has been consistently regarded as unacceptably compromising a nation's ability to defend itself. Enemy leaders in war may be killed as opportunity arises, with a few exceptions (during peace parleys, after surrender, and so forth) extraneous to our discussion. Killing enemy soldiers and their leaders without benefit of arrest or trial is not an offense in war. The status of the individual enemy soldier, whether he has killed anyone yet or violated any laws of war, is not the issue in battle. The outcome of the battle is the central issue. Killing enemy leaders is not particularly aimed at them; it's nothing personal. It is just one of the best ways of prevailing on the central issue, which is the contest between the two armies.

Israelis understand their struggle against suicide bombers to be part of the global war on terrorism, justifying targeted killing of leaders connected to bombings. Israelis argue that their approach to Palestinian bombers is the same as the American response to the September 11 attack on New York and Washington, which President Bush has always described as an act of war. If the war against terror is global, and if Israeli targeted assassination is a legitimate tool in such a war, then it is not at all far-fetched to imagine the practice spreading to all corners of the globe. The Israeli principle—that terrorist operatives, including leaders, are like military enemies and thus can be killed whenever opportunity arises—is now a candidate for universal application. Can we accept it?

Here the Israeli-American analogy to war begins to falter. We need a limiting principle, but none appears in their approach to terrorism. Can we define terrorism sharply enough so that we know who is and who isn't a potential target? Can we define culpability well enough to know who has sufficient in-

volvement to merit assassination? Israel has targeted organizational leaders, bomb makers, and others who recruit and equip
suicide bombers. But what is the limit? Will the mechanic who
repairs the car the suicide bomber is going to drive be facing a
penalty of summary assassination? What about the father who
feeds the suicide bomber and kisses her goodbye as she heads
out for her day? What about people riding in the taxis Israelis
have rocketed? The taxi driver? Do they deserve death, or are
they acceptable collateral damage (another topic we take up before this chapter is over)? All of these people, with varying
amounts of knowledge of what is afoot, may be contributing
more or less intentionally to the suicide bomber's enterprise.

How certain must the defenders be about a suspect's involvement before they attack? American forces in Afghanistan
and Iraq have made tragic mistakes, occasionally killing noncombatants (including a wedding party) in the mistaken belief
that the targets were Taliban or Al-Qaida terrorists, or Baathists.
In retrospect (and one hopes, in the future) the standard of proof
should be quite a bit higher before the trigger gets pulled and innocents die. In wartime soldiers are readily identifiable, by uniform and insignia. These clearly mark legitimate targets. But
terrorists are not readily distinguishable from innocents, which
is why fighting a war without these markings is considered "illegal warfare" and a war crime. The fact that terrorists try to
pass themselves off as noncombatants makes their actions even
worse, but that does not mean that those who defend against
them are thereby authorized to kill innocents by mistake or
recklessly.

The problems of making reliable distinctions when assassinating suspected terrorists leave us with no firm limitation on
the practice. Perhaps the Israelis and the Americans are doing a
good job of being careful about their targets. We will probably
never know, since these are not matters of public record and
there seems to be no effective legislative or judicial review. That
is a significant problem in itself. But the worse one is that once
the precedent has been set it is available for wider use. Vladimir
Putin can use it in Chechnya. Indian leaders can use it in Kashmir. Maybe we can trust the Russians and Indians not to stray
too far from the rule of law, but what of the Slobodan Milose-
viches of the world? The American and Israeli principle is that

"Whoever the security apparatus thinks is a terrorist can be assassinated."

The dangers in such a principle are manifold. As long as targeted assassinations are not accountable to an objective standard, judged by impartial and independent judges, and subject to sanctions suitable to the scope of the offense, then they are lawless. Targeted assassination as practiced today has no limiting principle. A different conclusion might follow if civilized nations worked together to define the limits of the practice and if participating nations were scrupulous to subject practitioners to accountability under the law. But until then, targeted assassination is just another form of terrorism when practiced in such a systematic and repetitive way that it amounts to the government's policy.

A similar conclusion is easier to reach when we consider the Israeli practice of collectively punishing entire populations for the crimes of the suicide bombers and the minority of people who aid them. Again there is no limiting principle. Innocents are punished for the actions of the guilty. Practitioners of house demolitions are not accountable to independent judges for the determination of who is guilty and thus worthy to have their property destroyed. The Israeli attempt to root out the terrorist infrastructure in the West Bank has not been constrained to the task at hand, unless one considers the civil records that were destroyed, the entire cities closed by curfew, the students prevented from going to school, and the workers prevented from reaching their jobs all part of the terrorist infrastructure.

Because the Israelis have not disciplined themselves to make judicial determinations of who is involved in the crime, they have had to interpret "terrorist infrastructure" almost as the entire social structure of Palestinian life. They have been rooting that up with vigor, all right, but at what cost? At the cost of the respect for rule of law, democracy, and transparency that forms the backbone of the Israeli dream for their country? Perhaps. At least many observers think so, and I am one.

We cannot afford to have this principle extended into the entire world. The Israelis and Palestinians cannot afford its extension to their territories. They will be even worse off if they cease to be an island of misery but find themselves awash in a world-spanning ocean of unprincipled reprisal.

So the answer is "Yes, governments can be terrorists." Governmental violence does have an added line of defense against setting a precedent for pandemic terror, since governments are marked by a legitimate monopoly on coercive force. But when governments as a matter of systematic policy act in ways not constrained by any limiting principles, generating arbitrary and unaccountable violence, they can be terrorists if they meet the five criteria developed in Chapter 1.

We could summarize this discussion by proposing a Golden Rule of Nations: Any government that regularly does to others' citizens what it would never accept having done to its own may be guilty of terrorism. Would the Palestinians accept having Israeli extremists blow up markets with the goal of killing as many Palestinian civilians as possible? If not, suicide bombing is terrorism. Would the Israeli government accept having the Palestinians assassinate officers in the Israeli army whom the Palestinians were convinced had exceeded the limits of just warfare in the occupied territories? If not, targeted assassinations are terrorism.

What About Collateral Casualties?

Killing civilians as unintended victims of an attack on soldiers, which we have come to call "collateral damage," presents another hard issue. If the first civilian casualty turned the entire attack into terrorism, legitimate national defense would be impossible, given the unfocused lethality of modern warfare and that some attackers hide among civilians. Nor can the presence of one off-duty soldier justify the bombing of a shopping mall. So what is the principle governing civilian casualties that could be reasonably universalized to all governments?

Collateral damage meets two of the criteria for terrorism—it is violence against civilians. But it doesn't necessarily meet the other three. It is not intended to cause political effect, nor does it try to achieve its aim through fear. If I am aiming at a military target but, because my maps are poor, I hit the Chinese Embassy, I have done harm to noncombatants, but it was accidental. I was not trying to scare the Chinese, nor was I using the civilian staff at the embassy as suffering-generators to amplify my message. It might not even be lawless, although even the laws of war might not countenance such gross negligence.

So the standard cases of collateral damage probably don't qualify as terrorism. However, cases in which civilian populations are bombed to sap morale may qualify. Civilians are the targets, they are killed as a means to a political end (reduced support for the enemy's war policy), and the tactic operates largely through fear (although also perhaps through fatigue or despair). Richard Nixon ignited significant controversy in the U.S. when he bombed Hanoi to put pressure on North Vietnamese negotiators in Paris. Perhaps protesters sensed that a line had been crossed when civilians were made targets, as pawns in a grand strategy. And we can put our finger on that line: bombing civilians on purpose is terrorism. So if Nixon's bombing was aimed at civilians, it would count as terrorism.

Now we come to the tougher cases. What of those military activities not officially aimed at civilians, but in which military planners know many civilians will die? According to the standards of Christian just war theory (discussed more fully in a later chapter), such a tactic would be sinful, and tacticians should cross it off their list of options. So it may be wrongful, but would it constitute terrorism, or some other sin?

One way to answer the question is to inquire why decision-makers decided to go ahead with the attack despite knowing many civilians would perish. Were they hoping to make some use of the suffering? Presumably, planners would hope to reduce enemy military forces by causing casualties among soldiers, destruction of weapons, or maybe even disruption of military production, supply, or transport. Did they also note as a positive byproduct the deaths of civilians, or the effect their deaths would have on morale or public opinion, either in the target country or back at home? If the latter counted in their counsels, the attack begins to take on the character of terror.

Here is another place where we might apply our Golden Rule of Nations. Did the Allies in World War II pass off the blitz of London as one of the unpleasant side effects of war? If not, then how did they justify the even more destructive fire bombings of Dresden and Hamburg, or the nuclear bombs in Hiroshima and Nagasaki? Note that the response "they did it first" won't wash as a defense against a charge of state-sponsored terror. The rule we are proposing is *not* "do unto others only what they have done unto you." Terrorism in response to terrorism is only more terrorism—it only spreads even further the lawlessness and pandemic violence which are at the heart of terrorism's evil. The rule is "do unto others only what you would accept having done to you under similar circumstances." Anything less is hypocrisy and, if it involves lawless killing of civilians, terrorism.

Many Americans argue that the atomic bombings in Japan were justified as measures intended to avoid the need for a land invasion, which may have caused many more casualties than the bombings did. In deference to this argument, we might want to reframe the context before we apply the Golden Rule of Nations: Would the U.S. have accepted two atomic attacks causing tens of thousands to die if it were necessary in time of war to convince an American military government to step down, end the war, avoid an invasion, and allow a democratic enemy to occupy the country? This is at least an intriguing question, one that would be somewhat easier to answer in the affirmative if the attacks had been calibrated to minimize civilian casualties while still maximizing their intimidating effects on the Japanese leaders. It was a time of war, and imperfect execution of a legitimate goal does not by itself make an attack terrorist, so it may be possible to acquit the U.S. of terrorism in this case, especially if American decision-makers did not know how devastating the attacks would be. We will leave that judgment to historians.

The Shape of Terrorism

We are finally ready to summarize a coherent definition of terror, one we can use throughout the rest of this book as we look for Christian options in dealing with it. Terror is lawless violence (in the sense that it is not connected to a legitimate exercise by a government of a monopoly on lethal force) directed at civilians to bring about a political objective through the operation of fear.

Far beyond the suffering inherent in violence, terrorism adds several layers of calamity. It introduces to society an unlimited principle justifying private violence which would make life impossibly miserable even if invoked by only a few. Those committing terrorism dehumanize their victims, and thus themselves, by reducing them to vehicles for making suffering a factor in political influence. And terrorism disrupts a society's ability to decide public issues on their merits, through the democratically expressed will of the people in combination with the rule of law.

In addition, now that terrorism can reach anyone anywhere, we can no longer rely on geographic firewalls to keep it confined to tolerably distant places. Terrorism is in everyone's backyard now. Christians have to give it serious thought and prayerfully seek God's direction as we explore ways to bring Christ's love to bear on the problem. I offer this book as one believer's attempt to begin developing such a response.

Chapter 3

....

Tyranny and Other
Forms of Political Misery

Paying Attention to Politics

For many Christians, political systems are little more than backdrops to the main dramas of life. Their focus is on personal relationships with God—nurturing their own, and working to bring others into salvation. With these human struggles and their eternal implications at the center of these believers' attention, they treat political systems as being a part of the environment with about as much spiritual importance as the weather.

This is a natural attitude. The Bible, for example, does not say much explicitly about political change, especially not as a Christian field of ministry. Some zealots hoped Jesus would overthrow the Romans in Judea, but his ministry did not go in that direction. And when Paul refers to governments in Romans 12, he seems to pass no judgment on their forms. Government is "ordained" by God for preserving order, according to Paul, but he makes no distinction among types of government. Paul seems to be ready to deal with whatever forms of government he may encounter, giving it deference as the agency responsible for preserving public order.

There are passages in the Old Testament describing regime changes (1 Samuel covers the switch from decentralized theocracy to a classic monarchy, and subsequent books describe dynastic turmoil in the ruling houses of both Israel and the seceding tribes in Judah). However, other than God's wistfulness over the Israelites' refusal to stay in a direct theocracy, the biblical record is not long on proof texts for political reformers, to say nothing of regime-changing revolutionaries.[10]

On the other hand, the Bible does have quite a bit to say about what constitutes good government. One might read the books of Judges and 1 Samuel as an account of God's attempt to install an ideal direct theocratic government for the Israelites. God gives Israel what amounts to a constitution in the Law recorded in the books of Moses, and God explicitly warns Israel that it is taking a major step backward by insisting on a human-style monarchy instead of the theocracy God established for them. Then, as the monarchies in Israel and Judah steadily stray deeper into corruption and violence, God speaks through the prophets to criticize the two kingdom's decadent politics and to call them to radical reforms. God even goes so far as to use foreign armies as scourges to enforce discipline when Israel and Judah do not heed the call to make their governments right.

Thus, judging from the biblical record taken as a whole, God does care about what kind of government people live under. And Jesus reinforces the point when he uses a passage from Isaiah to announce his ministry as the coming of the day of the Lord, when not only will individuals be healed but captives will be released and the poor will get good news. These are, in part, political messages.

Consider what damage bad government can do to people. To begin with, governments can harm people by taking wrong actions. For example, some governments actively deprive their citizens of freedom of speech, assembly, and religion. Most Christians have long recognized this as a theological and moral issue worthy of their attention and opposition. Without freedom to preach and hear the gospel, and to meet together to discuss it, how can people find a relationship with God? It may still be possible, but for the ordinary person distracted by the concerns of everyday life, finding God without the help of others is exceptionally difficult and unlikely to happen.

Even beyond direct attacks on religious freedom, there are an infinite number of bad policies a government can choose to enforce against its citizens. North Americans, used to stable governments, may be accustomed to focusing complaints about government on various ways specific policies may chafe. Believers may be called at times to work for changes at the specific policy level, but this is not our focus for the moment. As hurtful as individual bad policies can be, if they are set in a context of generally good government, citizens can usually work around the resulting problems.

In some countries, however, people do not have the luxury of complaining at length about the details of their governments. Their entire political environment is toxic. Our interest here lies in these worst-case scenarios, when governmental systems fail catastrophically.

Political System Failures

Three broad disorders in a political system can be a source of misery to its citizens: anarchy, corruption, and tyranny. We will examine each in turn, keeping in mind that there are cases which combine elements of more than one disorder, creating their own sets of sufferings.

Anarchy

Earlier we described a government as the agency with a legitimate monopoly on coercive force in a particular society. When that monopoly dissolves, anarchy results.

We have already glimpsed some of the problems people face living in anarchy. Personal physical security becomes a private good, available only to those who can employ guards and build walls. This leaves most people in an anarchy too poor to build their own security systems, with no defenses against criminals and thugs. Even those who can buy some security for their homes share in the general insecurity of their fellows when they venture outside their little islands of safety—and may find that their protected wealth makes them especially attractive to thieves and other predators.

Without personal security, productivity plummets. Once you accumulate equipment or other assets with which to produce things, you are a target for looters and thieves, as Iraqis discovered in the aftermath of Hussein's collapse. Resources have to be "wasted" on additional security measures. People break contracts, trespass, swindle, and steal with impunity. Even waiting for a crop to harvest becomes a desperate adventure, as the farmer worries about his neighbors sneaking into his fields at night and helping themselves. Crops may be harvested before they are at their ripest, even, as either farmers or their thieving neighbors try to get the jump on someone else they think may try to take the crop for themselves.

If a simple strawberry field becomes a free-for-all of almost-ripe berry poaching, consider the practical impossibility of reaping benefits from other kinds of creation. Inability to enforce patents and copyrights will drive most inventors, writers, and composers into other lines of work. Manufacturers will tend to want to avoid large inventories and large production runs, due to inability to count on customers honoring their contracts, to say nothing of how hard it is to keep inventory safe in a lawless environment. Even charitable relief organizations find their warehouses and equipment vulnerable to pillage in anarchy, so that many will not venture into lawless areas where need is often greatest.

A society which has accustomed itself to such chaos will teach its members to look out for themselves. These lessons will be passed on either directly and explicitly or unconsciously through a process akin to "survival of the fittest." The more ingrained this approach is in a society, the harder it will be even to find colleagues of good will with whom to do business in private arrangements of amicability and trust. Trust in an anarchic society is not a winning strategy. Sooner or later you get wiped out.

Private compacts designed to create islands of order amid the chaos will not have much chance of working for long. Even the best-intentioned will find it difficult to resolve major disputes without a functioning legal system and no police to enforce its decisions.

Anarchy, then, leads to lives of constant desperation. Specialization disappears as people lose the ability to rely on networks of contracts to supply their needs and thus have to meet more and more of them directly through their own labor. Disputes turn into blood feuds as other means of conflict resolution become unavailable. Work becomes less productive due to lost specialization and resources redirected toward maintaining private security. People live in constant fear for their physical and economic well-being. No wonder Thomas Hobbes called the state of anarchy the "war of all against all" in which everyone's life would be " solitary, poor, nasty, brutish, and short."

Anarchy is a spiritual, physical, and social predicament. We cannot pretend to love our neighbors if we are content to leave them in a state of political anarchy. To leave another human being in anarchy is to meet him on the lawless road to Jericho and pass by on the other side while he remains in the ditch, wounded by robbers and easy prey for others.

Anarchy is, thankfully, a rare condition in modern life. There are countries with weak governments where aspects of life are anarchic. Somalia, a lurid example during the 1990s, drew an international response in the form of peacekeepers. Anarchy proved stronger than international peacemaking in that case, and before long peacekeeping troops fled, leaving Somalians to work things out for themselves. Recently Iraq and Liberia, and to a lesser extent Afghanistan and Colombia, have all experienced extended bouts of anarchy.

Corruption

More common than the complete collapse of government is its corruption. Whereas anarchy consists of the absence of functioning government, corruption is government that has rotted. The forms are there, but they ooze and smell of putrification.

A government should operate to serve citizens as a whole, making choices based on the merits of each situation. Corruption occurs whenever systems abandon merit-based decisions to serve instead the private interests of one or a few.

This is a pivotal concept for the argument I make in this book, so let's pause to examine it more closely.

Key is the notion of "merit-based" decisions. I assume that in each situation better and worse can be chosen. Making decisions on their merits would involve examining available choices and choosing the best option (or as close to it as possible) on the basis of good reasons.

So what would make one choice "better" and another choice "worse"? Good choices meet three criteria:

- They are consistent with *truth*;
- The decision-maker, in making the choice, fulfills *duty* to others he is representing; and
- Where possible, the decisions adhere to *fair laws*—that is, to a settled pattern of similar decisions rather than being based on the whims of one person or even a transient frenzied majority.

So far, these criteria for merit-based decisions may seem to come out of nowhere. Who cares if all the criteria are met? Aren't there other possible criteria? For example, might we say that a good decision is one that "works" at some level?

My response is to consider what it means to say a decision works. If we mean that it "sticks," so people adhere to it, then certainly many decisions made every day do work. Yet I would contend that decisions not meeting these criteria cannot "work" in any sense acceptable to Christian believers.

Consider the requirement of "truth." It calls for decisions to be based on an accurate grasp of reality. If I accuse you of hurting me and insist you should pay my medical bills, the decision about whether you should pay me should turn in part on whether you actually did hurt me and whether I did have medical bills as a result. There are questions of fact, of the type we often resolve in trials before juries, whom we charge with the task of finding the truth about what happened.

If decisions are made regardless of the truth, injustice and misery result. Innocents go to jail, while the guilty go unpunished. Officials may arrest without cause. Informants make up charges against the innocent; cheaters and secret cartels dominate markets, siphoning off much of their customers' purchasing power without delivering any goods; the unproductive and unreliable get entrenched in positions of power and privilege since no one can effectively call them to account.

When it comes to making policy, the situation is just as bad if truth is not a fundamental feature of governmental decisions. Rulemakers, even those with good intentions, who do not know what life is like for their people will pursue imagined needs and ignore real ones. They will enact regulations that create unforeseen results, including inadvertent destruction of livelihoods.

To connect government decisions to truth, the government almost has to be democratic in some form. Decision-makers must know how possible policies affect citizens, since their complaints and aspirations are key factors in coming to the truth about what a government should do. Given the failings of human nature, unless a government official depends in some way on popular approval for her position, laziness or venality will interrupt the official's diligence in learning about the conditions of his constituents' lives. A crucial benefit of democracy is the strong incentive it gives to elected officials to spend time seeking out and listening to citizens. Another benefit is the incentive it gives citizens to communicate needs and wishes to their representatives. Between the representatives' eagerness to know what constituents want and constituents' confidence that representatives will listen, a context arises in which information about the truth can flow where needed.

Democracies also tend to encourage public officials to fulfill their duties faithfully. Failure to serve constituents well threatens to inspire public rejection at the next election. With political leverage in their hands, voters have less trouble reminding office-holders to fulfill their duty to constituents.

Democracy is not enough by itself. Pure democracy, where every decision has to be submitted to the people for a vote, can still be unpredictable and inconsistent. Hasty majorities may be vulnerable to their prejudices and may jump into action without learning much about the truth. Minorities may be treated unfairly, and may have no one to represent them.

To combat these ills, and to provide all citizens with a measure of predictability and order, governments need to constrain themselves to be accountable to law. In a sound governmental system, law essentially serves as the record of decisions on the merits about various issues a society faces. Legislatures which are well-connected to their voters are making decisions on the merits when they vote on legislation. Judges who painstakingly write out reasons for their decisions are recording how they weighed the merits of the case.

If cases get decided wrongly, or ill-advised legislation begins cluttering the scene, a good government corrects the problem. New cases allow court to limit or overturn errors. New legislation can do the same. In neither case is the decision made by someone who stands to directly benefit personally from the outcome.

Corrupted systems cut these connections and limitations. Officials find they can benefit more from selling their services to the highest bidder than from listening to their constituents as a whole and working to serve their interests. Without vital two-way communication with average citizens, officials lose access to information about their lives. They no longer can act from a grasp of the truth and have little incentive to serve constituent needs. Such needs get lost in the wheeling and dealing officials do with those willing to pay them off. And when laws fall into disrepute and irrelevancy, officials can act with impunity—at least so long as the government doesn't collapse so badly that turf wars break out among rival officialdoms.

This effect is not confined to elected officials. A corrupted system leads to breakdowns throughout government. Many countries have suffered losses, for example, in earthquakes caused by failure of building officials to enforce building codes because they had been paid by builders to look the other way. In these cases, building code enforcers have sold the safety, even lives, of future earthquake victims in exchange for kickbacks lining their own pockets. And the effects run well beyond the public sector. In a society accustomed to corruption, the blight spreads to businesses, schools, non-profit organizations, and even to the church.

The effects are devastating. Investors lose money to corrupt managers, and thus have less incentive to invest, impoverishing the capital markets. Customers get shoddy, overpriced goods because their suppliers ignore value and quality in pursuit of private gain. Companies lie about their finances to avoid taxes or secure investments. Even non-profits suffer, losing donors and effectiveness in the general expectation that everyone will cheat. This is a self-fulfilling expectation, of course: If you think everyone else is cheating, it may seem foolish not to do so yourself. A corrupt system rewards clever, relentless cheaters at the expense of those who play fairly and by the rules, and thereby tends to spread throughout society.

Christians who pay bribes, even in some cases to promote the gospel, are lending strength to the corrupt regime. I am not sure how much love it shows one's neighbor to bribe a government official to get the gospel into the neighbor's hands. Bribery and other forms of corruption cost lives and cause other miseries, and the more practiced the firmer its hold and the wider its spread. Bribing to spread the gospel is like trying to liberate prisoners by building extra walls around them.

Corruption in government is a spiritual, physical, and social predicament. We cannot pretend to love our neighbors if we are content to leave them in a state of political corruption. To leave a fellow human being in a corrupted political system is to leave her on the lonely road to Jericho in the custody of kidnappers who hold her for ransom.

Tyranny

Anarchies have no functioning government. Corruption eats away at the structures of government. Tyrannies have, in some senses, governments that are too strong.

Consider again our brief discussion of merit-based government. Governments ideally make policies and carry out functions based on the merits of each case. They try to serve the welfare of their citizens, seeking the truth about their needs and conditions and giving them stable, tested, and reliable guidelines and protections under law.

To accomplish these things, governments need to be connected to their citizens, accountable to them, with every incentive to listen to their needs and to respond to them. And governments need to be restrained by the rule of law, both to prevent arbitrariness and corruption and to take advantage of the law's role as a record of previous deliberations about the merits of things. That is, government needs to be a conversational process among officials and citizens, within the bounds of law.

Tyranny interrupts this process, substituting the monologue of the tyrant for the infinitely complex dialog of democracy. The tyrant cannot tolerate dissent and comes to distrust dissenters. Tyrants lose track of truth as they stifle all voices other than their own. Even so-called "benevolent" tyrannies lose their ability to operate effectively as their worldviews drift more and more from reality.

Tyrannies by definition break the bounds of the law. Since the tyrant's "law" is subject only to the tyrant's will, and that will can change at any moment, few of the benefits of law reach the citizenry. The tyrant's "law" is unpredictable, unfairly applied (since the tyrant's minions are immune to it), and does not protect citizens from attack or loss. There may be some protection from being victimized by other common citizens, but the benefits of this kind of lateral protection are lost when the regime's thugs can act with impunity, and thus have everything to gain and nothing to lose by stealing from and abusing defenseless citizens. The breakdown of la, and the loss of accountability to the citizens eventually erodes the chances that a government official will feel any incentive to do his duty to his fellow citizens.

Citizens under tyranny lose hope. Public life serves only the interests of the tyrant and his coterie. Whether citizens thrive is not a matter of concern for the tyrant's regime, whose overriding concern is that the citizens be kept quiet. Intimidation, imprisonment, torture, exile, "disappearing," and death are among the tools used with varying effectiveness at keeping the people quiet.

Tyranny is a spiritual, physical and social predicament. We cannot pretend to love our neighbors if we are content to leave them in a state of tyranny. To leave a fellow human being under tyranny is to leave him on the stony road to Jericho being beaten by thugs.

The Scourge of Evil in Political Systems

All three of these broad types of political evil fail in a variety of ways. First, they all fail to carry out the most fundamental purposes of government, according to Paul in Romans 13: They do not restrain evil and provide order. In fact, each in its own way tends to promote evil and break down order in social life. Thus each is illegitimate under the basic test for a governmental system and does not fit the description of a "governing authority" to which Paul urges us to be submissive.

Nor do any of these perverse systems of government provide any reliable means for resolving disputes and policy debates on their merits. Anarchy provides no forums for such work. Corruption transforms processes of policy making and dispute resolution into tools for bilking people heedless of the merits of the situation. And tyranny destroys meaningful conflict resolution and policy debates to impose a uniform point of view and stifle unrest. Without the means of reforming the system to serve the real needs of the populace, citizens of tyrannies are doomed to misery. The misery is compounded by the loss even of functional private dispute resolution processes, especially for disputes between the average citizen and rampaging members of the regime.

Lawlessness and oppression are contagious. For example, if anarchy arises in one country, it provides a haven for ruthless elements from all the countries in the region. Law enforcement in countries with functioning governments becomes much more difficult if the lawless can easily slip across a border into an anarchic area, making themselves immune to capture or extradition. And conditions in the lawless country breed more lawless people who must learn the ways of anarchy to survive. All these factors tend to encourage the spread of anarchy into previously stable areas.

Corruption spreads in a similar way. If anything, the cross-border influence of corruption is even greater than anarchy. Individuals have many incentives to adopt corruption. They may learn while trying to do business in a corrupt society—to get along there, a foreign trader has strong profit motivation to learn and adapt to the local ways. Having seen how some individuals thrive (even if at others' expense) in a corrupt system, those who return to a stable society from a corrupt one may be motivated to bring back with them expectations of payoffs and the techniques of the shakedown.

Even tyranny is contagious. For one thing, tyrants themselves tend to be expansionist. This may be motivated only by self-defense, an attempt to expand borders to move threats farther from the seat of power. But tyrants, having cut off dissent, often come to believe in their own invincibility and even indispensability. From the point of view of the tyrant, it is easy to conclude that neighboring populations need your rule, or at least that their objections to your rule are misinformed or irrelevant. So the tyrant himself may try to expand his empire directly.

But tyranny expands even without direct help of the tyrant. Often tyranny is wed to an ideology. Those who believe the ideology may conclude that they have license or even duty to spread it by any means, including violence. Violent revolutions, if successful, naturally lead to violent government, and thus to tyranny. (The historical counterexamples are depressingly rare.)

Or tyranny may expand merely by stimulating defensive responses among the tyrant's neighbors. Feeling insecure with a noisy dictator on their borders, previously stable nations may feel a need to crack down on destabilizing elements within their own population or leaking over the border from the tyrant's realm. Liberties may be curtailed and security forces beefed up. If the process goes on long enough, or if the tyrant's threat is seen as great enough, constitutional rule in a neighboring country can erode or even collapse in a coup d'etat. The original tyrant may not have won, but tyranny will have spread nonetheless.

The Links Between Political Misery and Terrorism

My original plan for this book did not include much reference to tyranny. Terrorism of the 9-11 kind was a new thing in the world, and it seemed to dwarf all other political concerns in the international arena. While the United States invaded Afghanistan, I ignored the role that political misery had played in nurturing Al Qaida.

The Talibani regime in Afghanistan was a clear case of tyranny, although perhaps in a form a little different than we are used to seeing. We think of tyrants as dictators, rule by one man, or at most a small cabal. The Afghani government looked different. It was true that no dissent was tolerated, and the government considered anything its people did to be within its jurisdiction; Afghans didn't vote for their governors; and there were no recognizable legal restraints limiting what the government could do to its people. But the regime did have the support and approval of a significant part of the civilian population, especially those who adhered to a strict reading of their Islamic faith. The Taliban's organizational strength drew from some hardy grassroots, especially among the Pashtun people. If you squinted a little, it almost looked like what America would be if a fundamentalist political party won a few elections—but in a foreign, male-dominated Islamic version.

Thus the war in Afghanistan did not clearly connect classic tyranny and terror in many minds, including my own. So it was that President Bush, when he decided that Iraq also had to be attacked as part of the war on terror, had a massive public education challenge on his hands. In retrospect, it seems that Bush mishandled the task, allowing his case for invading Iraq to rest too heavily on its supposed possession of weapons of mass destruction and on poorly documented allegations of connections to Al Qaida. Others made his central case much better than he did: Tyranny and terror are inextricably linked.

As we will see later in this book, tyrants help breed terrorists. They contribute to the spiritual deformation that brings people to the point of being ready to lash out against others they see as their enemies. Tyranny deprives people of nonviolent alternatives while reinforcing the widespread belief that only violence can be counted on to work as a last resort. These factors are all present even when tyrants don't foster terrorism as a matter of state policy, as Iraq under Hussein did in Palestine and elsewhere.

We can never rid the planet of terrorism as long as tyranny is tolerated. Our anti-terrorist struggle has to also be an anti-tyranny project. But tyranny is not the only breeder of terrorism. Corrupt polities and anarchies, each in their own way, also spiritually deform their citizens and deprive them of nonviolent means to redress their grievances. As long as any of these forms of political misery are permitted to endure in our midst, we will never rid the world of the seedbeds of terror.

I do not want to overstate my case here. Terrorists have grown, albeit rarely and typically not in great numbers, even in the most advanced democracies on the planet. However, these have been cases where, to the budding terrorist, the political system has not seemed to be as the rest of us see it. They have seen the system as a tyranny covertly running things behind a democratic smokescreen, or as corruptly favoring a select few, or as undermining our moral foundations. That is, in the world they perceive, the Tim McVeighs believe they are living in political misery.

It is also true that some of the world's most dangerous terrorists seem to have suffered a great deal of their moral collapse when they have come out of native lands steeped in political misery to spend time studying or working in more democratic systems. This seems to have been the case, for example, for the leader of the September 11 terrorist, Mohammed Atta. His descent into terrorism began with disillusionment about the state of his native Egyptian society. That the West should be so far in advance of the Arab world, while Western morals and faith were so depraved by Islamic standards, must have shattered something in Atta's soul.

Conclusion

Up to now North American Christians have been reluctant to consider someone else's political situation our business. Conscious of the evils of imperialism, we have worried that we should not intervene and trample others' rights to determine for themselves what their political system should be. We have worried that we had no right to tell others how to govern themselves.

Such worry may once have been understandable. For most of our history, those of us living in North America and Europe have enjoyed the luxury of being far from the influences of the worst anarchies, corruptions, and tyrannies. But this old world is long gone. As September 11 demonstrated so graphically, the world is now too small for anyone to be considered other than a neighbor. What happens in Somalia and Afghanistan, two of the places on the planet most remote from North America, now clearly affects us here at home.

The members of Al Qaida, from countries all over the globe, have declared themselves our neighbors, in the sense that we cannot pretend any longer that what they do does not affect us. Now it is time for North American Christians to declare ourselves to be their neighbors—along with all people anywhere—in the sense that we will no longer pretend we do not have to care what happens to them. Their suffering is our concern, no matter where on Earth they are.

We can no longer pass by on the other side of the road while they bleed from wounds inflicted by their political captors. Their salvation is our business, including their salvation from anarchy, corruption, and tyranny. We are called to help relieve their political suffering just as surely as we are called to help relieve their physical and spiritual woes—and this is a central part of the fight against terrorism.

Chapter 4

The Military Option

The Dissolution of Human Groups

Probably the most common first thought on the minds of those who watched the live video on September 11, 2001 was revenge. My own Quaker pastor admitted that this was his first immediate reaction, so perhaps I can safely acknowledge that there was a race for first place going on in my mind, too, and I can no longer recall whether "vengeance" nosed out "end the cycle of violence."

President Bush started calling the fight against terrorism a "war" almost immediately after the attacks on the World Trade Center and the Pentagon on September 11, 2001.[11] A few days later, French President Jacques Chirac, standing beside President Bush at the White House, was pointedly reluctant to use the term war.[12]

Chirac acknowledged the enormity of the September 11 casualties, as he had to. Those deaths were more than America suffered in some entire wars, more than on D-Day in 1944 leading to liberation of Chirac's homeland. And he agreed the fight would be long and require cooperation of all civilized nations, against an enemy in many ways unprecedented. But he seemed to be seeking new language to describe what we faced. Ever since those first days of horror over September 11, we have been debating what our responses should be.

Certainly the world is in a battle, so maybe it would work to call the anti-terror struggle a "battle," although that term usually denotes a single engagement. On the other hand, military historian John Keegan describes the objective of battle to be "the dissolution of human groups," especially military units and governments.[13] Extend the notion to terrorist networks and corrupt or despotic regimes, and we have a perfect description of the goal of the campaign: the dissolution of groups who represent a threat to modern civilization.

So it seems natural that military action might be a route we ought to choose to achieve our goals. Warfare is, after all, an attempt to smash human groups by obliterating some members and coercing the rest. We have thousands of years of experience with this approach to eliminating opponents.

But modern military power, and the defensive tactics created to withstand it, spread destruction profligately. Noncombatants have a hard time staying out of the way. We also have a hard time defining who is a noncombatant when modern warfare is so dependent on complex technological production and support. Modern mass armies rely on mass production for supply, massive industrialization for weapons, and mass governments for funding. The war machine extends well beyond the boundaries of the military itself, reaching deeply into the civilian population.

In conventional warfare these problems complicate matters, but they are not insurmountable. When the opponent is trying to play the same game, trying to dissolve your military and government through military means, it has to have some easily identifiable vulnerabilities: bases, massed troops, ships, and so forth, in the military sector; and factories, depots, and supply lines that stretch into civilian zones. The capital city might also be a crucial military target, since its capture will remove or displace the political leadership that coordinates the enemy's war effort. Conventional war gives you something to hit, someplace to have an impact with your concentrated coercive and destructive force.

But the struggle against terrorism is a different game. Terrorists avoid massed forces, have no conspicuous support or infrastructure facilities, and don't use visible lines of logistical supply or support. Terrorists often don't even have bases worthy of the name. They spend a lot of their time living in communities rather than barracks, making it difficult for their enemies to find them or to distinguish them from their innocent neighbors. If we do locate them, then we may not be able to confine the effects of our weapons to their intended targets. Civilians, including children and, often, adults who in no way intend to support terrorism, are likely to be within the lethal zone in our attacks.

So military tactics, while they might help to dissolve the terrorist group existing at the time of the attack, are likely to generate bitterness and despair among bystanders. If those who survive end up ripened for recruitment as future killers, the attack may destroy all or part of a terrorist cell while planting the seeds for its rapid recovery or replacement. There's not much gain in destroying your enemy as a fighting group if the immediate result is to replace it. Like Lewis Carroll's Red Queen, we may find ourselves running faster and faster just to stay even with the growth of terrorism.

Perhaps this sounds too pessimistic. But we already have a large body of experimental evidence that the most consistent and creative policy of retribution is useless as a way to eliminate terrorism, courtesy of the Israelis. Their long battle against Palestinian terrorism shows no sign of abating. Instead, the Israelis and Palestinians seem to be enacting a classic destructive conflict cycle,[14] as each tries to deter attacks from the other by retaliating in kind and then some. Neither side seems able to escape the maelstrom of violence their policies have stirred up. But the myth persists that "the only language terrorists understand is violence" and thus the only way to stop terrorism is lethal retaliation.

Since watching the Israelis and Palestinians suffer has not been enough to deflect the rest of the world from this belief—and since the parallel experiences of the residents of Northern Ireland, or of Sri Lanka, or who knows how many other places seem to have had no effect, either—we need to take another look at terrorism. How can we get past the mirage of retribution to a policy that will offer some hope of doing justice and ending terrorism?

Guidance from Christian Teachings About War?

One possible source of insight might be Christian ethical teachings about responding to violence. Can we mine some practical ideas, ones that will work, from Christian thinking about warfare?

I know there's no future in second-guessing an omnipotent God, so that's not what I am advocating. But the universe is designed to leave room for our creative input. We didn't start history knowing how to prevent polio, for example, or how to build a good sewer system. We had to develop science as a way of discovering the principles behind God's design of the universe, then use those principles to discover some of the technologies for relieving suffering and extending justice. I have no doubt that preventing children from getting polio is in God's will, but it would not have come about had we not studied God's ways, so we could learn to live within them better.

The same thing, I suspect, applies to warfare against terrorists. If we can discern some of God's basic principles guiding our response to warlike situations, perhaps we can then creatively apply them to the situation at hand.

However, there is a problem. Christians do not agree about what God is trying to teach them about war. Most modern Christian theories of war fall into one of two camps: pacifism or just war theory. However, the earliest biblical model of warfare—the one we will start with here—was neither.

Holy war

The Old Testament seems to depict God as a warrior. God endorses several Israelite military adventures, sometimes explicitly instructing whom to fight and when and where to fight them. And some of those instructions are startling.

On some occasions God commanded the Israelites to wage wars with a minimum of violence. Gideon's battle against invaders, defeating tens of thousands with only three hundred men, is one of the classic cases.[15] So is David's one-boy battle against Goliath.[16]

At the other end of the spectrum are those occasions when God told the Israelites to wipe out entire populations, including women, children, and even livestock. Saul lost his blessing as Israel's first king when he disobeyed God twice: once by making an offering to God when Samuel had instructed him to wait, then by failing to kill some inhabitants of a town God told him to eliminate and allowing his troops to carry off the town's wealth as plunder.[17]

God was disappointed in Israel many times in the Old Testament, including often in Israel's choice to go to war or its tactical decisions during the war. But the problem, apparently, wasn't that Israel went to war or that it sometimes used tactics we normally call barbaric. Anything could go in one of God's wars, as long as the Israelites adhered to the one crucial standard. They had to stick strictly to God's commands. If God commanded a genocidal war, that was the war they had to fight. Or if God commanded a minimal war effort, just enough to provide a vehicle for a convincing display of divine power and faithfulness, then any deviation from those rules of engagement would bring God's disapproval.

For Israel's early days, then, at least up to the time of Saul, God used war as an instrument for arranging human affairs. But the consistent lesson is that, under God's direction, there do not seem to be rules for conducting wars that we can discern in advance and use as a guide to preparing for the next war. Instead of designing rules of military engagement, the Israelite response when a fight loomed was supposed to be to resort to God and diligently seek specific guidance about how to fight this time. God might ask every Israelite tribe to send troops for a mass battle, or for an emergent leader like Gideon to assemble a few dozen people capable of breaking pots and making a lot of noise. Or God might insist on not fighting at all . . . one could never know.

Before Saul became king, Israelites did not put much effort into preparing for war. There certainly was no standing army. Imagine the difficulties you would have faced if you had been asked by one of the longer-standing judges (such as Samuel) to be a military planner. In a time when the national military preparedness budget was next to nothing and God decided the tactics, what would you make the first priority in your spending plan? Bows and swords, shepherd boys' slings, or torches and pitchers?

And that seems to have been the point. One of God's laments when Israel insisted on "replacing" God with a king was the warning that, under the new government, Israel would have a standing army.[18] Soon Israel would err by putting its reliance on chariots and horses rather than directly on God.[19] That is, Israel would take upon itself planning ahead for the next war. Then, having armed itself to the best of its ability, Israel would build its military strategy around its equipment rather than direct obedience to, and trust in, God. Human wisdom would take the place of radical faith as the cornerstone of Israel's national defense.

Soon after Saul makes this clear by second-guessing God's operational instructions in battle, the age of divine war leadership comes to an end for Israel. God quits ordaining wars when the Israelites begin pragmatically planning for war. As far as one can tell from the Bible, the holy war option is limited to the conditions of direct theocracy and operates under conditions that defy military planning and preparation. Citizens of the ancient theocracy could expect God to act to protect them, and to give them marching orders as part of that protective plan, but they could not anticipate God's tactical plans. They could only prepare by carefully tending to their spiritual lives, disciplining themselves to listen for the voice of God, and being ready to do whatever God commanded, no matter how silly it might look to the wisest military veterans.

Some people believe the conditions of direct theocracy may reappear on earth and open the way for resumption of holy warfare. For example, medieval Crusaders seem to have been operating, more or less, on this theory. They thought it their duty as Christian princes and citizens to rid the Holy Land of Moslems. Most Christians are now convinced the Crusaders were off-track, bolstering this view on an examination of the Crusades' tragic "accomplishments." In the last few years, many Christians have even gone to the Middle East specifically to apologize for the evils done there in the name of God during the Crusades.

And here is a poignant irony: Modern Islamic terrorists twist their faith in ways similar to the Crusaders. So they have convinced themselves that God is ordering them to rid the world of secularized Westerners whose lifestyles and politics threaten to corrupt "true" Islam as they see it. To most Moslems, and of course nearly the entire non-Moslem population of the planet, this view seems grossly mistaken. For example, the Taliban's policies in Afghanistan seemed so unjust and oppressive, especially toward women, that it was hard for observers to see how anyone could mistake such practices for the will of God.

The Taliban is not the only group to have deluded itself into thinking it has a divine mandate for Holy War. The wars accompanying the Reformation were frequently described in holy war terms, by both Catholics and Protestants. Both sides in America's Civil War included some who thought of their cause as divine. Christian Hutus and Tutsis in Rwanda and Burundi may have had a sense that killing members of the other ethnic group was part of God's plan to rid their lands of evil. Radically paranoid groups in America today include some who think of themselves as being God's scourges against a corrupt society and an evil government. As a result, they are willing to bomb federal buildings, even if it means killing toddlers in day care centers there.

Judging by the biblical evidence, the planet's holy wars might have ended about the time of Saul. But later passages in the Old Testament still record God's use of war as an instrument of divine policy. The prophets rail against Israel's sins and warn that God will punish the wayward people. Foreign invaders deliver some of these punishments and even carry much of the population off into exile.

These corrective episodes aren't exactly holy wars, since the Babylonians and Assyrians don't subject themselves to God's commands and no doubt use tactics not blessed with the divine seal of approval. But when Israel needed disciplining for its injustice and unfaithfulness, God let the violence swirling in that dangerous neighborhood do divine work. On the other hand, as Jonah indicates, repentance and correction can ward off military disasters.[20]

So what principles can we derive from the Old Testament record of warfare?

1. War is another occasion, among the many in a community's life, where the crucial thing is radical dependence upon and obedience to God.

2. God might command a theocracy to go to war but would insist on its soldiers fighting in the ways and for the ends God commands. Specifically, human military planning is not al-

lowed to lead the way or even modify the specific commands God has for a particular campaign.

3. In cases other than direct theocracy, God does not seem to command warfare. Holy war, in the biblical record, is confined to the pre-Christian situation, unique in human history, when God had chosen a specific people as the vehicle for demonstrating covenant life. As the kings of Israel and Judah moved away from functioning as a theocracy, holy war faded as an option. It may have ceased altogether with the ministry of Christ, after which God has been working through the kingdom community of all disciples wherever they are, rather than through a particular national group.

4. Although there seem to be no more holy wars, warfare, even if outside of God's operational direction and thus in general an evil, can be a vehicle to chasten or punish a rebellious people. As the prophets urged in ancient Israel and Judah, God's people should see war against them as an invitation to self-examination dedicated toward finding and eliminating injustices and unfaithfulness in their lives.

Pacifism

While the Old Testament record seems to support the notion of war as a holy instrument of God's will, the New Testament strikes a contrasting note. Beginning with the Sermon on the Mount and running through the epistles, Jesus' message emphasizes a different theme that also has its roots in the Old Testament: love for neighbors and enemies.

Jesus contrasts his teachings with some of the pillars of Old Testament theology. Instead of an eye for an eye, the fundamental "lex talionis" of Old Testament justice, Jesus tells us to turn the other cheek and to go the extra mile. Justice hasn't dropped off the Christian agenda, by any means; rather, it is now in radical creative tension with grace and forgiveness. The early Christians believed Jesus' new instructions superceded the lex talionis just as His death and resurrection superseded the need for animal sacrifices. Thus the early church was predominantly pacifist.

In our day, Christian pacifism has at least two variations. We can trace them, at least in part, to two slightly different readings of the Sermon on the Mount.

One interpretation focuses on suffering. Pain and injustice are a part of human life. Christians are to take as much suffering upon themselves as they can to save others from it, even in cases where the others may "deserve" it. Christians who understand the Sermon on the Mount this way sometimes conclude that their response to evil is to be *nonresistant*, drawing on Jesus' injunction to "resist not the evil one."[21] Justice will be at God's hand, not ours. Nonresistant pacifists are trying to do their part in God's overall plan by demonstrating in their own lives the kind of sacrificial love Jesus showed by dying for us. The nonresistant Christian remembers how her own realization of the scope and depth of God's love transformed her life. She wants to be a visible reflection of that same love to those who would harm her.

The nonresistant Christian makes a powerful point. The church is God's body, the physical continuation of Jesus' ministry to every corner of the globe. If nonbelievers are going to understand the gospel message, they need to see it being lived out in the lives of believers. If Christians allow their lives to be governed by human pragmatism, the image of God will be obscured, not revealed. Jesus asked us not to resist the evil one, and to give our cloak as well when someone asks for our coat. How can we second-guess these instructions based on our human calculations about what will work? In doing so, say the nonresistant pacifists, we are making the same mistake Israel made when it insisted on a king—and his horses and chariots—for humanly pragmatic national defense rather than relying on our omnipotent, creative, and incredibly surprising God.

It is possible to read the Sermon on the Mount differently and still remain committed to pacifism. Why are we instructed to go two miles when the Roman guard asks us to go just one? The guard had the right under Roman law to insist that a civilian help him carry his pack one mile. If the follower of Jesus carried the pack only one mile, he would just be complying with an onerous and unfair civic duty as defined by those who had conquered his country. By going two miles, the Christian made it clear that his service was not just a way of complying with Roman law but was actually intended as service to the soldier himself. It was voluntary, even proactive, a way of loving the soldier by meeting his needs.

The *proactive* pacifist agrees with the nonresistant pacifist that his response to provocation must not sully the clarity of the gospel message—that God loves us enough to come and die for us. The proactive pacifist emphasizes her availability as one of God's tools to bring love tangibly into human lives. In this, the proactive pacifist provides a nice counterpoint to God's use of invaders as scourges: The proactive pacifist is, in a sense, one of God's own invaders, but this time to act as a gift of grace, bringing surprising mercy and service into the lives of oppressors and evildoers.

Neither the proactive nor the nonresistant pacifist can make the old Israelite mistake of relying on horses and chariots. Jesus urges us to be like the sparrows, ready for each day's miracles, not cowering in cages constructed out of our own worries and plans. God is still going to act in the old stunning ways and we don't want to mess up the plan by being an obstacle. The nonresistant pacifist tends to stay out of the way; the proactive tries to get into the way to help push along God's work. In neither case does the believer try to make the way, nor choose it—God is the main actor for all Christian pacifists.

Sometimes we will need to go two miles, or turn cheeks, or give cloaks and go practically naked. Other times we will need to give sermons, help heal wounds and diseases, or stay in jails even when the bonds have been broken (maybe even when those jails are in Kabul, and the accusation was evangelism, and the earthquake is the shock of a cruise missile). God's next move may be as surprising as any of these, and we have to be ready to hear our marching orders right away and get moving. And we do all these loving things even with those who have already killed our fellows and are threatening to kill us, too.

Furthermore, the pacifist Christian remembers some of the other lessons from the Sermon on the Mount. We are to pray for forgiveness and to forgive.[22] We are to seek out those who have grievances against us, and work at reconciliation.[23] We will always pray for those who wage war against us, celebrating God's grace which rains on the just and the unjust alike.[24]

So what do we learn from pacifists? They reinforce the holy warrior's lessons about radical dependence on God to direct the details of our operations and the need to be ready to learn about our own failings when we suffer the scourge of violent opposition. The pacifist adds a fundamental concern for the spiritual—and perhaps also the physical—needs of the opponent, even when he is a violent oppressor. We are to—

1. love our enemies, even the violent ones;
2. pray for our enemies, and celebrate the blessings God bestows on them and us alike;
3. forgive and seek forgiveness;
4. work sacrificially to ensure their needs are met.

Just war doctrine

Pacifism was the majority Christian view of war until the Roman Emperor Constantine converted to the faith in A.D. 312. It is hard to tell from this historical distance how long the transition took, but before long the majority of Christians had undergone their own "conversion" from pacifism to what eventually came to be articulated as the "just war" doctrine.

Pacifism, already a difficult ethic to live out, becomes even more so for a secular government official. The early Christians had the luxury of deciding only for themselves when they took on the risks of relying on God and not on weapons. If the local Roman governor executed them for their beliefs, or a passing army marauded through their households, it was the Christians' own loss.

But once Christianity reached the higher offices of the Empire, the luxury of nonresponsibility was gone. If Constantine had converted to pacifism, his apparent defenselessness would not have affected only him or his family. When a public official chooses a defensive strategy, she is choosing not only for herself, but for all the people she is supposed to defend.

Indeed, Constantine's conversion occurred on the eve of a decisive battle in one of the frequent civil wars of succession that beset the Empire in his day. Restoration of civil peace was Constantine's first great achievement. If Constantine considered adopting a pacifist stance, it must have seemed an impossible option. It could have exposed the entire empire to invasion or, more likely, the same kind of devastating civil war he was just about to end. Constantine's old duty to love his Roman neighbors, certainly endorsed by Christianity, would have seemed to be in serious tension with his new Christian duty to love his enemies, too.

The vast majority of public officials facing this dilemma have tried to choose the policy that seems most likely to "work" using the best advice they can get from human experts. In practice, as God predicted to Samuel so long ago, this means having to make plans in advance, anticipating the likeliest threats by studying neighboring powers, and preparing to meet them. So we come back to the seemingly universal rule of human governments: reliance on chariots and horses, or whatever is their contemporary equivalent. Radical direct dependence on God seems at least as foolish now as it did to Saul, or Constantine.

St. Augustine did much of the work of trying to find a way for political leaders to negotiate the dilemmas in love for enemies and neighbors. His solution has come down to us as the just war doctrine. Starting with the premise that there is a legitimate role for secular government in maintaining order and national security, Augustine worked out a set of guidelines for governments contemplating warfare. Various versions of these guidelines exist, but one of the classic versions lists seven factors for government leaders to consider before going to war:

1. Just cause. You can't have a just war if your reasons for fighting it are selfish or frivolous. War involves killing people. The Christian is never excused from the command to love his enemies. We can't start killing our enemies until we are clear that doing so is, on the whole, at least in some way an act of love for them as well as their victims. Here we stop the enemy from carrying out a program so evil he would be better off dead.

This is, of course, the root of the problem for pacifists, who generally cannot see how one can kill while loving. The just warrior understands the dilemma but insists that at times it is a loving act to kill someone to prevent her from committing a grave evil. At least it is a loving act toward potential victims of a menacing injustice, and maybe that is enough when someone in the grip of evil has forced us to choose between him and his victims. Yet even when we pull the trigger to kill the terrorist just before he kills innocent victims, we are to continue acting in genuine love for the terrorist.

2. Just motive. Anyone familiar with sibling rivalries will recognize that sometimes the "victim" of an injustice will cry "just cause" at the top of her voice, while inside she is rejoicing at the opportunity it offers to get back at her opponent. But "go ahead, make my day" is not a Christ-like utterance according to just war theory. Rage and revenge are destructive to both sides in a conflict; they form no part of loving one's enemies.

The war must be undertaken for just purposes, as well as out of just provocation. Wars of retribution don't pass this kind of muster, nor do wars of conquest. Many Christians balked at supporting the Mexican-American or Spanish-American wars once their expansionist aims became clear. Woodrow Wilson tried to make out a just war case for World War I by arguing it was a war to end all wars and make the world safe for democracy. George Bush the elder argued that the first Gulf War was needed to defend the principle that nations cannot make war on their neighbors to seize territory. His son described the anti-terrorist "war" as aiming at eliminating terrorism as a threat to peace and freedom anywhere. Reports circulated of meetings at which key defense department officials tried to sort out how just war doctrine might apply to the conduct of armed struggle in Afghanistan.[25]

Perhaps the acid test for just motive is this: Would this war be worth it if my side had nothing to gain, and had never been among those injured by the aggressor? And will my side forego any gain for its own particular interests when the war is done? These questions come into play in a complex way in the second war in Iraq. While the justification before the war emphasized the danger of weapons of mass destruction, the postwar rationale for the invasion sounded more like the U.S. really went to war on behalf of oppressed Iraqis—that is, that we should have been willing to invade even though we had nothing to gain directly in terms of our own security. It may be years before it is clear whether Americans and Britons have avoided the temptation to appropriate oil wealth to their own profit, which would undermine the altruistic rationale for the war.

3. *Just means.* How will the war be conducted? While just cause and just motive limit the initiation of a war, just means defines how far we can take it and how we go about it.

We can only conduct the war in ways proportionate to the cause. We can't drop a nuclear weapon on someone as a response to their seizure of hostages, for example. Nor can we invade their country and settle in for a long occupation. We have to take into account the disruption we will cause by our conduct of the war, including enemy casualties as well as our own. It does no good to respond to just cause with just motive and then end up doing more harm than good.

Also, when the just cause has been answered, and the just motives attained, the war must stop. George Bush senior seems to have been aware of this restraint in the Gulf War, when he halted the allied operation after the Iraqis were expelled from Kuwait and driven in disarray far enough into Iraq to eliminate any chance of a counterattack. The war's just cause was the prevention of expansion by conquest, and that goal had been achieved. Even though one could predict further trouble from Saddam Hussein if left in power, his regime's existence was not by itself just cause for a war to oust him, so trying to overthrow him was not just means.

George W. Bush seemed also to realize that the mere existence of Saddam Hussein was not enough to justify an invasion. He emphasized Hussein's lack of cooperation with weapons inspectors and his ambitions to acquire weapons of mass destruction. When Hussein persisted in obstructing inspections (according to the intelligence Bush reported using), just means extended to removing his regime so inspections would no longer be thwarted. At least this seems to have been the rationale.

Had the war been primarily justified from the outset on the basis of the oppressions carried out by the Hussein regime, perhaps the just means argument could have been stronger for the devastating violence the "Coalition of the Willing" used. Uprooting the elements of the regime that were oppressing Iraqis probably called for a more thoroughgoing campaign than would have been needed merely to change attitudes toward weapons inspectors.

4. *Last resort.* As an additional protection against forgetting our duty to love our enemies, war can only be undertaken as a last resort. Perhaps the evil threatened is so great that it would be a loving act toward our enemy to kill him to prevent him from doing such an enormous thing. But it is also loving to give the villain every chance to repent of his plans and swerve away from them.

The requirement of last resort is especially difficult in application. The passengers who attacked the hijackers on United

Flight 93 over Pennsylvania probably were pretty well within the scope of last resort. Once they knew of the attacks on the World Trade Center, they recognized the probable intent of their hijackers and that there was not likely anyone else who could do anything about it. From a just war perspective, it would have been best if these passengers had tried a non-lethal response first . . . and perhaps they did.

The "last resort" provision was designed to prevent wars in all but the rarest cases. Diplomacy, the ever increasing "arsenal" of nonviolent tactics, and so forth, extend the range of other resorts, which should be pushing war ever deeper into a true last resort status. But how can a responsible decision-maker know when the last resort line has finally arrived? There are always more nonviolent things you can try to do, even after it's really too late, because you don't always have the clear markers the passengers in Flight 93 had.

5. *Reasonable chance of success.* Even if the war is just in cause, motive, and conduct, it has to have a reasonable chance to succeed. There is no respect in just war theory for the lost cause. War kills. And it does much additional harm as well. If we have no chance of achieving our aims, we have no justification for adding to the world's sufferings. Surrender is better than useless resistance!

This sounds so offkey to American ears, attuned to "Never give up! Never surrender!" But if we start with an ethic of love for enemies, informed by the Sermon on the Mount's teaching that we meet our enemies' needs and accept suffering that may not be our due, then we can see the wisdom in abandoning the methods of killing when the cause has no reasonable chance to succeed. To impose suffering without real hope of gaining our goals is to forget people in the pursuit of ideas—i.e., to commit idolatry. Instead, under just war theory we should shift to accepting suffering in pursuit of our just goals.

Redemption's power is not ended by military defeat. We can still live our lives of discipleship, quietly or defiantly as God may lead, even under foreign occupation. The Hungarians surrendered in 1956, and the Czechs in 1968, and the Poles in 1980, preserving their nations from further devastation. People continued to live, albeit under repression. They were ready to seize the next opportunity in 1989 and finally achieve their liberation.

6. Legitimate authority. Under just war doctrine, only the legally authorized agencies of legitimate governments can initiate lethal violence. The crucial text supporting this view is Romans 13:1-5, where Paul asserts that the civil authorities are used—or perhaps even commissioned—by God to secure public order. The implication, according to just war thinking, is that God had given to the state a task denied to individuals: the power to use lethal violence when necessary for the public good. No private vendettas are justified, nor any illegal covert operations. Wars of rebellion are only justified when the existing authority has so corrupted its administration that, on the whole, it has ceased to be an improvement over anarchy. Just war doctrine does recognize state sovereignty, so traditionally there has been no requirement for international cooperation. How the modern activity of international agencies might affect this standard is unclear.

According to most just war thinking, once a legitimate government has assured itself that its actions fit the just war tests, Christians have a duty to support the government's efforts, including military service. Classically, the individual Christian doesn't have a role in determining which wars are just—the decision is, after all, to be made by an appropriate authority. Individual decisions don't have some of the safeguards available to government leaders, who should have more and better sources of information and, hopefully, communication with the foe. Out of love for our enemies, and for our neighbors who benefit when there are no ongoing violent vendettas, individuals cede war making power to the government exclusively.

Furthermore, according to Christian just war theory, it is not the Christian's place to resist the state's decision that violence is needed. Just as an individual cannot initiate lethal violence on her own, she cannot on her own refuse to join in lethal violence commissioned by a legitimate government, at least not when that government has tried to be faithful to just war standards in deciding to go to war. If preserving public order is exclusively the state's divinely appointed duty, it follows that citizens cannot justifiably refuse to cooperate with the task without defying God.

Modern Christians may differ with this view in part, arguing that each believer has responsibility to determine for himself whether a war is just. I suppose this idea would follow from suspicion that modern governments are not overly reliable in seeking out God's will or limiting themselves to just war constraints. The American government has so far disagreed, only offering conscientious objector status to those who oppose all wars. And according to strict just war principles, the government's position is the more easily defensible.

Part of making sure that war is under legitimate authority is making sure an adequate declaration of war outlines the grievances giving rise to the fighting. This public explanation of why the war is being undertaken allows other nations to scrutinize the bellicose nation's motives and methods, setting up a form of accountability. If the declaration of war does not state a just cause for the war, other nations may move toward military opposition, on their own just war grounds.

The other reason for requiring a declaration of war grows out of the principle of love for one's enemies. Just war allows for killing enemies but requires that the warrior give the enemy every opportunity to abandon its evil course of action that gives the war its justice. Declaring war formally notifies the enemy that attempts will soon be made to kill some of its members and perhaps to destroy the enemy as a political unit. This provides one last moment of grace, one more chance to repent before the job is undertaken.

The United States Constitution seconds this requirement by granting Congress the power to make war. Until the second half of the twentieth century, this provision operated in most of our country's foreign conflicts. In the last two generations, however, under pressure to allow the president to respond more quickly to the immediacy of modern threats, Congress has acquiesced in the obsolescence of the declaration of war. Nevertheless, before the first Gulf War, President Bush tried to lay out his case for the war (along just war lines, as it happened) and sought (and got) a congressional resolution authorizing the beginning of the allied counterattack against Iraq in Kuwait. This kind of procedure probably fulfilled the main goals of the requirement of a declaration of war.

7. *Noncombatant immunity.* Love for enemies means that we take risks on ourselves to avoid killing people who are not part of the fight. This means taking pains to keep our actions from

reaching civilians who are not members of the fighting machine—i.e., are not making, managing, or using weapons, or actively engaged in acquiring intelligence for those who do. If there are lethal spillover effects on civilians, they have to be minimized.

Some have argued that just war requires there be no "collateral damage" at all among civilians, but most just war theorists believe that the requirements are met as long as civilian casualties are kept to a minimum. Under either view, if too many civilians are dying, the war no longer fits the "just means" test, and tactics have to be altered, even if it means more casualties on our side. If we cannot conduct the war by just means, including noncombatant immunity, then the war cannot be fought. Or if minimizing civilian casualties means we can only fight the war justly in ways that eliminate a reasonable hope of success, the war cannot be fought.

This restriction gets more important and confusing as technology develops. For example, many Christians who otherwise subscribe to just war theory have concluded that there could be no just atomic war, because it would cause so many noncombatant casualties that it could not possibly be just. The same might be said for biological or chemical weapons of mass destruction.

Just war theory deserves respect even from those who disagree with it. Its proponents have done some careful thinking about how to resolve the dilemmas created when we are commanded to love our neighbors *and* our enemies. If just war criteria had been applied to every human war, there would have been many fewer wars, and the ones we have had would have been far less devastating. Perhaps with fewer and less frightful wars in our history, there would have been less alienation, and (for example) the world's second largest religion (Islam) would not have so many members tempted to hate the West. And perhaps there wouldn't have been such intensity in pursuit of greater lethality in weapons, and maybe we would not be facing the nightmare of nuclear destruction.

In fact, it is possible that just war ethics, even applied as unevenly as they have been, may have already had positive effects in reducing war's frequency and severity. Perhaps we are still here only because just war has taken some momentum out of the escalation of violence! Of course, this is hard to prove, since we cannot know how history would have been different. On the other hand, there are three problems with just war theory that do stand out: one *political*, one *practical*, and one *theological*.

The *political* problem is evidenced in the prevailing public debate each time America—or perhaps any country—considers going to war. Just war, to be internally valid, requires that the governing body makes its decisions with the just war criteria in mind. But the public discussion at times of war ranges widely, with hardly a reference to just war notions. Vengeance takes a prominent role. Enemy casualties weigh little in the public mind, at least compared to American lives. Swift, strong responses are valued, and the patient search for more loving alternatives is devalued if not ridiculed or deemed unpatriotic. If our leaders refer to just war criteria, it is more likely to be in defiance of rather than in response to, political pressure. At none of these points does American political culture cohere with just war criteria.

Instead of just war rhetoric, we seem to have a penchant for a sort of civil religion version of holy war talk. God somehow ends up on our side, endorsing what we are doing. The war pits good against evil, and with good on our side, any hesitation about means or methods is easily mistaken for lack of will to eliminate evil.

This leads us to the *practical* problem: Just war criteria don't seem to be reliable in diminishing the frequency of war and have also been disappointing in modulating its conduct. World War II and the first Gulf War are perhaps the only two of America's previous wars that could withstand just war scrutiny of the decision to go to war. All the other wars probably fail right at the outset—violence was hardly a last resort in any of them. In most of our wars, decision makers never made any careful reference to just war criteria. And even our most outstanding example of a "good" war—World War II—ended with the Allies joining their adversaries in the widespread targeting of civilians. The niceties of "just conduct" are hard to sustain when your people are dying and you could save some of their lives at the cost of faceless people in a foreign city.

Furthermore, as my colleague, historian Ralph Beebe, has often pointed out, in most of America's wars, both sides claimed to have God (or at least good) on their side.[26] This is most remarkable in our own Civil War, when religious leaders on both sides, with all apparent sincerity, assured their flocks that God smiled on their cause. But both sides can hardly have just cause, or even just motive, for their war effort. Just war is supposed to eliminate this problem but seems to fail at least half the time.

One suspects that human agents are as unreliable at judging their own cases when it comes to going to war as they are at judging their own cases in law or in athletic events. If there were an international just war tribunal, perhaps we could give just war criteria some teeth. But the international system, and the very notion of sovereignty which plays such an important part in just war theory, prevents us from resorting to neutral, dispassionate judgments about whether war is just. As long as we rely on passionate, aggrieved, pressured political leaders to judge their own cases, we are going to be disappointed in just war's ability to affect our war conduct.

In practice, then, just war opens the door to lethal violence, but once we get to the threshold, just war's careful criteria seem to give way to a different ethic. At best, while we espouse just war, we usually operate in some form of pragmatic cost-benefit ethic. At our best, we give some weight to the costs and benefits for everyone, including our enemies, but more often we only count the effects we expect (or fear) on our own people. The decision to war, and how to conduct ourselves in war, is usually based on what's in it for us or for our ideals. Human lives are reduced to a sort of currency, with American lives given high value and enemy lives heavily discounted—but all to be traded for something we might value more. With our dreams and way of life at stake, theories about just war don't deflect us very far once we get to the brink.

Finally there is a *theological* issue. Assuming for the moment (as many pacifists do not) that just warriors read Romans correctly, it does not comfortably follow that a Christian is to have two masters. That is, if it is true that the Christian, in her private life, is to turn her other cheek and love her enemy, does it seem likely that she should abandon that ethic in public life? Does she cease to be a disciple of Christ when she puts on her uniform? Can she wash her hands of the effects of her actions on the grounds that she was only doing the bidding of a secular state? Are the victims of her weapons less dead than they would have been had she shot them on her own authority? If there are two kingdoms—the private and devotional realm of the Sermon on the Mount and the secular violent one of the state—how can a Christian be an active adherent to both without compromising her single-minded devotion to Christ?

Yet just war theory has some consistent lessons for all Christians. We must be willing to take risks, to go to the last resort, out of love for our enemies. We must not make idols of ideas and ways of life, and hold them as more important than the souls of human beings. We can't succumb to the temptation to forget about our enemy's humanity even when his actions may give us just cause to kill him. We can't consign whole peoples to worthlessness because of evil done in their name by their leaders— our response should be tailored to save their lives even if it costs more of our own. And most importantly, decisions about national defense are not pragmatic matters, nor are they to be handed over to motives of vengeance or even heroism. Instead, they are to be subjected to divine standards, and taken in obedience to our best understanding of the will of God.

Summary: Lessons from Christian war ethics

Each of the theories we have looked at has its problems. Holy war would lead us to throw away all of war's "rules" and let anything go—but only insofar as God leads. And it makes modern security policy impossible, since it discourages humans from making preparations for war as if they knew in advance what tactics or strategy God would command them to use. Pacifism leaves national leadership in an awful tension, trying to love neighbors while also loving enemies. So far pacifists have not figured out how to have reliable national security policy without retaining the option of killing. Just war has a poor record in its goals of preventing nations from engaging in wrongful warfare and assumes that Christians may need to lead ethically bifurcated lives.

I am convinced we have not yet stumbled on God's final answer in the area of war ethics. But I am confident there is such an answer. An omnipotent, loving God would not leave us with permanently insoluble problems in such important ethical areas. Perhaps the answer will come when we better understand nonviolent methods of social control. Perhaps we will find ways to make just war calculation more reliable and binding on our actions, which would, of course, eliminate warfare among ethical nations (since it takes two to fight, and the side in the wrong would be prevented from fighting).[27] Perhaps we will find our way back into theocracy, and let God take control of our national defense. Or perhaps there is a new ethic to be developed that transforms our thinking in unforeseen ways.

We must be diligent in searching out God's will for us on warfare. We might start with the areas in which all three of these theories of war agree. In our intense debates over war ethics, we too often overlook the questions that really are already settled among us, regarding which we have already reached secure common ground. Consider these common themes in all three systems of Christian war ethics:

1. *We are never released from our Christian calling to love our enemies.* Whatever we do, their welfare (including their eternal souls) has to have full weight in our decisions, along with the welfare of their victims.

2. *We do not have the right to offer careless, vengeful, or enraged responses.* Patience to wait until God's way clearly opens is not too much to ask from those who love possible victims of war.

3. *When we are attacked, we must use it (in part) as an occasion for reflection.* God may be using the attack to chasten us for our injustice or disobedience. Or God may be calling us to undertake to meet the attackers' real needs, regardless of what they are asking us to do. Or we may be called to suffer as substitutes for our attackers, or even seek them out to offer and receive forgiveness. At least we must examine our motives and goals to ensure they are just, including subjecting them to the scrutiny of others.

4. *In everything, we must be wide open to God's creativity.* At least in our personal lives, according to both holy war and pacifism, the proper response is to renew our sense of radical obedience to whatever God may have in store, striving to prevent our preconceptions (and our investment in them) from blinding us to what God has in mind. Even as a nation, even under just war thinking, we need to be sure we have exhausted God's surprising creativity before we prematurely declare "last resort" and kill people who should be living out full lives with every opportunity to know and serve God.

Chapter 5

....

If Not War, What? Tools for Christian Peacemakers

Our study of Christian doctrines about war revealed areas of consensus but didn't go as far as we might like toward inspiring creative, positive suggestions about where we might look expecting to find nuggets of God's direction for these times. So now we begin a positive search for ideas about how we can do our part as believers to contribute to the elimination of terrorism and the relief of political misery in ways that leaven the worldwide struggle with the love of God and its attendant hope.

I am still mindful of God's grumpy comments about ancient Israel when it insisted on a human king. I think we should scout around for ideas, but we have to avoid coming to rely on our own cleverness and creativity (or worse, pet notions) rather than God's surprising on-the-spot leadership. I am working here toward brainstorming a sizable list of promising ideas for what we can do to fight terrorism and political misery while loving the terrorist and the tyrant and their victims. But the list we come up with has to be seen as a sort of rough draft, an attempt to see through a glass darkly toward what God might actually lead us to do.

We aren't going to reason our way reliably all the way to God's will, only to an attitude of waiting and expectation for it, and a place where we are as ready as we can be to leap on God's Word for us when it comes. We may stumble directly onto something God would like us to do, or thrash around in the bushes

95

somewhere near God's will, or maybe just thrash around in the bushes. The moment must come, however, when we can hear God speaking through all our chatter, including the chatter in this book.

I recommend, then, that you read what I have written with a certain reserve, listening the entire time for God's direct nudging in your ribs. Even better, take ideas this book inspires to a group of believers you trust, and ask them to help you discern the actual will of God for you. For some of us, at least, the actual command direct from God will be a lot farther from conventional thinking than anything I mention as a possibility.

We don't have to start from scratch in this search for ideas. Quaker peacemakers John and Diana Lampen suggest three different approaches we can take to a conflict if we want to help build toward peace. Veteran church consultant C. Douglas Lewis describes three levels at which we might address a conflict. And Quaker economist Kenneth Boulding identifies three different types of influence people use in conflicts, each of which can be drawn on by peacemakers to transform conflict into something constructive. Since we will be using each of these ideas in our discussion of terrorism and political misery, let us spend a little time now exploring them and making an initial estimate of how they can help build peace.

Three Angles for Promoting Peace

When John and Diana Lampen moved from England to Northern Ireland to find ways to work for peace there, they faced a daunting task. The conflicts ran deep among those loyal to the British government, mostly Protestants, and those who considered themselves Irish, mostly Catholic. Issues were very complicated, given the hundreds of years of history that lay beneath the late twentieth-century dynamics in the region, and relationships among members of the two communities were strained, often to the point of violence. Where could two well-meaning but unknown English Quakers find a way to make any difference?

The Lampens recognized that the Northern Irish conflict offered three broad avenues for possible action, each tied to a particular aspect of the conflict. For example, one might try to address the *issues* over which the two sides were disputing.

Should Northern Ireland be attached to Britain, or to Ireland? Should changes be made in how the Catholic minority was treated by the Protestant majority, and vice versa? What sort of government structure should Northern Ireland have? Should various groups be permitted to hold marches that tended to inflame other groups?

All these and many more were questions people in Northern Ireland debated. Perhaps someone could intervene in these matters and help the parties develop ideas and negotiate agreements to resolve them. If this were possible, it would be crucial work, since it would help the people in Northern Ireland remove many of the points of irritation between them.

But discussing issues was difficult if not impossible in Northern Ireland. People did not trust one another. Many leaders on each side didn't even know important people on the other side. Even among ordinary people, relationships across party lines were scarce. Perhaps the Lampens could do their best work by helping build more and healthier *relationships* between Catholics and Protestants. Better relationships could help lead to more productive discussions of issues.

Of course, the opposite is true, too—progress on issues could help improve relationships and make further progress easier. However, a third factor came into play here, to complicate matters: The way in which each side went about trying to achieve its goals had a powerful effect on relationships and even tended to create new issues and color the old ones. Some of the Northern Irish conflict was being waged with violence. Irish Republican Army members might set off a bomb; Protestant hardliners might respond with violence; the British troops posted in Northern Ireland might also play a violent role. In addition to violence, other destructive tactics were used, including intimidation, discrimination, dehumanizing rhetoric and behavior, and more. Perhaps the Lampens could be of help by helping the parties create better *processes* to confront each other in more constructive and nonviolent ways.

Borrowing from the Swedish peace scholar Johan Galtung, the Lampens came to think of their peacemaking options as falling at the three points of a triangle, as depicted below:

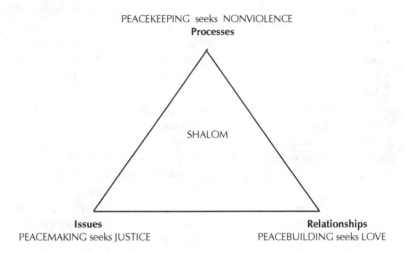

PEACEKEEPING seeks NONVIOLENCE
Processes

SHALOM

Issues   **Relationships**
PEACEMAKING seeks JUSTICE   PEACEBUILDING seeks LOVE

The Lampens used different terms to describe what they were doing when at work on each of these three angles of the conflict. When they worked to help develop improved processes for managing the conflict and having the parties deal with each other, they considered themselves *peacekeepers*. As peacekeepers, they were trying to avoid violent, alienating approaches to the conflict, pushing instead for nonviolent tactics.

When the Lampens focused on fostering improved relationships across partisan lines, they considered themselves to be *peacebuilders*, in that they were building the conditions for productive processes and sustainable resolution of both current and future issues that might come up in the Northern Ireland community.

And when occasions arose in which they could help the parties sort through issues and find good solutions, they thought of themselves as *peacemakers*, since they were helping the parties work out the terms for their future together.

Peacekeeping to improve conflict processes might focus on nonviolence. Sometimes this might involve finding ways to separate fighting parties, at least until they can cool down. Or, if enemies won't disengage, perhaps all the peacekeeper can do is monitor the fighting, and report on what it sees, as a way of trying to keep things from escalating any further. But when a peacekeeper's work can be more constructive, he might find himself looking for methods of dealing with the conflict that emphasize resolving issues on their merits, or by developing free and informed consent among the parties to the dispute. She might advocate mediation, elections, constructive negotiations, joint projects, or the like. The UN has done much peacekeeping, separating warring factions and helping them find ways to move forward in resolving disputes. NATO forces in Bosnia have played a similar role. A parent who sends sparring children to their separate rooms is being a peacekeeper.

Peacemakers working directly on the issues help the parties find just and enduring solutions to the questions that divide them. Peacemakers might help research conditions on the ground, brainstorm ideas, convene negotiations, or even draft possible agreements for the parties to comment upon. When President Clinton tried to help Israel and Palestine work out the boundaries of a Palestinian state in East Jerusalem, he was playing the role of peacemaker as the Lampens would define it. The same might be said for President George W. Bush when he promoted the multilateral roadmap for how the Israelis and Palestinians could make progress toward a final agreement and peace.

Peacebuilders work to establish human connections among disputing parties. Dehumanization and demonization are routine in serious disputes. Peacebuilders might begin by helping each side see the humanity in the other, to help each empathize with (that is, understand the point of view of) the other. Trust and cooperation are major goals for peacebuilders. But for Christians, the ultimate objective includes repentance, forgiveness, reconciliation, compassion, and even love between the (soon-to-be) former enemies.

Of course, these three aspects of the conflict overlap, and they affect each other. Trust helps reduce the appeal of violence. On the other hand, trust does not grow at gunpoint. Finding a just and acceptable solution to part of a conflict helps disputants empathize with and trust one another. Working for methods of addressing conflicts on their merits both diminishes the incidence of violence and increases the chance of achieving justice.

The ideal situation is often having peacemakers working from all three angles at once. Then improving relationships can strengthen constructive processes and help generate richer, more creative, and fairer ideas for resolving disputed issues. And with enough people involved in promoting peace, perhaps all three angles could be addressed in a coordinated way. But even if this is not possible, even if only one or a few are working for peace, the Lampen's model has a big advantage: It clarifies that good work can be done even by those who only have access to one of the angles of the conflict. If I know people on each side of a dispute, I can do things to help build stronger, humanized, empathetic relationships even if I can't do anything else. And this work, as modest as it may be, is still important and useful in helping the disputing parties move toward peace.

The Lampens' adaptation of Galtung's model has some important and exciting implications for Christians. For one thing, taking all three aspects of our peace work together—nonviolence, love, and justice—the entire model resonates very strongly with the biblical concept of *shalom*. Although we traditionally translate shalom as "peace," the biblical concept is much richer than any of the meanings of the English word. Shalom certainly invokes an expectation of nonviolence, of course. But nonviolence by itself is a sort of pasteboard peace. One could almost "make a desert and call it peace"[28] if absence of violence was the only criterion. This simple form of peace, marked by the absence of killing, might be called "irenic" peace, after the Greek word used in some New Testament passages.

The Old Testament Hebrew concept of shalom goes much further. It includes justice and right relationships in its vision for human communities. A shalomic peace adds to nonviolence notions of reconciliation, righteousness, harmony, and faithfulness to God's moral law. To get to shalom, we need work on all three of the aspects of conflict in the Lampens' model—violence has to be replaced with a rich array of nonviolent processes; hatred and dehumanization must give way to reconciliation and love; and contest over issues must move toward just outcomes. This is why I put the word *shalom* at the heart of the triangle.[29]

The Three Levels of Human Behavior

People do not act at random. If we want to understand human behavior and have a chance to change it, we have to grasp a simple concept: People act for reasons that seem good to them.

This is not really a new insight. Since the Enlightenment in Western thought, leading theorists have repeatedly made this point in some way or another. Some have begun with the assumption that humans are rational, and can be relied upon to make the choice that most benefits them. This was the working assumption for many as far back as the eighteenth century. Adam Smith assumed people would be rational actors when he described how the market is a powerful tool for harnessing greed to do good.[30] James Madison had in mind a similar mechanism in arguing for the different levels of government and separation of powers built into the American governmental system in the Constitution he helped write.[31] The assumption carries down to today, in a variety of disciplines, including (for example) modern economics, and the game theory approach to understanding human behavior.[32]

I am uncomfortable with the notion that humans always act rationally. Maybe this is just because I myself don't always do the sensible thing! But I do think we can safely say that humans nearly always act purposefully. That is, our behavior is goal-oriented. Roger Fisher and William Ury distill this more realistic approach to human rationality in their leading works on negotiation.[33] They start with the observation that behind every position a person may take in a dispute lies a set of interests that drive and explain that position.

This point was made even better by C. Douglass Lewis.[34] He uses the following diagram to give a basic and simplified explanation of human action:

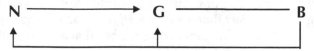

Here, B stands for behavior. Behaviors are all outward manifestations of human conduct, including actions, words, and so forth. G stands for goals. Goals are the immediate or direct motivations for the behavior. If you were to ask someone, "Why did you do that?" she would probably respond by describing a goal. We might want to include "fears" as a recognition that many goals are in the negative. People often act to stop the unfolding of something they don't want, rather than to bring about something they do want to happen.

So far Lewis' model looks much like Fisher and Ury's. But Lewis does not assume that all motivations are equal. Underlying the goals that directly drive behaviors are needs, the underlying basic requirements of human existence. These are identified in the diagram with the initial N. The difference between needs and goals is subtle. Needs are the most basic of human motivations. They are essentially noncritiquable. That is, one could not select an alternative to the need identified. Goals, on the other hand (as well as fears), can be critiqued. They still need justification, which people might debate. One could possibly select other goals, or could learn new goals that are improvements over current goals. Not so with needs.

Here is an example. Imagine that we are roommates. I am trying to sleep while you are trying to study. Our behaviors (B) are in conflict. I ask you to turn off the light or quit typing on your computer. This is also a "B" on my part, embodied in a position I am taking, a demand I am making—you should stop studying. Your studying is a behavior, and if you resist my suggestion that you stop, your resistance is also a behavior. So might be your snide comments about my being so lazy.

Behind both of our actions lie goals (and fears). I want to get some rest, maybe because I had a late night the night before. You are hoping for a really good grade. You may worry about whether you can stay in school. I might be worried about getting sick. If we each succumb to the temptation to treat the other's behavior as the problem, we are in for a nasty fight. But if we can recognize the goals and fears involved, we have a much better chance of finding a constructive solution. For one thing, the mere fact that we give weight to each others' motivations and desires is a humanizing act, one that inspires trust and gives a good basis for creativity.

But my desire to sleep in and your desire to get a good grade are not the fundamental needs in this situation. We can still ask "why" of each other when we express these desires. Even your fear of flunking out of school, and my fear of getting sick, are open to investigation. We may be unrealistic in our fears. But underneath these motivations are some basics that are not open to question. You cannot very well say to me, "Ron, your life would go so much more smoothly, and you'd get so much more done, if you'd just kick that sleep habit of yours! Think of all the extra time you'd have each day if you stopped sleeping." I cannot legitimately say to you "You don't need an education. Literacy and all that is not what it's cracked up to be." When we get down to those fundamentals, the things about which there really is no debate, we have reached the level of needs.

Lewis' model also includes arrows pointing from B back toward N and G. These represent the internal feedback loops we use to roughly assess how well our behaviors are doing at serving our goals and needs. In theory, if we are perfectly rational beings, we will recognize when our behavior is leaving us short of these objectives, then we will adjust the behavior until the results are more to our liking. But Lewis does not assume perfect rationality. He recognizes that often our self-assessment and feedback loops are sloppy. We misperceive our needs, we don't fully recognize or articulate our goals and fears, and we frequently misjudge how well our behaviors are tuned to meeting our objectives. This might be due to sin, or to pathology in our mental health or personality, or even to just being too busy to spend enough time in personal reflection and prayer.

Nevertheless, this model predicts that once a behavior has achieved some stability in our lives, it is probably due to an internal feeling that it is in some sense "working" for us. *Tried and true behavior is stable behavior*. On the other hand, when someone else threatens our ability to continue in stable behaviors, we feel the threat going more deeply than just the behavior itself. The needs and goals (or fears) to which it is linked are also at risk if we suddenly have to cease one behavior and adopt another. *Imposed behavior is unstable behavior*, since it is unlikely to connect with our internal feedback about what works for us. If you have ever tried to repeatedly force a child to do something he doesn't want to do, you know firsthand what Lewis is talking about here.

If I force you to stop studying, the outcome will be expensive. Your internal feedback, not recognizing the imposed behavior as meeting your needs, will bring about psychological pressure on you to resume your studying habits at the first opportunity. This urge will be reinforced by any feeling you may get that my unilateral imposition of my will on your life, if it turns into a pattern, will leave you with untold numbers of other goals unmet and fears in fruition. The issue can easily take on symbolic importance for you, related to your entire well-being and your ability to find a place in our relationship where you will be okay in the long run. Every time I succeed in forcing my will on you, your *personal powerbase*—your sense of security that you will be okay in the end—erodes. More and more of your internal feedback will be raising alarms. Your incentive to defy my orders will grow.

If I want to keep my will imposed on you, I am going to have to spend effort and resources. I will have to police you, monitoring your actions and suppressing revolts. You will have to spend extra energy finding ways to cope or to rebel. Ultimately we could descend to becoming pathological adversaries, expending huge amounts of time and energy in our battle for dominance.

But all is not lost. Having warned us against blithely assuming that forcing new behaviors on others is a quick and effective way to proceed, the N-G-B model suggests more promising avenues for reaching agreements in times of conflict. If I avoid exercising pure coercion, and instead spend some energy up front listening to you until I get a good sense of what are your needs, fears, and goals; and if you come to see that I take those motivations seriously and am working in good faith to find ways to meet them while also meeting my own, our dispute over study and sleep times does not need to take on overtones of vast personal threat. You will be affirmed as a person of worth to me largely to the degree that I convey to you that your needs and goals matter to me, and that I am unwilling to leave you without means to meet your needs.

At the behavior and goal levels, this might mean we discuss alternatives. A cooperative creative process, where both sides' needs and goals are held high, and both sides' behaviors (and possibly goals) are up for discussion, allows us to proceed with our personal powerbases intact, and thus without anxiety. Lowered anxiety helps us perceive one another more accurately, frees up creativity in looking at alternatives and creating new ones, and allows us to make more realistic assessments of our own behaviors, goals, and needs. In other words, when needs and goals are taken seriously by both sides, conflict can become both a wonderful learning experience, helping us to adapt better to our environments, and a trust-building example of interpersonal integration. We can come out of such conflicts closer, with relationships stronger and more resilient in the face of future stresses.

The N-G-B model accommodates us when we approach conflicts from other angles. For example, one fruitful way to look at the dynamics of conflicts is in terms of social *narratives*. Human groups tend to develop mythologies. That is, to explain to themselves who they are and why they do things the way they do, humans in groups tell each other stories. These explanatory stories may be objectively true, or they may be fictions (either "true fictions" that accurately represent how the world works, like Jesus' parables, or "false fictions" that do not). Whichever they are, the group uses them to understand itself and its values.

If we assign "narratives" to the intermediate level of human motivation, as a compilation of a group's fears and goals, we can immediately see their power in driving human behavior. The narratives themselves structure a group's internal feedback. People consult the narratives as they try to determine if behaviors are working or not. To the degree that the narratives (and the myths embedded in them) are in some sense "true," they probably will not mislead the group. But false myths and dysfunctional narratives can lead groups seriously astra, and tragically complicate the process of resolving conflicts, whether within the group or in relation to outside groups.

To discern whether narratives are functional for groups, then, we have to get below and behind them, to the *merits* of the situation. Just as goals represent attempts to translate needs into action plans, narratives represent attempts to embody the merits of a group's position, or even to dress up as merits things that might not be. If I tell myself that I am a weak person, in need of extra sleep, and that others cannot reasonably demand of me the kind of energy or wakefulness most people have, I have created for myself a narrative. It expresses and explains my goals and fears surrounding the issues of sleep, industriousness, and possibly even underachievement. If you challenge my sleeping patterns, and my overall lack of productivity, I will defend myself with some part of my narrative. The only way to get beyond such a defense, and in the process to take my needs and goals seriously, is to work with me to explore the merits of my narrative.

Do I really have some kind of condition that requires of me more sleep than others get? Have I ever experimented with going to bed at a regular time? Eating right? Getting good exercise? These and many other questions might be fruitfully investigated in a noncoercive environment.

Of course, if I am seven years old and you are my mother working on your doctoral dissertation, we might conclude that my self-narrative is badly out of whack, and you should coerce me into going to be at a reasonable hour. We might trust parents to do better than most at understanding their children and prescribing sound solutions for them. On the other hand, if we are both adults, or even in some cases if you are a parent and have not given me the attention I need (and so are less likely to hit on just the right coercive solution to meet my needs), some kind of process that explores things on their *merits* is warranted. Or, to put the case slightly differently, a process based on our mutual *consent* is more likely to take full account of both our needs than is an outcome imposed by one of us on the other.

Before we update our model of conflict, I want to point out one other deep implication in Lewis' approach to human behavior. I have already discussed the kinds of conflicts that arise between one person's goals and behaviors and another person's goals and behaviors. But I have left unaddressed the possibility that two people's needs might be in conflict. This would be the kind of situation where, for one person to get basic, appropriate needs met, someone else will have to go without having equally vital needs met.

I have a basic faith problem here. I believe in a loving omnipotent God. I am not alone in this belief—it forms a basic pillar in the theology of all three great monotheistic faiths, Judaism, Christianity, and Islam. If God is loving, what does this mean? Can it mean anything less than that God wants all of us to have means to meet our needs? I think we might with good reason make a much more expansive claim about God's love, all the way up to desiring for each of us "life and more abundantly" as promised in Scripture.[35] But for now I would like to stick to the minimum: God, out of love for us, wants each of us to have means to meet our needs.

What does it mean if God is omnipotent? Again, we might want to say that God makes everything happen, as some Christians do. Being all powerful certainly includes the possibility of making everything happen. However, as I understand the faith, humans are in God's image, and thus also are free moral agents. That means we are capable of choosing things God does not want, and of accomplishing at least some small things on our own power. So I don't hold that God makes everything happen. But certainly an omnipotent God *could* make anything happen, consistent with God's own character. God has the power, then, to make happen anything that fits the divine will. And if God wants all of us to have means to meet our needs, then God has the power to make that happen.

In other words, with an omnipotent loving God in the picture, it is always possible for all of us to have means to meet our needs. God, if no one else, knows of a way to make it happen. No matter how badly we disappoint God, no matter how massively we fail, God is sill omnipotent, and still loves us. God is, to say the least, resourceful.

For a believer in an omnipotent loving God, it follows that there can never really be an irreconcilable conflict at the level of basic needs. God knows a way, so one exists, whereby everyone can have means to meet their needs. I do recognize there is much evidence that people do not always have means to meet their needs. People die horribly, they suffer basic deprivation. Some people are chronically in a condition of need. All of us at some time or other experience at least temporary lack of access to things we would have to call basic and appropriate needs.

So I admit deprivation happens. But I deny that it is ever necessary. If humans could stumble into the path God knows exists, needs would always have a supply. Obviously this is a stark faith statement. It does not follow inevitably from the Lewis model of human behavior. One has to have a firm faith in the existence of a loving omnipotent God. But if one does, then it seems to me the conclusion is inescapable: in any human conflict, there is always *hope* for all sides. There is a way, it is available to us, for all to have means to meet their needs—or even, if your faith is greater than mine, for all to have life abundant.

I recognize that not all readers will agree with me about this unshakable hope. I have lived a relatively privileged life, spared all but a small amount of the vast scope of human suffering. It is easy for me to say there is always hope, there is no necessary conflict among human needs. If I did not have faith in a loving omnipotent God, I don't see how it would be possible to arrive at this faith. (Here is one of those places where belief makes an unmistakable and radical difference in one's life!) Some readers may not have this faith about God. Others may, but still may disagree, perhaps because of all the suffering that does exist.

Nevertheless, even if ultimately there can be cases where despair is in order, at least believers in God should be the last ones on the scene to abandon this kind of hope. Christians bring many things to conflicts, but one of the most valuable is hope. With hope, it is easier for people to maintain a personal power-base, a conviction that they will come out okay. With hope, then, it is easier for people to listen to one another; to take the risk of taking their opponents' needs, fears, and goals seriously; to question and revise their own narratives; to see the world around them more accurately and spot more of the creative opportunities that lead to God's paths through the conflict. So I invite those who are ultimately skeptical about my conviction that it is always possible to find means to meet needs, to at least go with me this far: In more cases than we are likely to imagine, even when all who are in the situation seem to have every reason to despair, hope has its reasons, and those who hold it high are doing God's work.

Now we are ready to tinker with our model, to reflect some of the value that the N-G-B model brings to our understanding:

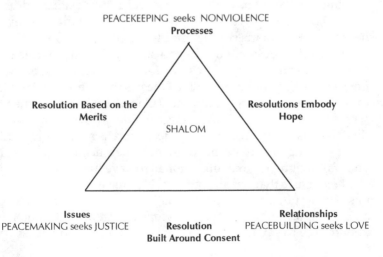

PEACEKEEPING seeks NONVIOLENCE
Processes

Resolution Based on the Merits

SHALOM

Resolutions Embody Hope

Issues
PEACEMAKING seeks JUSTICE

Resolution Built Around Consent

Relationships
PEACEBUILDING seeks LOVE

The Three Faces of Power

C. Douglas Lewis encourages us to be skeptical of coercive solutions to conflicts, because they are unlikely to result in behaviors that match people's internal feedback, and thus are unstable and expensive to maintain (and unlikely to be based on the merits of the case, or on parties' consent). Then what can peace workers do?

First, let us not too hastily dismiss constructive uses of coercion. For example, in cases where people have made clear that they do not give weight to the effects of their actions on others, coercion may be required to protect innocent people from predators. The police are an example, as are criminal and civil courts. Where coercion is a tactic in an overall strategy of deciding things on their merits, according (for example) to the rule of law democratically enacted, it can be an important tool for peacemaking and peacekeeping.

Physically restraining an angry person, or interposing between fighting parties, are mild forms of coercion, since they are attempts to impose on someone a restraint on their action that they would not otherwise accept. Economic sanctions, including boycotts, strikes, and embargos, are often coercive, although it is possible to cast them in such a way that they are not purely coercive. Many forms of coercion would not be considered violence, any more than restraining a child from running into the street. Police work is a mixed case, since violence is sometimes required of almost all modern police officers.

But coercion is not the only, nor maybe even the most effective, way of influencing others to change their behavior. The late Quaker economist Kenneth Boulding gives us some hints about where to look for alternative strategies.[36] He points out that *coercion*—the medium in which armies work—is not the only way we influence each other. In fact, humans spend only a small fraction of their energy trying to influence one another through coercion. Although we often instinctively think otherwise, coercion is only one of at least three possible mediums of influence, or as Boulding puts it, one of three faces of power.

Most of our time and energy is spent relating to each other on the bases of two noncoercive types of influence. For example, we spend much more of our time trying to buy others' cooperation than merely force it. We offer things they want to get what we want, seeking mutual consent for mutually beneficial *exchange*. Many of these exchanges occur in market-like situations and can be thought of as commercial transactions. But exchange also happens in politics, where competing interest groups make mutually beneficial deals so that each can get some of what it wants. Politicians in democracies offer their best efforts for their constituents in exchange for votes. Families use exchange to agree on how to allocate chores, neighbors swap tools, friends reciprocate with invitations to dinner: the opportunities for mutually beneficial, consensual exchanges are almost infinite.

Boulding noted that exchange has some serious advantages over coercion as a way to get things done. For one thing, maintaining control over others' behavior through coercion can be very expensive compared to voluntary cooperation bought through exchange: the coercer suffers a constant drain on resources to maintain the apparatus of coercion. Governments relying too much on coercion to secure citizen compliance are weakened thereby, tottering on the edge of nonviability, as all the communist regimes in central Europe suddenly discovered in 1989. The same discovery awaits a youth soccer coach who tries to force a dozen of his eight-year old charges to run a drill in which they have no interest.

Another advantage of exchange is that it leads participants into *positive sum transactions*. Coercion often is a zero-sum transaction. We call these episodes "win/lose" competitions, because one side's gains are at the cost of the other side's losses. If we fight over the last cupcake, only one of us can win. Every bit of cupcake I take for myself is equal to the cupcake you lose for yourself.

Not all coercive transactions are zero-sum, win/lose affairs. When the parent keeps the toddler out of the street, both sides gain. But because coercion between adults is often resolved with no regard to the merits of the situation, very often coercion results in a negative-sum outcome. That is, either both sides lose, or the gains of one side are smaller than the losses on the other. One would think that rational people would stay out of negative sum conflicts, since the losing parties would always be better off making a deal with the winning parties to minimize their losses. But in real life there are a lot of barriers to making such deals in a coercive environment, both practical and sometimes moral, as we shall see when we discuss whether one should ever give in to a terrorist.

When we move into the realm of exchange, however, we avoid most of the danger of negative sum, lose-lose transactions. Because exchange is based on exercise of each party's free will, and can only happen when both parties consent, exchange offers the promise of positive sum win-win outcomes. Both sides are better off when you enter the store and buy a gallon of milk. As long as the transaction is voluntary and thus consensual on both sides, your willingness to buy the milk is based on your estimate that you are better off with it than with the money. And the store owner's willingness to sell the milk means she is better off with the money than with the milk. Because resources are finite and not uniformly spread among the population, the opportunities for mutually beneficial exchange are practically infinite.

Although some people disagree—notably egoists who believe all our actions are self-interested—Boulding says that coercion and exchange are not the only ways we try to influence each other. Much of what we do for others requires no coercion against us and doesn't even need to be bought. Sometimes we do things for people because we care about them as people—we identify with them, we give them power over us by making them important to us. This is the dominant means of influence in families, where children lack coercive power and have almost nothing with which to exchange, and yet are able to secure the help, attention, and devotion of their parents at levels unreachable by anyone outside the family.

Boulding sometimes called this form of influence "affiliation power," but he also referred to it as "love." Each term seems to identify a different aspect of the phenomenon. When Michael Jordan's face goes on a cereal box, people are induced to buy it because they want to identify with Jordan, that is, to affiliate with his skill and charisma. But we might more easily call it love when a World Trade Center office worker stays behind with a wheelchair-bound colleague even though it is likely to mean his death. Both affiliation and love are on display when Americans proudly raise their flags and hearty cheers in honor of New York firemen and common passengers on United Flight 93.

Those of us who belong to churches should find the power-ful mix of exchange and affiliation/love a familiar one. We pick churches to attend, often, with exchange in mind—will the pastor's sermons be worth my time? Will the youth program provide what my children need? Then as we get to know people and move from newcomer to insider, we begin to care about our brothers and sisters in the congregation. Prayer requests flow from the phone through our quiet times, and we attach to people's faces. The day comes when someone in the congregation is in trouble, and we can't stand not to help. We still might complain about the style of music on Sunday morning, trying to nudge our chorus-besotten worship leaders to let us sing more hymns with parts[37], but once we get inside that warm community, its members have power over us far beyond the value of resources we can ever expect from them.

Note that as we move along the spectrum of human influence from coercion through exchange to affiliation, we encounter many situations in which the faces of power are mixed. When I vote, I am participating in an exchange with candidates, in a sense: my support in exchange for their promises, both to support certain policies, and to do their best for the polity. In another sense, I am exerting coercive power, since my vote (in combination with others) can keep someone from taking office. In still another sense I am involved in a vast affiliative exercise, as I and my fellow citizens renew our commitment to the welfare of our country, state, and communities.

We also note that the tenor of the relationship necessary for each face of power changes as we move along the spectrum. Coercion is based on a balance of power and requires very little if any understanding among the parties. Exchange requires that I at least recognize one need or goal you have and that I tailor my actions toward meeting that objective on terms that make you better off. Affiliation demands even more—at least a level of identification that approaches empathy. In many cases of affiliation, the influence is based on intimate familiarity with, and tenderness for, one another.

The most powerful person in my life right now is my wife. I am bigger and stronger (although she is faster), but coercion plays almost no role in our life. We do make deals with one another, explicit and implicit, so that consensual exchanges of resources play a complex and important role in our relationship. But if one of us were to be crippled so as to be unable to contribute much to the support of the other, that person's power would hardly be diminished. In fact, the other one of us would probably find that the impaired one took even more time and attention than before the accident, and might even be irritated from time to time by how much the injured one's needs dominated her or his life. This is because affiliation at a deep and powerful level is the dominant feature in how we, like spouses everywhere, influence each other.

Reflecting on Boulding, we see immediately that warfare isn't the only coercive option available to us. Something on the order of law enforcement also invokes coercion but vastly deemphasizes its lethality and indiscrimination. We also might begin to wonder, however, if the doors marked "exchange" which open onto democratic politics and markets, and the ones marked "affiliation/love" which open onto families and communities, might themselves serve as gateways to opportunities in the fight against terrorism.

The Alternatives to War

Already we have seen enough to hint at the possibility that there are many ways to counteract terrorism firmly, relentlessly, and effectively. We can approach the problem from one or more of three angles—process, relationships, and issues. We can address the problem at any of three levels—the surface level of actions and demands; the intermediate level of goals, fears, and narratives; or the fundamental level of needs—that is, the true merits of the situation. We can redress wrongs and restrain wrongdoing with coercion, exchange, and affiliation. Combinations among all these options are possible, giving us wide scope for creativity as we seek out God's preferred path.

With so many rich possibilities before us, we can bring to bear some of the deepest and strongest themes of our faith. We will build our response to terrorism and political misery on a foundation of careful listening, to each other and to God's will, and energized by the hope we have from our faith in a loving omnipotent God. Our approach will focus on nonviolence, justice, and love. Our work will buttress righteousness and the rule of law on one hand, and repentance, forgiveness, and reconciliation on the other. The entire project is directed toward seeking out truth and building a beloved community in the highest meaning of shalom.

Does all this sound too idealistic? If we stopped here, then it would be hard to rebut such a charge. These are Christian ideals, surely, but they are little more than that . . . so far. We now turn to the task of fleshing out these dreams, exploring how to put practical feet to Christian ideals in the struggle against terrorism, tyranny, and other forms of political misery.

Chapter 6

···

Corrosive Grievance: The Spiritual Side of Terrorism, Part I

We are looking, now, for practical steps we can take to follow Jesus and respond to terrorism and tyrants and their newly global reach. We have defined terrorism, explored the main varieties of political misery, consulted Christian ethics about war, and drawn from the wisdom of people with rich experience in human conflict. To put these insights to practical work, we need to understand not only what terrorism is, but how it is linked to political misery.

Our response to terrorism can't be developed in the abstract. If it is, we are likely to find that, even where we manage to suppress or deflect terrorism, we don't really eliminate it. Instead we may spatter it, sending it cropping up all over. Someone else in another place or time will pay for our failures. Only by correctly analyzing the factors that bring about terrorism can we be confident that our responses are well-designed to remedy the problem.

In fact, as we shall see, when we correctly analyze terrorism's sources, we will find that terror and political misery are closely related. Tyrants, anarchists, and officials on the take all breed terrorism.

In the next four chapters we will look at terror and its roots in political misery by focusing in turn on each of four key factors that give terrorism its energy. Terrorism has both a spiritual and a political dynamic, each of which has an experiential and a responsive dimension. That is, terrorism has its spiritual roots in a sense of *corrosive grievance*, and practical political roots in an experience of *political despair*. The terrorist responds to corrosive grievance by slipping into *dehumanizing hatred*. She responds to despair over her ability to exercise political influence by *embracing the myth of effective violence*.

I explain each of these four elements in opening each of the following chapters. For now let me offer a simple summary of the dynamic that drives terrorism: The terrorist, nursing a corrosive grievance against a dehumanized enemy and despairing of political effectiveness, puts faith in the effectiveness of violence to remedy or avenge the grievance.

Starting at terrorism's taproot—the sense of grievance—in each of the next four chapters we will first do our best to describe how the element arises, how it is linked to political misery, and how it operates on the terrorist. Then we will explore what we can do to correct the problems that give rise to terrorism, while at the same time counteracting the destructive dynamics arising from terrorist attacks.

Among the problems to be addressed in each chapter are the aspects of political misery relevant to that chapter. Throughout we will do our best to be sensitive to the Holy Spirit's leading, responsive to guidance of Scripture and human experience, and open to creativity and new ideas for practical steps we can take as individuals, members of our communities of faith, and citizens.

Terrorism As a Spiritual Issue

It might seem odd to start our examination of terrorism and political misery with a look at terrorism's spiritual dynamics. Terrorism does not strike us as a particularly good example of how to live a spiritual life. We rightly think of terrorism as evil. So how does it have a spiritual dynamic? Terrorism certainly is not a sort of spiritual discipline, at least not in the sense we usually mean. If anything, the terrorist is starving spiritually, having ingested a steady diet of spiritual poison.

This does not mean terrorists are demon-possessed. Terrorism is well within human capacity. We don't need to blame some outside power for terrorism (or for anarchy, tyranny, or political corruption). There are simpler human explanations that account for the entire phenomenon.

Terrorism is a spiritual problem because it is a depraved response to conditions that do not warrant depraved responses. Of course, this puts the point too mildly, since the description could apply to all human sin, but it's a worthwhile place to start. Terrorism is the extreme product of a process that applies to every human being: the destruction we wreak (through our sinful natures) on the beauty God created.

Terrorism is a case of sin, and terrorists are people who have allowed themselves to be sucked into practicing this sin. They are accountable for their sins just as we all are. All of us have allowed ourselves to do evil. We are all sinners.

I am not trying to minimize terrorism; it is one of the grossest evils human beings can inflict on each other. But when we say that terrorism is sin, we are connecting it into a continuum of human behavior all of us have participated in. Since terrorism is sin, and we all have sinned, in a sense there is that of the terrorist in all of us. No, we are not going to kill people en masse. So I suppose, in a sense, that most of us are better people than terrorists. But Christians know this is no cause for self-satisfaction. There but for the grace of God go we.

The terrorist aligns himself and his entire life to a cause and an organization willing to make people suffer to get its way. After September 11, it is clear that neither common decency nor any other ethical restraint limits what some people choose. Nothing is too enormous, too destructive, too monstrous. When they get a nuclear weapon, they'll use it, in the place and at the time it can cause the most suffering.

Now a clearer distinction emerges between the terrorist and you or me. I do not set my hand to any of the tasks associated with killing innocents. I am lazy and insensitive; I manipulate others to get my way; I shade the truth to avoid being held responsible for my actions; I lose my temper and then justify it by blaming others; I forget meetings; I don't keep some of my promises; I neglect my friends and my family; I am brusque with my neighbors; I often don't listen; I am stingy with the resources God has given me; I forget to say "thank you." I do these troubling things and more.

But I don't kill innocent people. I have adopted limits; there are things I would never do that a terrorist does apparently without remorse.

My choice not to terrorize makes a moral difference in the world around me. But it doesn't save my soul or remove me from the dynamics of sin that have so mangled the terrorist. I am not all good.

The terrorist is not all bad. I would guess terrorists often work hard, are good friends, keep their appointments and promises, are generous, subject themselves to rigorous self-discipline, remember to thank people for kindnesses, and love their families tenderly. Just as there is that of the terrorist in me, there is also that of God in the terrorist.

By what path does the terrorist, saddled with the same spiritual disease I have but also sharing in the image of God, succumb to seductive sin in ways that take the infection of evil within each of us and turn it into such a hideous malignancy?

Corrosive Grievance

The path to a terrorist heart starts with a corrosive sense of grievance.

We all suffer wrongs. The world is a fallen, imperfect place and we are imperfect people. Even the smallest errors cause others to suffer. Some suffering seems to come without any human cause.

How we respond to the wrongs we see in life is one of the core spiritual issues every person faces. Some people abandon their faith because they can't reconcile wrongs with the idea of a loving God. Others fall into depression, or freeze into immobility out of fear. A few find new direction or strength in life.

But sometimes people nurse bitterness over injustice and pain. They suffer, or they see their families and communities suffer, from poverty, oppression, personal failures, cultural disintegration under pressure from modern life, or any of a variety of ills. Despite their best efforts to fix the wrongs in their life, progress is agonizingly slow or nonexistent. Their vision of a better life haunts them but seems beyond their reach.

When someone has reached the point of being haunted by the wrongs done to him or his people, he has begun to nurse a *grievance*, by which I mean an ongoing sense of having been wronged. A person with a sense of deep grievance no longer looks at all the evils he suffers as being unconnected. Some of them, at least, are related to one another in what the aggrieved perceives to be a pattern. Commonly, some or all of the wrongs come to be seen as connected to a single cause, a person or agency where all the trouble began. As long as the suffering or loss continues and the person blamed for it is not punished or otherwise escapes "justice," the grievance intensifies. The aggrieved rehearses the wrongs he suffers, searing into his spirit a catalogue of injustice.

When we nurse grievances we narrow ourselves. The wrongs done to us fill our vision, dimming our ability to appreciate the beauty in life or to seize opportunities to grow. Other interests fade; we find less joy in our activities and spend less of our energy on them. The grievance, dense and bitter, cuts its way toward the center of our personality. Our lives begin to orbit around the hot black hole of bitter grievance. Everything else in our universe starts to bend in toward this new all-consuming center. We may even recast our understanding of the meaning of our lives in terms of the grievance.

One does not have to be a terrorist to recognize this pattern. Many of us have tasted the bitter springs that flow from grievance. Whenever we fail to forgive wrongs done to us, preferring instead to cling to our righteous indignation, we plant in our souls the seed of corrosive grievance. Perhaps our own sojourn in that place was temporary, and we were rescued from it by the grace of God, working through friends or family. But not everyone is so fortunate. Whether due to their own gritty and stubborn choices, or because no opportunity seems to present itself amid their suffering, some people do not find release from their sense of grievance.

Of course sometimes grievance is fed by people who actually are harming the aggrieved. I am *not* saying that a person with a grievance is unjustified in feeling wronged. Most grievances are actually at root about something real—some pain that really has been suffered, some wrong that actually has been done. But when the sense of injustice transforms into grievance and acquires the added mass of accumulated resentment, it also begins to grow, often developing aspects of what conflict theorists call *unrealistic conflict*.[38] The aggrieved may begin to notice "evidence" of wrong without being too particular about where the evidence came from, or its reliability, thus connecting things to his wrong that are actually disconnected from it.

Humans instinctively try to explain why things happen. People in pain are no different. In fact, they often intensify their desire for explanations. But just when they most need all their powers of perception, including self-criticism, to help them find a powerful and effective response, the overwhelming stress of living under harsh conditions cuts into their ability to see themselves and the world around them accurately. For one thing, if they are really suffering (as they often are), they have to work harder and longer to survive. For another, feeling one's back to the wall tends to inspire defensiveness and to erode creativity and the ability to correctly perceive the motives of those who may be threatening.

The desire for explanations is always going to be met. If we do not have good information to help us discover why things are happening to us, we will construct an explanation out of whatever pieces we can find. Consider times when a public figure—a politician, say—has declined to offer an explanation for something he did that looked questionable. While the public awaits his full explanation, people speculate wildly about what might be true. People are left to try to piece from rumors what actually happened. Sooner or later it dawns on all but the densest public figures that they have lost control of the story of their own activities, because people who aren't given a satisfying account will make one up. Once the story has begun to gel in the public's mind, out of whatever ingredients the press and talk show hosts have at hand, the politician may find it impossible to repair the damage. It would have been better to come clean in the first place.

By delaying, the politician falls afoul of what psychologists call the *primacy principle*: people tend to organize information to fit their current view of a topic or person. Thus, people who have had no exposure to issues or persons are likely to be the most open-minded about them. Once a first impression has taken hold, it takes much more information to change the impression than it took to make it. And once we settle into a "permanent" impression of someone or something, it becomes even harder to change that view.

The terrorist is also subject to this pattern. But he faces still another barrier to accurate perception of his environment. The terrorist is under severe threat. Once he joins the terrorist organization, if not before, he is in danger of prison or sudden death. If he is preparing to be a suicide bomber, the stress levels would elevate even more—or so we would expect. Feeling threatened usually reinforces the primacy principle because it tends to undermine our ability to think clearly and creatively. We tend to lose some of our ability to form dramatically new worldviews.

In particular, once we have identified an "enemy" who is at least partly at fault for our condition, the greater the threat we feel and the easier we find it to blame anything we can on that enemy. We have already done the mental work necessary to label him an enemy. It's much easier to toss new evils into the same old mental trashcan than to go to all the work of trying to discover the complex factors that cause each real world event. Soon we see our enemy's hand at work in things that are far beyond his powers.

An enemy is useful for beleaguered people. Life gets simpler. When we have an enemy, we no longer have to spend energy looking for explanations. The enemy is behind most of the evil that besets us. We can curtail the draining work of self-examination. Things are not our fault anymore! What a huge relief this is when our lives are not going well.

If I share my enemy with others, our common sense of being threatened will draw us together, give us a bond that can withstand many stresses, and give us many avenues for working together. If the enemy is widely shared, its very existence will create new allies and friends for us.

The more we invest in our enemy—the more evils we blame on her—the stronger our enemy grows in our eyes. We build a myth around our enemy. This doesn't mean we deliberately tell ourselves lies about our enemy. Here myth means a story told to explain something, not a story told that is untrue. Some myths are true. What makes them myths is what we do with them. When we use the story to help us define who we are, explain how we got here, or embody our ideals, then we are using the story (true or fictitious) as a myth.

When an enemy becomes mythic, we are in danger of losing all sense of proportion between the real enemy and our mental image of him. We may still be telling ourselves some true stories about what our enemy has done to us, but the most important thing about those stories has ceased to be whether they are true in the sense of being factual. Instead, we are willing to settle for stories that are "true" in the sense of being faithful to the myths we have constructed about our enemy.

The role of political misery in corrosive grievance

Corrosive grievance can arise in any political context, especially in individual cases. No political system can ensure that all its citizens always feel justly treated. Part of our fallen nature is the ease with which we lose perspective about our hurts.

But healthy political environments offer powerful antidotes to corrosive grievance. For one thing, a political system able to respond well to citizens' needs will leave fewer people with the wounds that breed corrosive grievance. The system itself will inflict fewer wounds, provide more means for redressing hurts, and equip its citizens with more adaptive self-healing skills.

Anarchies, tyrannies, and corrupt governments are all unable to meet their citizens' needs. Hunger, ignorance, hopelessness, and poverty abound in such systems. In addition, the individual is under constant threat of abuse by neighbors and people in power. The sheer volume of suffering is much higher in situations of political misery, making the incidence of corrosive grievance many times more probable there than in healthy polities.

There are also other, subtler effects. Free flows of information about others' lives can give hurting people a chance to escape from their narrow interpretations of their life experiences. But these fountains of information are dry in systems of political misery, or their waters are brackish. Without a free press, and without an atmosphere of free speech and free assembly, information must flow through back channels. What little gets through is subject to all the routine distortions of any word-of-mouth information: exaggeration, gossip, and omission all go uncorrected.

Consider the case of the rumor that Jews were warned away from the World Trade Center on September 11. These tales get little credence in free societies, because there are too many sources of corrective information. We know where to look for corroboration about such lurid stories. Since no corroboration has appeared, most of us confidently dismiss them. But citizens of politically miserable places have no such reasons for confidence. Wild stories run through those societies not only without correction, but without any possible means of independent verification or debunking. Since no reliable information exists in these places, people no longer expect to get reliable information. All information is unreliable, and none of it can be trusted. One is left with one's own prejudices and limited world experience, along with the personal trustworthiness of one's source, as the only tools by which one can measure the credibility of any report, no matter how far beyond the pale. If one has been taught to distrust Jews, and one lives in the information wasteland that accompanies political misery, that distrust is the only relevant test of verification one can bring with which to assess reports of Jews being warned away from the World Trade Center.

Or consider the remarkable performance of the Iraqi Minister of Information, denying the invasion of Baghdad even as American tanks are practically visible over his shoulder. Such a thing is unlikely outside of systems experiencing political misery.

On the other hand, vibrant civil society, rich with opportunities to spend time with those who share one's interests, gives potential terrorists a chance to avoid such isolation. And if members of the terrorist's group also associate widely in other groups, they will be somewhat inoculated against joining the terrorist's corrosive view of life, since they will be in touch with other points of view. Unfortunately, vibrant civil society is impossible in anarchy, tyranny, or (to a lesser extent) corrupt political systems. The extreme insecurity of anarchy saps the energy needed for forming and sustaining private organizations, or even hobbyist groups. And tyranny cannot tolerate the potential for sedition that arises when people associate freely with one another. Only those organizations which submit to governmental monitoring (and probably control) can be allowed to function in a tyranny.

In such an impoverished civil society, groups that do manage to function become especially vulnerable to being infected by grievance. Members of these groups do not have many connections to other groups that might provide a counterbalancing perspective. Any vivid myth propounded by one member of the group will be hard to resist when all other members of the group are equally cut off from a wider view of reality, huddled down as they are amid the storms of anarchy or oppression in which they constantly live.

Summing up: Corrosive grievance

So grievance is corrosive in more ways than one. First, it corrodes the soul. As it gains spiritual mass due to its power to explain the wrongs in one's life, it sinks like a rock through the corroded personality to the person's core, whence it can make the person's entire life orbit around a sense of injustice.

Second, grievance corrodes the person's vision. He can no longer see (or admit seeing) facts that would explain or justify the pain suffered. He can no longer excuse or exonerate the people who caused it. In their places, he "sees" facts which confirm the myths he has built and add weight to his grievance, even though some of these "facts" are untrue.

Third, grievance corrodes the grievant's community. If others share his pain, they are susceptible to sharing his explanatory myths. Grievance is contagious. It draws adherents and distorts their souls, until entire communities have succumbed and put their worldviews into orbit around their shared grievance.

Grievance is not confined to terrorists, of course. Not every one with a lump of resentment at the foundation of her personality becomes a killer. It is not a crime, other than against God and oneself, to resent something intensely, nor to let one's personality fall into grievance's thrall. Some people just become cantankerous. Others fall into paranoia. Others succumb to the allure of conspiracy theories, with all their liberating power to shift blame for one's own failures onto someone else.

There are those who, while acknowledging the severity of an injustice done to them, and insistent upon bringing perpetrators to justice, avoid trudging down the path and through the prison gates of corrosive grievance. Perhaps these people know more about forgiveness and grace than the rest of us. Maybe they have a clearer vision of the debilitating power of grievance and decide to embrace other powers instead. Perhaps they are just easier-going, people who do not feel quite as deeply, or maybe people who have found cheerfulness to be good medicine and just don't want to give it up.

Those who choose bitterness are not excused by its explanatory and self-exculpatory allure. They have not given themselves over to terrorism by this act alone, but they make themselves into little factories of the poison of corrosive grievance every terrorist imbibes in large doses.

No matter how large the doses, though, corrosive grievance is not by itself fatal. It can be treated, and every victim can be given the opportunity to choose healing. We can offer two powerful antidotes to the toxins in corrosive grievance: *empathetic listening* and *loving service*.

Responding to Corrosive Grievance: Empathetic Listening

Let's begin with empathetic listening. This is almost an individual-level response to the problem of corrosive grievance. It is not going to be enough by itself, of course—we have just explored some of the broader social context that can trap people into corrosive grievance. Later we will look at how we can directly address the broader political system with societal-level work. But we need not begin at the level of nations to start having a real effect at healing corrosive grievance. Following the Lampens' lead (see ch. 5), we can begin with individuals, working through relationships to create new possibilities for the seriously aggrieved.

Perhaps an example will help. I see grievance-bound people routinely when I serve as a mediator through my church or my local community mediation organization. Even though mediations are generally not the worst cases of corrosive grievance, people in mediations are really quite brave. They go to mediation because they are willing to risk meeting with their enemy to try to find a peaceful resolution to their conflict. This is difficult work for many. Their entire history with the other side may have been marked by failed attempts to communicate, which often have led to painful outbursts and searing life disruptions.

As a mediator, I usually come laced with hope, ready to watch the nearly miraculous transformation I have seen so often in previous mediations. I am eager to push ahead to resolution. But I know from experience that it will not work if I try to hurry the process. No matter how prepared they are for the mediation, the disputing parties still need the mediator to perform an essential service at the outset: the mediator has to listen to them. Neither party can move far until someone has heard her entire story, has heard the opponent's story, still accepts both parties as people, and treats their fears and aspirations with respect. The path to cooperation between the disputants in a mediation runs straight through the mediator's ability to listen with empathy to both sides.

I am choosing the word *empathy* with careful calculation. I do not mean sympathy, where the listener comes to share the speaker's feelings. I don't need to share the feelings I am mediating; if I do, I lose my value to that person as a mediator. If I sympathize, I have taken her point of view, abandoning my role as an intermediary between two parties, and have taken up the role of ally, joining the community surrounding that person on which she relies for support in her ongoing battle with her foe. And I cease to deserve the trust of the other side, who also has a story. I cannot be fully in sympathy with both sides in a mediation. But I can be passionately in empathy with both sides—that is, I can come to a place where I understand much of what they feel, fear, and dream.

Of course, I am often privately in sympathy with one side in a mediation—or at least, it is rare when I am equally in sympathy with both. I am a human too, after all, and I have my own reactions to the parties who walk in through the mediation door. But my sympathies are not of much value in the mediation. My empathies are what the parties need: my ability to connect with what they are seeing and feeling.

They need me to listen until I can state their views to their own satisfaction, then do the same for their opponent. And, equally important, I have to show both sides that, even having listened to them and to their foes, I still take their needs and goals seriously.

Taking needs and goals seriously is crucial. If any disputing parties think there is a risk their needs are going to be sacrificed for the sake of an agreement, the mediation becomes untenable for them. As a mediator I don't have to agree on the parties' first draft descriptions of their needs, but I do have to demonstrate that I haven't merely dismissed them as invalid and unworthy of consideration. I invite the parties to mutually explore what their needs actually are without imposing my own definitions on them.

Then suppose that, having demonstrated empathy with each side without taking sides, I still doggedly pursue reconciliation and resolution and obviously still think it is possible. That is when a breakthrough is often possible. That is when the lights begin to go on for the disputants.

But that is only half the work of a mediator. The other half is creating a setting in which the disputing parties, despite animosity and pain, begin to listen to and find empathy for one another. Part of the job is done when I can empathize with both. Then they can imagine doing the same for their opponent and may even be able to notice when their opponent does it for them. The key is the mediator's ability to *embody fully informed compassion,* to *hold in suspension two opposing views of reality,* and to *expect the parties to be able to find a peaceful way* when they haven't yet trusted themselves.

When the disputants in a mediation see the mediator living out the promise of empathy and reconciliation, they begin to believe in it, too. In their newborn faith, they take small steps themselves toward acting as if peace were possible. And usually they find it is.

Consider the power unleashed when we can listen to our enemies and communicate empathy with their pain and concerns. Empathy with the enemy cuts into our enemies' myths about us, especially notions about our arrogance and implacability. When we demonstrate genuine concern for the needs and goals of our opponents, we make dialog possible. And when we refuse to discount out of hand their own understanding of their needs and goals, we begin to unravel the cords of distrust that hold a grievance together.

Of course, what I do as a mediator is usually much easier than listening to terrorists, let alone tyrants, especially now that it is clear how intensely many regard us as their enemies. For one thing, we are a party to the conflict. It is extremely hard not to insist on making enemies listen to us. They do need to listen to us, but they are going to be able to do that only when we have broken the mythic mold by listening empathetically to them first.

So now we move to our practical question: In struggling against terror and political misery, how do we embody fully informed compassion; hold in suspension two opposing views of reality, theirs and ours, until we can find a way to move toward a common understanding of the truth; and expect the parties to be find a peaceful way when they don't yet trust themselves?

A mediator embodies compassion by listening empathetically, and refusing to discount anyone's sense of their needs and fears. Here are ways we can play an analogous role in the struggle against international terrorism and political misery:

Start where you are. *Consider your own soul and whether you are nursing any grievances.* You will understand much better what it is going to take to dissolve the lump of grievance in the pit of another's soul if you honestly undertake to dissolve your own grievances. This need not be limited to political grievances. Working on our most intimate personal grievances can be even harder than our political ones, and might be the best possible way to prepare oneself to be constructive as a healer. If we are serious about empathy, it will not do to isolate ourselves from our own experiences of grievance.

You can also *invite people who share some of the background of terrorists, or have lived in anarchy, tyranny, or corruption, to tell their stories.* Find someone who has connections to the group you have the most trouble understanding. For example, if you are concerned about Islamic extremists, go out of your way to get to know Moslems in your community. Most followers of Islam are not terrorists, of course, but they can introduce you to their faith so you can be more intelligent about your concerns. Along the way, your listening to a non-terrorist Moslem may be a small act of healing for him, since under current conditions he may find it hard to get an empathetic hearing from Christians.

Or if your concern is domestic terrorists, from either the left or the right, find some people who share views similar to terrorists'. Listen until you can state their views to their satisfaction. Pay special attention to the places where they feel vulnerable— listen especially closely when they touch on their fears, needs, and goals. Try to go entire sessions without giving in to the urge to argue or even explain your point of view.

If seeking out people with links to such groups seems to be more than you can do right now, then start even closer to home. *Listen to your neighbors*, coworkers, fellow church members, or others in your community, practicing empathetic focus on discerning their underlying needs, fears, and goals. Perhaps you can find people who disagree with you on some key spiritual or political issue. Listen until you can state their version of the issues to their satisfaction. This might be good practice, after which you would feel readier to try listening to people connected to terrorists or tyrannts.

One can do similar listening to those who might be ideologically attracted to anarchy or totalitarianism, or someone who does not think of corruption as being a particularly significant moral issue. These points of view do not have much to recommend them, but a way must still be found to grasp what motivates people to perpetuate political misery for themselves and their community. In the process of listening to gather this kind of information, you will also be building a bridge of trust and concern to those with whom you may be working someday on other, more immediately practical tasks of political reform.

Between opportunities to listen, you can prepare yourself with a little studying. *Read up.* A number of excellent books are out that describe the experiences of people in areas where corrosive grievance develops or political misery prevails. For example, there are several books dealing with the experience of Christian Arabs in Israel and the West Bank.[39] Others cover the situations in Bosnia, Northern Ireland, Burundi, Rwanda, and many more.[40] There are innumerable ways to read what terrorists or their sympathizers are saying, especially on the Internet. Reading isn't complete without also listening in person. You can't do much to show you have heard, and you can't catch as many nuances in what is being said, or to explore further when something just doesn't add up for you. But it's much better than nothing, and in tandem with listening it can be a powerful tool to help you see the big picture that goes with the individual stories you can hear in person.

Letter writing is a wonderful tool, and now that it can be done instantaneously via the Internet, it is even better. Make opportunities to *correspond at length with people in areas that are suffering political misery or are otherwise seedbeds for terror.* Urge your church to help you make contacts with people in those areas who would like to practice their English (or give you a chance to practice your Urdu, Arabic, Spanish, or Serbo-Croation). Focus your correspondence on listening. In your first few messages, confine yourself to asking questions and offering your best summaries of what you have been learning from your pen pal's letters. Work at it until you hear from your contact that you have done a good job of expressing the point of view of people in her community.

Travel with open mind and heart. If possible, visit places suffering political misery and where terrorists recruit new members. Have a local host. Ask her to help you make your visit a success as a listening tour. Try not to go home until you can reflect the point of view of a possible terrorist recruit to your host's satisfaction. This is not an easy step for one person to take. Consider joining a study tour being organized by a church group or college you trust. Or join one of the Christian Peacemaker Teams' short-term delegations to Hebron on the West Bank, or to Colombia.[41]

Of course, the whole point of traveling like this is to listen with compassion. You will need to take special care to gain entry into the communities you want to listen to. Working with a local host is crucial, as is listening to your host's advice about how to conduct yourself to make your respect clear. Humility is key.

Most Americans will find it difficult to make these kinds of connections directly with the people they're most interested in. One way around this problem is *networking*. Find the point at which you do have access—perhaps a mission or development organization active in an appropriate area. Then create an opportunity to listen to a representative from that group. As you listen to more people involved with the community you are concerned about, offer to help them make contact with each other.

Networking doesn't necessarily give you a chance to send feedback that you are listening. But it does give you at least some of the perspective-building benefits of more direct contact. And the organization you connect with may be of help in other aspects of your peacemaking and healing ministry.

Initiate formal links with groups in regions where politics are miserable or grievances are becoming corrosive. Take networking another step, and celebrate a particular connection your group has with another group from a region descending into corrosive grievance. Sister congregations, pen pals, visitor exchanges, and the like can be powerful tools for relieving isolation and its misery- and grievance-magnifying effects.

Reward the media. Mass media outlets have a major role in the creation of grievance, when they feed its conditions by discounting the needs of a group of people or feeding into stereotypes. But the media can also help soften grievances by helping various groups in the world communicate with each other. And media coverage of political misery can be therapeutic, as it puts pressure on corrupt officials and autocrats to be more responsive to the needs of their people. Reward media outlets when they do a good job of listening to our enemies—or helping enemies listen to us. Praise them publicly, write appreciative letters to local station managers, and reward them with a greater share of your media patronage.[42]

Reward public leaders when they do a good job of empathetic listening. In American political culture, with its tendency to boil discussion of issues down to their most simplistic level, it is almost impossible for a political leader to show empathy with an enemy. Any move in that direction opens the politician up for an attack from an opponent, who can quote the empathetic language out of context and portray the speaker as potentially lacking zeal for the American cause. But there aren't many things more damaging to a political culture than loss of ability to discuss all sides of a problem, especially in times of crisis.

It will take a deliberate effort on the part of many to change this pattern. Some of us will have to be the first in our localities to publicly and boldly commend a political leader for listening empathetically to an enemy. We will have to work to make clear the distinction between listening empathetically and sympathizing. But Jesus called us to love our enemies. If you love someone, you listen to them, even when you disagree—especially when you disagree—because there is no other way to reach them.

Empathetic listening doesn't sound like a blow against political misery, but it is, in its quiet subversive way. Take the reactions of various totalitarian regimes to Internet e-mail. No one message over the Internet is going to bring down the Chinese communist regime, for example. But China's leaders realize that they take a huge risk when they allow their people to use the Internet. Individual connections with outsiders infect Chinese Internet users with other points of view than the one propounded by China's dictators. Multiply this individual effect by all the connections each user can make, and all the millions of users, and China is constantly in danger of having its hold on its own people eroded away, just as happened in Eastern Europe half a generation ago. When you empathetically listen to someone, you liberate them just a little.

Responding to Corrosive Grievance: Loving Service

Empathetic listening begins to dissolve the hard lump of grievance by giving the aggrieved a hearing in which needs and fears are taken seriously. However, even though listening is hard to do, it is relatively cheap. That is, I can listen until my heart bleeds for you, but that doesn't mean I will make any changes to help you meet your needs.

Even if we can soften grievance by listening well, something more needs to happen. We may be able to identify some kernel of injustice, or at least perceived injustice, at the heart of the grievance. And once a seed of apparent injustice is found, if we love our enemies we will want to remedy the injustice.

There is a real danger here. If we tailor our response to fit the terms of the terrorists' or tyrants' demands, we begin giving in to them.[43] However, if we have listened well, we do not need to take these demands as the best measure of justice. We can look behind the demands, moving past objectionable parts (the right to continue treating women as subhuman, perhaps), to the points that are grounded in needs not vulnerable to critique. That is, we take these demands not as a "to do" list but as the cry of a community in pain. Then we look behind the demands to their fears and goals, we listen to their narratives, and we take them as signposts to the valid needs upon which peace can be built.

In fact, if we assume out of faith that no ones' needs are incompatible with any one else's (at least as a general rule), we can also consult with the victims of terror and political misery and with the people a terrorist might hope to influence through victims' sufferings. What we hear from victims will help us draw boundaries around our search for the perpetrators' underlying needs. For example, since terror victims deserve a chance to live without fear of being bombed at the railway station, we can assume from the start that the terrorist cannot possibly need to bomb the railway station. The same is true in life apart from terrorism. If a Haitian needs to be able to feed her family, I cannot possibly need (as opposed to "crave" or "consume") so much food so as to leave too little left over for her—or, perhaps more tellingly, I cannot need to have my country prop up a political or economic order that deprives her of a reasonable opportunity to meet her needs.

One of the most basic needs in any conflict is often more clarity about the facts of production, distribution, and consumption of goods, whether they be economic, political, social, or spiritual. The parties to the dispute, including ourselves, are prone to getting the facts wrong, either because we misperceive, or can't perceive, or willingly won't perceive the truth. In particular, we are likely to subtly filter what we see to help it fit our existing theories about the shape of things. We make ourselves partly blind. No one is immune to this malady.

This leads to the first recommendation for loving service: *Encourage independent, reliable fact-finding.* We can send in the doctors (and professionals in missions, public health, development, education, appropriate-scale commerce, and political institutions) to find out why the patient is in such pain and then guide us to do something about it. Actually, if we love our neighbors, we should constantly be monitoring their condition, ready to help when they get into trouble. Individually we can only pay attention to a few people around us, but as the body of Christ, the church as a whole needs to have someone listening to all the major social groups in the world. We need to be ready to help redress wrongs, heal hurts, and alleviate political misery, before terror can begin to make its twisted appeal to a critical mass within any society. But given the difficulty of monitoring conditions everywhere, we should promote reliable fact-finding at least in areas where widespread grievance is in danger of becoming corrosive and political institutions are collapsing, corrupted, or controlled by despots.

We can pursue the truth about problem areas through many channels. Scholars, including those at Christian universities, are one valuable resource. Missions and development groups could do more to document social, economic, and political trends. My colleagues at George Fox University, Lon Fendall and Ralph Beebe, have done excellent work by helping write the life stories of Christians who live in turbulent areas and work for peace there.[44] Tony Bing of Earlham College has done the same.[45] More of this work needs to be done.

Church groups can also organize helpful fact-finding teams. An example I know of is the Quaker Working Party on Middle East Peace, of which I am a part. This group visited Israel and Palestine in June 2002, and is publishing a major report describing the dynamics and current conditions in Israel and Palestine, and recommending ways to be constructive in promoting a just peace there. Conferences involving scholars, missionaries, development workers, and people from the region of concern can be quite helpful.

As needs emerge, we need to be ready to *channel funds and other support to those agencies already active in missions, development, political reform, and other fields of service*. If missions organizations could include this broader vision of peace work as a part of their vocation, they could enhance their impact in helping bring the love of God tangibly into people's lives.

Perhaps some who would never have considered themselves missionary material might find they are called to *go to another country to look for opportunities to serve needs*, both through their professions and by sharing the gospel. Many missionaries work under some version of "lifestyle evangelism," meaning they go into the country to carry out a secular profession and look for opportunities to share the gospel that will arise naturally out of the flow of their lives. The work they do serves both as a vehicle for meeting people and making friends, and as a "tentmaking" source of financial support for the missionary effort. The missionaries imprisoned in Afghanistan during summer 2001 were practicing a form of lifestyle evangelism, with a German development agency providing their official reason for being in that country.

Lifestyle evangelism seems to hold promise as a format for delivering genuine service to those who might otherwise be our enemies. Tentmaking missionaries with international connections can bring many spiritual, economic, and even social benefits to their host societies.

In fact, we can go another step, and *practice honoring these kinds of workers as heroes,* with recognition equal to any that we already give to those who serve in the military or police. Our culture needs to see the development worker as sacrificing on the front lines to prevent terrorism and relieve political misery. They are just as valorous as the firefighter who works on the home front to respond to an attack.

Fact-finding and service are crucial. Not only will they help meet needs and thereby avoid political misery and corrosive grievance, they can help burnish credibility and credentials in vulnerable regions of the world. As I toured the Middle East with the Quaker Working Party, I was amazed to see how often doors were open to us everywhere we went by the service Quakers have performed in the region. Some remembered Quaker efforts to help Jews escape Nazism in World War II, others recalled Quaker work with Palestinian refugees from 1948 until the United Nations took over the job in 1950. Some were educated (or had family members educated) at one of the two Quaker schools in the area. And I, who had nothing to do with any of this work, found welcome in surprising places thanks to those who had gone before me.

But even in the area of meeting needs, we cannot expect to solve everything from outside. There are limits to what outside help can do. One risk is that outside help can create a sense of dependency and inadequacy among the people being helped.

As a partial antidote, we ought also to *support indigenous institutions that are ready to help meet needs.* For example, relief and development work channeled through nonviolent Islamic agencies, or through indigenous churches, could be a powerful tool in the Middle East for shrinking the opportunity for resentments to arise or harden into grievances. The Quakers in Burundi have set up a college-level training school and a trauma healing project, both as part of a wholistic healing response to the horrific ethnic violence that has flared up there from time to time. These programs were initiated by Burundians, and are largely staffed by them, but as new organizations in a poor country reeling from ethnic violence, they are drawing on Americans and Europeans for funds and expertise.

Another possibility is to *invite people to come to us to find resources they need,* providing scholarships and fellowships as appropriate. David Niyonzima came to George Fox University from Burundi to supplement his counseling background so he can work more effectively in the Burundian trauma counseling program. His travel, tuition, and other expenses were covered by donors. Guilford College in North Carolina has a scholarship program for Palestinian graduates of the Friends School in Ramallah. Churches, denominations, colleges, and others could initiate peacemaker retreat centers, offering sabbaticals for reflection and rejuvenation to indigenous peace workers. I have long dreamed of such a center at George Fox, where peacemakers like Jerusalem's Jonathan Kuttab, or a Mennonite pastor in Colombia living in political misery and violence from four sides (the government, the paramilitaries, the drug cartels, and the leftist guerrillas), can come to renew their visions in a retreat-like environment.

In recent pages, we have been looking at what might be done privately, by individuals, churches, and nonprofit organizations. In so doing we have been emphasizing the tools of exchange and affiliation. As another form of using exchange power to meet human needs, Christians can be careful to find ways to buy products they need from those who most need their business. *Promoting creative international trade* is a good way to contribute to the expansion of resources in economically underdeveloped areas, and thus indirectly help meet needs there. It is good for us to remember that there are people around the world who need our business, not just those in our own communities. Our neighbors are not just local. In a global economy, we may have as much impact on a family in Asia whose income depends on the car we buy as we do on the family who lives next door. Chauvinism in our economics is hardly loving.

On the other hand, Christians should *avoid exploitive international trade in personal consumption.* If we benefit from goods made by people who are not paid enough to live on, we are essentially being subsidized by the shortened lifespans and misery of others. This would be most obvious in the case of a worker who makes so little he can't even feed himself a subsistence diet. That worker is trading away days off his lifespan when he labors. Those who pay a starvation price for his products are essentially killing him. But subsistence in diet is not the only need a human has—we truly to do not live on bread alone.

A worker who eats enough but is taking an uncompensated risk with her body, through exposure to dangerous machines or toxins, is relying on luck to survive. The unlucky ones injured in unsafe conditions are trading away parts of their lifespan to make your product as surely as is the starving worker.

Similar analysis applies to ability to afford shelter and health care and to feed, house, and educate a family. Or if a worker cannot participate meaningfully in her political system because she cannot spare the time or energy, then the price of what I buy is being subsidized by her political enslavement—which may include many other effects, such as the poisoning of her environment, the impoverishment of her children's schooling, or any of the other wounds by which people suffer when their political systems run without popular participation. Furthermore, if a worker cannot spare the time and energy for her spiritual life, then when I buy what she produces, my price is being subsidized at part of the cost of her eternal soul.

Participating creatively in international trade while avoiding exploitation of other children of God is a hard thing to do well. It is unlikely that we will ever get it just right. But there are some who can help. For example, Ten Thousand Villages is a Mennonite-inspired business that pays Two-Thirds World artisans a decent income for products, then imports them to the United States for retail sale. Shopping at Ten Thousand Villages and other fair-trade importers is a way of helping to resolve economic misery and slows the growth of political misery.

For now, such outlets are not a practical means of meeting all our international trading needs. Christians can do much to help fight terrorism if they *enter the field of international business with a clear eye toward promoting fair international trade.*

Finally, we should not overlook coercion as a means of helping people in the shadow of political misery and corrosive grievance. We don't exercise much useful coercion as individuals when it comes to terrorism, but governments do. Citizens of democratic countries who can influence their governments should make it a consistent practice to *pressure elected leaders to deal fairly and humanely in their interactions with other nations.* Christians concerned about loving neighbors all over the world cannot afford to leave to someone else the task of holding their governments accountable to act fairly, with due regard for everyone's needs, including those who are in other countries. Without this kind of citizen pressure, our leaders will find it very difficult to buck the prevailing public pressure to put our interests first, even to the exclusion of others' needs.

Furthermore, citizens can *press for improved laws and policies regarding international relations, economic development, and commerce.* Whether the issue is international debt relief consistent with biblical jubilee principles; trade barriers that prevent poor people from having access to our markets; support for corrupt regimes that cripple moral, economic, and social progress; or holding international corporations accountable for how they pay and treat their workers: Christians in the developed world, whose economies drive the world economy, have a unique responsibility to make sure that their laws and policies are consistent with the spirit and example of Jesus Christ.

Dealing with Corrosive Grievance: Love and Hope

Already we have 21 broad actions that Christians might take to chip away at the conditions that generate corrosive grievance and political misery:

1. Consider our own souls and whether we are nursing any grievances.

2. Invite people who share some of the terrorists' backgrounds to tell us their stories.

3. Listen to our neighbors to practice empathetic discernment of underlying needs.

4. Read up on the experiences of people who might be nursing corrosive grievances.

5. Correspond at length with people in areas that are seedbeds for terrorism.

6. Travel with open minds and hearts.

7. Build networks with those working in our communities of concern.

8. Initiate formal links with groups in regions where grievances are becoming corrosive.

9. Reward the media when they help various communities communicate with each other.

10. Reward our public leaders when they do a good job of empathetic listening.

11. Encourage independent, reliable fact-finding.

12. Channel funds and other support to those agencies already active in missions, development, and other fields of service in regions where grievances are, or may soon become, corrosive.

13. Go to other countries looking for ways to help meet needs.

14. Practice honoring as heroes those who seek to meet needs abroad.

15. Support indigenous institutions that are ready to help meet needs where corrosive grievance is developing.

16. Invite and host people from other countries to come visit us, offering resources they need.

17. Promote creative international trade.

18. Avoid exploitive international trade when making personal consumption choices.

19. Enter the field of international business with a clear eye toward promoting fair international trade.

20. Pressure elected leaders to deal fairly and humanely in their interactions with other nations.

21. Press for improved laws and policies regarding international relations, economic development, and commerce.

Listening and serving; reflecting God's love more brightly into lives that find it hard to believe; embodying in a practical way the hope that there are ways to meet needs: though these may seem at first to be awfully idealistic goals, they are also intensely practical. They have the power to change the world, a little at a time. If believers concentrated their listening and loving service where political misery and corrosive grievance are beginning to do their worst work, a little change at a time could go a long way toward uprooting terrorism at its source and extending democracy to everyone.

Twenty-one possible actions is not bad, but it is only a fraction of the number of ideas an omnipotent, omniscient, loving God would have. Unfortunately, no human being can read the infinite book of good ideas God could write. On the other hand, we still have three more chapters to go in our own exploration of how the dynamics of terror and tyranny can suggest for us ways we can constructively respond.

Chapter 7

....

Dehumanizing Hatred: The Spiritual Side of Terrorism, Part II

Our task now is to consider how corrosive grievance affects its victims, making them readier to undertake violence against others. Corrosive grievance by itself does not generally lead to violence, even though it poisons the soul and embitters life. Nor does political suffering automatically cause its victims to be ready to do violence. But each in its own way weakens its victims' resistance to the temptation to kill. We will first consider how corrosive grievance can work on its victim to leave him ready to kill. Then we will examine the ways that political misery can do the same thing.

How Grievance Drives Dehumanization

As we have already seen, corrosive grievance is a powerful force for spiritual deformation. It begins the process of distorting the future terrorist's soul. It gives him a furnace at the core of his being, transmitting fierce energy. It provides him with a worldview that polarizes the world into friend and foe. And it helps twist his powers of perception, preparing him to lose the ability to see humanity in those whom he links with his enemy.

Of all the losses corrosive grievance causes, this last may be the most telling in the life of a terrorist. Such grievance dehumanizes. We have already seen how it causes its victim to wither and lose some of the joy and openness which marks the richest human lives. But it also leaves its victims with ever decreasing ability to see their foes as fully human.

Grievance is not the only path to dehumanization. Treating others as less than human is pervasive. People have always done it and continually find new ways to do it. Masters, in their own minds, had to dehumanize slaves, or they couldn't justify owning them. Races dehumanize each other to create mental space for the ways they treat each other. Religious groups discount others' faith and the resulting degree to which other religious groups attain a fully human nature. Men dehumanize women to reduce the spiritual dissonance that would otherwise make it inconvenient to treat them as beautiful things for sexual pleasure. Whether women have done equivalent things to men, I as a man cannot be sure, but my guess is that both genders find ways to dehumanize the other.

Grievance, however, seems to turbocharge the dehumanization process. To the other motives for dehumanization—ignorance, convenience, prejudice, and so forth—grievance adds a powerful supplement. When an enemy has emerged, and grievance has invested it with mythic significance in explaining how things have gone so bad, dehumanization offers crucial explanatory power. Who could ever be as bad as the myth claims the enemy is? No normal human being, of course, would have done such evil.

As the myth grows wilder about the influence of the enemy on a victim's affairs, it has a greater gap to fill in explaining how anybody could be so bad. The distinction between *doing* evil and *being* evil is one of the first things to disappear. Assumptions about an enemy's sanity also vanish. Already we are in the territory of "Great Satans," "madmen," "the Evildoer," but lesser labels also do dehumanizing work.

Soon the complex human motives we generally recognize in ourselves seem to boil away in others. The enemy ends up with only one motive, which must be as venal as can be imagined. The myth grievance constructs is exceptionally fertile in predicting (and therefore perceiving) immense evils from the enemy—e.g., a few Moslems remain convinced that the World Trade Center bombings were conducted by Israeli or even

American secret agents—but it runs out of creativity when it comes to recognizing complexity in the enemy's motivations. America's focus on Afghanistan as an initial target for military strikes against terrorist bases could be seen by some suspicious observers as just another case of American greed for oil—this time, to prepare Afghanistan as a site for a pipeline from Central Asia's deep reserves. There are even those who suspected the United States of staging the September 11 attack as a cover for American plans to invade Afghanistan and later Iraq.

These scenarios seem bizarre to most Americans. We recognize in ourselves complexity in motivation that we find hard to see in others. Certainly Americans crave oil, and our country might do some things it would not be proud of to acquire it. Each of our wars with Iraq has had its oil angles. But we understand that Americans also act for other reasons. We see our interventions in Bosnia and Kosovo, and Somalia and Haiti, as not having anything to do with oil. We remember that the first Gulf War was as much about deterring aggressors from marching across national borders as it was about oil. And in the minds of the American people, the second round of war against Iraq was about keeping weapons of mass destruction out of the hands of terrorists, or ending one of the world's worst dictatorships, or bringing democracy to the Arab world—or some combination of these factors. Since America is a democracy, our intentions as a people are as important in explaining the war as whatever private intentions some greedy oil interests might have had.

We can't imagine that our government would have a hand in something like the September 11 attacks, because we feel we have the power to hold it accountable for anything so heinous—after all, we almost kicked President Clinton out of office for lying about sex. We believe—hopefully correctly—that any party that had anything to do with something like a terrorist attack on our own citizens would suffer an immediate political destruction, and anyone who happened to be a leader in that party would find himself out of politics for life no matter how ignorant he or she was of the events.

But enemies don't see all these nuances. Their mythology has already made it nearly impossible to do so. Monolithic evil is a simple, powerful explanation of the type corrosive grievance demands. Once the myth is in place, every new fact must be turned over and over until it fits the picture. Actions that seem innocent to the actor look sinister to the aggrieved observer.

Terrorists aren't the only people who demonize and otherwise dehumanize their opponents. We can see our own society doing much of this in its turn, responding to the terrorists' attacks. Our fear in the face of a foe who is ready to kill as many of us as it can drives us to mythologize, too. American law enforcement officials see threats in dozens of directions and are often unable to tell which might be the next avenue of terrorist attacks. There is a basis of awful reality to their response, since our society offers so many targets for terror. But we have to be careful, because we are on the verge of ascribing to terrorists power to attack on all those fronts at once, when in reality they can probably only pick one or two at a time.

There is a countervailing tendency, also a form of dehumanization. This is the temptation to see all of one's own actions as kindly and innocent, even when an observer would be startled to know we thought so. Studies in "attribution theory" have shown a strong tendency for people to describe their own actions as exhibiting much more good will than observers give them credit for, and to describe the actions of others as being much more perverse than neutral observers rated them.[46]

In a sense we dehumanize ourselves when we persist in denying our own flaws and the elements in our mixed motives which don't smell so good. Dishonesty with ourselves about our own actions may not lead directly to hatred, but it sure helps prepare the path. The more we misperceive ourselves as being innocent, the easier it is to form harsh judgments about others when we see them as having succumbed to evil. Humans tend to try to maximize the contrast between their own behavior and others', which paves the way for justifying hatred of the other.

This may be why Jesus warned his disciples that, unless they forgave those who harmed them, they could not themselves be forgiven.[47] If I ask for forgiveness for my sins but am unwilling to forgive others, I am dehumanizing both myself and the others. I am assuming that my sins aren't really like other peoples', that is, that I am better than they, somehow a little above other humans.

Once we dehumanize our enemy, or superhumanize ourselves, we can take off some (or all) of the restraints that keep us
from wallowing in hatred. We achieve hatred when we wish
others ill and delight in their misfortune. We may even take
pleasure in imagining their suffering, which is only a step or
two away from taking pleasure in bringing about their suffering. Taking those steps gets much easier when we have succumbed to the temptation to dehumanize the enemy.

If a community shares the sense of grievance and agrees
about who the "enemy" is—that is, who is to blame for the suffering the community experiences—the spiral toward dehumanizing hatred tightens. If I rely on a group for support and
protection from my enemies, real or imagined, the views of
other members of the group will take on added power in my
life. My dependence on them makes me less likely to challenge
what they say and think. I will tend to echo their thoughts.

A nasty positive feedback sets in. As each member of the
group expresses something that justifies hatred of the enemy,
every other member of the group is given a strong incentive to
loudly agree. Doubts must be suspended lest they threaten to
draw some group members away, leaving them isolated and the
group weaker. Loud concurrence is the order of the day! Loud
concurrence elicits even more invective, which stimulates more
concurrence, and so on.[48]

Once set in motion, especially in a group that feels threatened, denunciation of the enemy, accusations about the evil in
his heart, and descriptions of his unworthiness to be treated like
a human all feed each other. Mobs are a dangerous thing, for this
very reason—it is extremely difficult to interrupt this kind of
feedback cycle once it has gotten under way. Attempts to mod-
erate things, to get people to calm down, threaten to weaken the
group in the face of its enemy. People lose a good share of their
ability to listen to opposing views.

Terrorist cells are not strictly mobs. Their group norms tend
to be more regular, for one thing. But the groupthink feedback
loop that makes mobs so dangerous is present, in a milder form,
in every group. My guess is that terrorist cells approach the
rawest mobs in how fiercely their members succumb to the
groupthink feedback cycle. Intensity of feeling can substitute
nicely for spontaneous physical proximity as a means of ampli-

fying cycles of response. And surely terrorists score near the very top in intensity of feeling.

It should be clear by now how dehumanizing hatred and corrosive grievance reinforce each other. They have their own positive feedback loop. The more I demonize an opponent, the more I have a reason to hate him. As he gets more demonic and hateful in my mind, the enemy's imagined capacity to do evil grows. His expected reach gets longer. So we can understand when an Islamic terrorist looks around his world and everything seems to bear the stains of contact with the West; or when a Timothy McVeigh concludes that all the evils in his own life are due to a vast governmental conspiracy against him.

Remember, these grievance/dehumanization/hate cycles are not confined to terrorists. If you think carefully over your life, you may eventually remember an occasion when you succumbed to some milder version of this dynamic. I know I have.

Usually there is some actual truth somewhere near the core of the terrorist's mythic understanding of his relationship with his enemy. For example, Western culture really is pervasive and has touched almost every aspect of Islamic life. When the Islamic extremist terrorist looks around his world and everything seems to bear the stains of contact with the West, he is not making that part up. And Israel really has at points extended settlements onto land no other country in the world (not even the U.S.) has deemed it to have a right to possess. The monarchies on the Arabian peninsula are badly marred by corruption, as bin Laden has pointed out more than once.

The extremist's mistake is in how he explains these facts and what conclusions he draws from them. Because he nurses a grievance, he finds it very hard to accept as fact anything that tends to challenge the grounds upon which it is based. He has to insist that elements of western culture are spreading because Moslems are being duped, not because people find them successful and useful. He has to disavow any notion that the Arabs helped create the conditions that leave Israelis feeling so extremely vulnerable. He has to blame what he sees as Islamic retreat on demons from outside his community, because he can't afford to focus on flaws within his culture.

I have used the Islamic extremist as an example here, but the pattern applies to anyone. We all dehumanize to some degree. I have a habit of judging people harshly on first impression then disregarding them, consigning them to the category of "not worth my trouble." I reduce annoying drivers to "buddy," "sweety," and worse. I work from stereotypes: thinking of smokers as self-centered; those with body-piercings or lots of makeup as having poor self images; those who root for the Yankees as having inferiority issues they are trying to work out. When I fall into these stereotypes, I dehumanize other people, losing sight of their individuality and unique characteristics. I also lose sight of reality, overlooking all those who don't fit the stereotypes. I save a lot of time and energy this way. Dealing with people as things, or as mere members of preassigned categories, is a lot easier than recognizing them as people.

We all simplify our environments this way. Categorizing and classifying things is, to some extent, adaptive behavior. We survive better if we recognize all moving cars, or anything glowing red-hot, as dangerous. We would be foolish to suspend judgment about each moving car or red-hot poker until we had in each case made sure it was indeed dangerous. And some of our prejudices about people may also be adaptive. After all, the writer of Proverbs does not encourage us to take loose women or corrupt men on a case-by-case basis.

Americans now are struggling with whether we should follow our democratic ideals and treat everyone with equal suspicion when they line up to get on a plane, or whether we should single out those who look like possible terrorists for additional scrutiny. Racial profiling is a form of dehumanization. Each individual is submerged into a mass identity. She is reduced to the variables she shares with a suspected population. Once the authorities have concluded she fits the superficial criteria they are looking for, none of her individual traits matter any more—at least, not until after she has been stopped, searched, questioned, or whatever.

Dehumanization by itself is pernicious, robbing color from our day by dimming that of God we might see in every person. We clear the decks for all kinds of petty, unremarkable harm to be done to one another when we have objectified each other. "Health and a beautiful environment for all are not worth my trouble to carry this trash to the garbage can," says the litterer. "The time I save doesn't cost anyone else much," says the line-jumper (or in my case, the one who is frequently late to meetings), who carefully avoids adding up those small slices of time for each person who must wait longer. "Everyone else is doing it," says the briber, who thereby avoids considering the suffering and waste he is helping to foist on a society beset by corruption. "Winning is the important thing," says the candidate who savages his opponent with an unfair last minute smear. Never mind that the entire polity suffers when self-serving politicians spread cynicism and untruth. In each of these cases, someone has decided to ignore the legitimate needs of those around him or has concluded that other people do not count in his moral calculations. This is the essence of dehumanization.

Jesus knew how easy it is for us to treat each other as means to an end, rather than as full human beings with all the richness of detail and imperfection that implies. This is why he summed up the Christian's duty with the Golden Rule. "Do unto others as you would have them do unto you" is a prescription for humanization. I am invited to imagine the effects of my action on the one person—myself—I am least likely to reduce to a shadow of humanity. This helps me see the other person as a full human.

Dehumanization in Political Misery

A person sinking into corrosive grievance loses track of the humanity of his adversaries primarily because he loses some of his ability to process information. Spiritual deformation mangles how he perceives his world and corrupts his thought processes. He isn't seeing or thinking straight anymore because of what has happened inside him.

Dehumanization happens a little differently for those in political misery. Whereas corrosive grievance operates primarily internally, interfering with how a person receives and interprets information, political misery operates primarily externally, leading to information starvation. People get little information, and what they do get is often decayed beyond recognition, because the environment around them discourages the free flow of the truth.

Tyrannies are the worst culprits in this regard. Tyrants fear truth. Especially in the modern world where democracy is a real option, and has done relatively well at providing prosperity and opportunity for its citizens, tyrants tremble at the threat of letting their people know the truth about life without tyranny. The Soviet empire fell because its westernmost citizens had access to direct, reliable information about how their lives compared to those in the European democracies just across their borders. Chinese tyrants walk a tightrope, trying to allow the flows of information necessary for modernizing their economy without giving their citizens access to the truth about political alternatives. And of course every tyrant must keep citizens from talking freely to one another, lest they organize their opposition and topple the regime.

Tyrants may succeed for a time at keeping the truth from their citizens, but they do so at tremendous cost. For one thing, to keep a lid on truth, tyrants must cultivate a culture of untruth. People learn to fear to speak their minds or tell unpleasant truths. Soon all politically sensitive information ceases to flow freely, at best trickling by hushed word of mouth. Instead, the regime fosters the spread of images and ideas that buttress the regime—one-sided or even false accounts of the leadership's deeds, equally distorted versions of the actions of the regime's foes and even of conditions in other places that might offer a different vision of how people can live.

With only contaminated "information" flowing in public, citizens lose contact with reality, both in their own country and in other places. Citizens as well as government officials lose track of real problems, which go unsolved. National policy, even with the best of intentions, loses its ability to address the real needs of the nation, and the private sector's ability to fill customer's needs steadily decays. The nation gradually but inevitably ossifies, no longer able to respond well to the reality within or outside its borders. Everyone lives with a fantasy image of the world, the one approved by the regime, rather than the real image, and sooner or later everyone pays the price for living in a fantasy.

This is a major reason why despotic regimes inevitably fall. Their ability to acquire and process accurate information is systematically destroyed by the regime trying to retain power. Despots may linger longer if they can shut their people off from reality nearly completely. But in the modern world despots are doomed to early demises, given the blossoming revolution in global media, including the Internet.

We cannot complacently wait for the fall of dictatorships. Tyrants cling to power at the cost of tremendous suffering among their people. And they also help cause the kind of dehumanization of others that can lead to terrorism. Some of this is the deliberate work of the regime, using its control of internal media to demonize rivals within and without. Images of the "enemy" are managed to make them look as bad as possible.

But some dehumanization of foreigners happens as the natural and inescapable result of information starvation. People in tyrannies have little opportunity to meet and get to know people from elsewhere. Even skeptics who distrust the official regime's dark descriptions of foreigners may have little reliable information out of which to construct a more accurate and richer picture. Thus leaving tyrannies alone not only condemns people to political misery but also accelerates the process of dehumanizing others so crucial to developing terrorists.

A different form of information starvation besets anarchies and corrupt political systems. After all, no government agency in any anarchy, nor in most corrupt systems, is going to suppress thought and speech like a tyranny does. But accurate and useful information about strangers is always hard to come by, much harder than the pre-packaged caricatures we naturally construct about others based on stray images and experiences. To combat the natural barriers in crosscultural and international relationships, we need high volumes of good information.

Prosperous people can get this information from travel and from connections built through professional, religious, and other international organizations. But poor people have fewer such opportunities. Anarchic and corrupt political systems do not tend to sustain large upper and middle classes. Most citizens of poor countries get no personal contact with foreigners, unless foreigners come to them. If those visitors are mostly rich vacationers who seldom leave posh resorts or cruise ships, the resulting cross-cultural contacts are unlikely to be rich opportunities for humanization. In fact, they may reinforce unfortunate stereotypes.

It is possible for mass media to play a constructive role in humanization across national and cultural bounds. But anarchic and corrupt political systems, like tyrannies, do not abound in opportunities for the transmission of rich intercultural humanization. Some segments of these societies have little access to mass media to begin with because they cannot afford televisions or computers nor the time to use them. And without a large and prosperous market for programming, there is little opportunity for media managers to create much that is of value in this area. Given how little good humanizing information we receive from North America broadcast media, is there really any chance that a typically poor citizen of anarchy or political corruption would find better fare?

On the other hand, in some markets American television series are readily available to foreign viewers, much more so than are foreign shows to North Americans. At least in the transmission of language, then, citizens of other countries have an advantage. When they do have contact with North American tourists, for example, people almost everywhere have a stock of images and even vocabulary upon which they can draw in trying to relate.

I do not want to downplay how important this is. But healthy persons in political misery develop skepticism as a basic survival skill, learning not to trust much of what they are told. This makes humanization via the media harder—in fact, it makes all communication harder and contributes to information starvation in such places. Even accurate images are likely to be distrusted and discounted. And one has to wonder how humanizing much of North American television is. Do the images others get about us from television portray us accurately, giving a window on our full humanity? At least in the case of Al-Qaida, which seems to have built its hatred for North Americans largely on media images, the results are not encouraging.

Counteracting Dehumanization

One of the connections between political misery and terrorism is thus dehumanization. We will examine more measures we can take against political misery in chapters 7 and 8. For the rest of this chapter we are going to look at how we can address dehumanization even though in some cases it may be in part only a symptom of political misery,

We also should note that, as toxic as dehumanization is, it does not always lead to terrorism. Much of our dehumanizing activity is practically instinctive, perhaps a residue of original sin. Some of it is learned from our culture or our families of origin, reflexive behavior rooted in self-centeredness or insensitivity. Dehumanization is cultivated, to be sure, in boot camps everywhere to ease the killing process in wartime, and perhaps inadvertently as a byproduct of violent movies and video games.[49] But even in the military, where dehumanization may help someone pull a trigger or drop a bomb from high altitudes, it doesn't always lead to political uses of violence against innocents. That hallmark of terrorism generally requires a combination of dehumanization with either corrosive grievance or an undisciplined "mob" group psychology.

If we do well at responding to corrosive grievance, we will already have in place a good part of our response to dehumanization. If we are creative and insistent about listening empathetically, we will make good headway toward helping others find psychological space to revise their explanations to fit closer to reality. If we serve lovingly we will challenge dehumanizing mythologies about us.

If we remember our own tendency to dehumanize others, including terrorists and tyrants, we will find it easier to empathize and serve. And we cannot empathize and serve without rapidly growing in our sense of the humanity in those we listen to and help. So in a sense, we have already begun to prescribe a response to hatred with the suggestions made in Chapter 5.

But there are at least two more broad strategies we can bring to bear when our objective is to remedy dehumanizing hatred: *creating human connections*, and *working toward reconciliation*.

Creating human connections

How do people overcome their prejudices about others? Consider a time when you had formed a vivid negative first impression of someone, but later changed your mind. What was it that forced you to reconsider your original evaluation of that person?

I can recall several cases where my bad first impressions of someone were corrected over time. I have also watched this process in others, especially in the context of mediations. Many, if not most, mediations begin with one or both parties actively distrusting the other. Part of what happens in a good mediation is a change (for the better) in how the parties to a dispute see one another. Usually one mediation does not result in a 180-degree turnaround in mutual perceptions, but there frequently is significant improvement—say a ninety degree change, or even more.[50] One of the important tasks for mediators is to help disputants make a human connection with each other to maximize the opportunity for such a revolution in their relationship.

Most people don't resort to mediation until their relationships are under serious stress. So at the outset, human connections are either nonexistent, or are under severe strain. We can diagram their predicament like this:

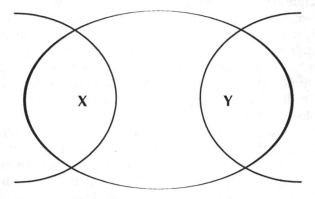

The oval is the arena of the dispute involving X and Y. The arcs are the areas where each side feels comfortable or safe—where they do not feel they have left behind their personal powerbase. The problem is that there is no place where X and Y jointly feel at ease. They do not believe, or maybe even cannot imagine, that they have anything substantial in common. Under conditions like these, each side will have little to restrain them from dehumanizing the other. Everything they know about the other is either alien, or threatening, or both.

In fact, people in a relationship like this are in a double predicament. As things stand, there is little hope for progress since they share nothing about which they are ready to trust the other. But if X wants to make some kind of move in the direction of Y, to push her zone of comfort toward Y's zone of comfort, it is easy for Y to misunderstand. Such a move toward her "space" may be perceived as aggression, as yet another attempt to invade Y's turf. For example, should a Protestant Unionist in

Northern Ireland go out of his way into Republican Catholic neighborhoods, even with the best of motives, his "incursion" may be viewed with suspicion—is he spying? Trying to co-opt someone? Trying to somehow claim territory? After all, every year zealous Unionists insist on marching through Catholic/Republican neighborhoods. And they do so not as a show of good will, but to remind everyone that Northern Ireland is British.

At this point, people tend to put stock in an assumption I call the "myth of the conservation of behavior." Physicists tell us there is a "law of the conservation of matter" describing the fact that matter never really ceases to exist, even when we lose track of it. Some people think the same thing holds for human behavior. Once people have established a pattern of doing something, according to this myth, they will always do it. Even when an enemy appears to have changed her ways, according to the myth it's a false front, or maybe even a clever scheme to lure us to our destruction.

Remember, by "myth" we do not mean "an untrue account." Myths are stories we tell ourselves to explain the world around us. Some myths are entirely true. There is an element of truth to this myth, as in most myths. After all, the N-G-B model of human behavior informs us that tried and true behavior is stable behavior. It will tend to persist until the person recognizes through her own internal feedback that the behavior is no longer "working." But even in the N-G-B model, change is possible, even inevitable under the right conditions. We can learn and adapt. It's what makes us human rather than machine.

How could a Christian believe that human behavior cannot change? At the core of the Christian gospel is the idea of conversion and salvation. If becoming a disciple of Christ does not involve significant changes in behavior patterns, then our understanding of our faith doesn't make much sense.

Christians know that the most basic response to an enemy, even one who is out to hurt us, is supposed to be love. So even if we find ourselves in a situation where the chasm between ourselves and our opponents is vast, we cannot in good Christian faith yield to despair. Philip Smith argues that this duty to love is not just for the benefit of the opponent. He urges us to adopt the "virtue of civility," a character trait which prompts us to treat our opponents well.[51] Smith bases his advice in large part on the insight that our opponents are a valuable resource—a treasure, even—if we are serious about growing toward truth.

MULTIPLYING CONNECTIONS

But none of this means changes are easy or easily predictable. Looking again at our diagram of conflict, we can see that with suspicions and past hurts reinforcing the "lines of safety," turning them into fortifications, human contact can steadily decline. Stereotypes and suspicions thrive with little contrary data. As lines harden, those on either side nursing corrosive grievances will continue to drain their enemy of human qualities, adding onto their edifices of dehumanizing hatred.

An early sign that lines are hardening against safe common-ground is the tendency to label the other in some dismissive or pejorative way. American whites calling others "nigger" is a classic case. But ugly racism isn't the only form labeling takes. Sometimes it involves sexism (e.g., not all soccer parents are moms, not all deadbeat parents are dads), ageism, denominationalism, and even political-persuasion-ism. Republicans referring to Democrats as "baby-killers" or Democrats calling Republicans "corporate fat cats" are dehumanizing each other.

One of the most subtle and damaging forms of dehumanization occurs when we reduce our opponents to one-dimensional figures, so that George W. Bush is only capable of acting for one motive (to protect the oil industry or whatever), inevitably nefarious, or Bill Clinton is only capable of acting out of one animal urge, inevitably lascivious. *Christians will avoid using or thinking labels* such as these, or even the ones we use in our daily lives to allow us to quit thinking about people in their richness and surprising complexity.

A related syndrome is the temptation to think of other groups as monoliths. We know our own groups are not. Even groups as intimate as nuclear families celebrate internal diversity. "She is nothing like her brother" is a refrain uttered by countless parents. I've said it dozens of times about my own children. But once the attention shifts away from one's own groups, the tendency is to lost track quickly of individual variations: "They" are suddenly "all alike."

I encountered this monolithizing constantly, and ironically, in my work as director of the Center for Peace Learning at

George Fox University. On hearing my title, some people assumed me to be a granola-loving, tree-hugging leftwing Democrat, reasoning (if that is what we want to call their thought processes) that anyone involved in peace studies has to be a leftist. On the other hand, an opposite set of assumptions crops up when people learn that I teach at an evangelical Christian university. One group cannot believe that I could be a Republican convinced of the moral power of the free market; the other is surprised I am a pacifist convinced of the moral error of militarism. It is just so much more convenient to assume that, once you find out what group people belong to, you know everything about them.

A parallel temptation is to assume that once you know one of a person's motives, you can explain all his actions from that one intent. Combine these two logical leaps, and it becomes possible to ascribe to a person evil intent just by learning what group she belongs (or has belonged) to. The awful explanatory power of monolithic assumptions enables one to leap tall buildings at a single bound (e.g., that all U.S. government policies are designed to benefit the multinationals, especially the oil companies, even though the federal government is a fragmented structure employing millions) to reach devastating conclusions. *Believers will resist the temptation to shortcircuit thought processes by assuming other groups are monolithic.*

A third related dehumanizing temptation is embodied in the allure of conspiracy theories. How comforting it is to ascribe problems to someone else, especially to hidden networks of nefarious operatives out to get us. The benefits are enormous, since belief in conspiracies simultaneously excuses us from taking responsibility for conditions around us and provides foolproof explanations for bad things that happen to us. We can be blamed neither for current conditions, nor for our failure to do much about it, since events are in the control of a cabal.

But when pressed to explain who the cabal is, or how it works, we can cite "conspiracy" to explain how the plot is invisible to others, and to excuse ourselves for not knowing exactly how it operates. Any attempt to show that there is no conspiracy is doomed to failure, since the most important evidence is hidden, as one would expect conspirators to do. The perfect self-exculpation along with the perfect defense: no wonder conspiracy theories are so powerful. All you need to do to believe them is to convince yourself that all the members of the conspiracy are so venal, so depraved, that they would knowingly sell you out for their own gain—and, in many cases, that the conspiracy has been successfully maintained and defended for generations with no one but a few ever knowing about it.

Christians will resist the allure of conspiracy theories and treat them with healthy skepticism. They will not willingly trade in their belief that there is that of God in every person, and that people act for a variety of motives, to take on a belief in someone's subhuman uniformity of motive and conformity in action persisting over generations.

Once we have ceased erecting the barriers of monolithic stereotyping, labeling, and conspiracy theories, we can turn to looking for ways to lower barriers and make it easier for people to hear one another.

Some peace workers, recognizing the need for foes to re-humanize each other, have worked in a variety of creative ways to *bring members of hostile communities together in a neutral setting to get acquainted*. The settings differ, from camps for kids to conferences for professionals and officials. Sometimes the meetings are arranged by third parties serving as conveners to bring people together, not to resolve specific issues as a mediator would, but only to give the members of mutually hostile factions a safe place to be together and talk to each other. Other meetings are arranged by members of one side who have invited the other to join them.

I know of no evidence that any conflict has every been materially worsened by such contacts, although there certainly is at least a theoretical risk that new offenses might be added to old ones when enemies are brought together. Much more frequent are reports of participants seeing something in their rivals they had never recognized before. That is, humanization at some level is, apparently, the most frequent result of cross-community meetings.

However, I don't want to overstate the positive effects one can expect from bringing relatively small numbers of people together for simple dialog. For example, I heard from several sources, both in Israel and among Palestinians, that they were disillusioned about the value of these kinds of meetings among

groups from either side of the 1967 border. Since the participants tended to be ordinary citizens, or perhaps community
leaders but not governmental officials, any improvements in
the personal relationships in the group did not translate clearly
into improvements in either side's political or military stance toward the other. What good does it do to have dialogue among
people who are not in a position to change policy?

Unless the hostile communities are small, so that even common people have significant influence over attitudes on their
side, any progress in rehumanization from meetings among
small groups is likely to vanish under the overwhelming tide of
national resentments. For humanization to spread, we need to
pursue three broad strategies—multiplying the number of such
contacts, multiplying their depth when they happen, and
spreading their effect to as many people as possible when they
do happen.

One way to increase the number of contacts is to encourage
them to happen in ways that grow naturally out of people's interests. *Encouraging the formation of international voluntary associations of shared interests*—churches, hobbies, professions, and the
like—can provide many opportunities for people to meet those
of other communities. The Quakers have an organization like
this, the Friends World Committee for Consultation, whose
main purpose is to create opportunities for Friends around the
world to meet and communicate on issues of interest to Friends.
There are international sporting organizations, of which the
Olympics and soccer's FIFA are only two of the higher-profile
examples. Hobby groups sharing interest in everything from
quilting to flower gardens can, and often do, have international
assemblies.

Christians concerned about the rise of corrosive grievance
between two societies should take special pains to organize targeted bilateral contacts on as many levels as possible involving
members of those two groups. *Exchanges among youth, possibly in
the form of camps or study groups* held once each year in each nation, can be very powerful. Many Christian colleges already organize service or study trips for their students to other
countries. These are good. They would be even better if the colleges invested in hosting service and study trips of college-age
students from those countries, so that information and human-

ization can go both ways more powerfully. Existing programs to support exchange students at high school level could expand if believers were to participate in them more.

To add depth to the humanization going on, these *contacts can be organized around projects of joint interest.* Peacemaking itself might be the point of common interest, but other projects would also do nicely. An Indian group might go to Pakistan to work with Pakistanis delivering health care to refugees. The Pakistanis might return the favor, providing health care to homeless people in Calcutta. Or an American college soccer team might travel to Iraq for a series of matches, and invite (and probably help fund) a return visit by an equivalent Iraqi team.

Much of this is already happening. Elise Boulding, Quaker sociologist (and Kenneth's wife), has written about the burgeoning global civic culture. A growing number of private nonprofit international organizations are flourishing, built around such communities of interest as faith, sports, hobbies, and professions.[52] I see expanding interconnections across national boundaries as evidence of God's provision for us, giving us a powerful but subtle tool to help manage conflict in a globalizing civilization. Believers wanting to implement the Good Samaritan's understanding of the command to love our neighbors should be at the forefront of building international ties, so we can more often actually be on the road to Jericho when someone needs us to be there, instead of at home glued to the television.

Actually modern technology does give some hope to those prone to stay at home. If, instead of being glued to the television screen, one's addiction is to the computer screen, it is possible to still be constructive in combating dehumanization. Internet and e-mail offer significant opportunities to build humanizing connections. For example, a friend of mine stumbled into an e-mail correspondence with a man from Bangladesh which has ranged across a wide span of topics, including important personal and spiritual issues. Modern cybercommunication has unmeasured potential to help people work together on projects of mutual interest.[53] Christians can do a tremendous amount to combat dehumanization by *actively corresponding via e-mail and through innovative uses of web pages.*

International adoption is an example of a mutual project—matching children and homes—that brings people together across cultural lines. If it motivates the adoptive family to get to know their new child's native culture, and if the family keeps in contact with that culture, it can have a powerful humanizing effect, at least on the adoptive family and others in its community. It can also help change the physical appearance of the adopting community, eroding stereotypes. My own home congregation is experiencing this kind of quiet transformation, thanks to a wave of adoptions from China, Southeast Asia, India, and Russia (among others). My wife and I have a new son, Benjamin Quan Mock, born in Vietnam in February 2002.

Hosting foreign exchange students is another superb way of building this kind of human connection.

One of the most important resources Christians bring to the project of humanization is their long experience in cross-cultural missions and development work. In tens of thousands of local congregations all over the world, churchgoers get a rudimentary education in what life is like in other countries when they read accounts from missionaries they support, or come to missions-week services. Of course, missionary and development worker families become intercultural in at least some sense, and bring those experiences with them when they come back home. Building on this good start on international humanization by *expanding on missions and development work, through more short-term service opportunities and other exchanges,* would multiply its counter-terrorist effects.

Some missionaries and development workers have not always succeeded in overcoming stereotypes; at their worst, some have acted as if host cultures had nothing to teach them, and were thus negligible. But no negligible person was ever born; every person has that of God in them, and thus has something to teach us. Nor are there any negligible cultures, with nothing to teach others. Even the most devout saint has something to learn.

John Paul Lederach went to Nicaragua in the 1980s as a sort of missionary of peacemaking. One of his goals was to help Nicaraguans strengthen their nonviolent responses to conflict, so as to deflect some of that nation's conflict from violence.[54] Lederach carried with him sophisticated models of conflict resolution drawn from his fellow Mennonites' groundbreaking work in North America. But before long, he decided that the North American models he had brought with him weren't perfect fits for Nicaraguans. Instead, Lederach experimented with an "elicitative" approach to conflict resolution training. He became a listener, prompting Nicaraguans to reflect on how they manage conflicts and how they might improve in areas Lederach suggested to them.

Elicitative conflict resolution training turned Lederach's Nicaragua work into a two-way humanizing experience. The Nicaraguans taught Lederach, and through him many of us in North America, that conflict can be successfully managed in ways we never would have thought of otherwise. In turn, Lederach took to Nicaragua reports of the results of many years of experimentation with innovations in conflict management in North America. Together, Lederach and his Nicaraguan hosts did a lot of work toward clarifying what is true about all human conflict and what might be truly general principles of conflict management, valid across a variety of human cultures. In the process, Lederach and those he worked with in Nicaragua came to know each other at levels they would never have reached had he spent his time teaching without listening.

This elicitative process, mildly revolutionary in my conflict resolution field, probably looks very familiar to good missionaries and development workers the world over. But we have barely begun finding ways to apply its respectful, cooperative approach, focusing on discerning anew how to apply timeless principles of faith (or even the more mundane principles of economics, art, engineering, or many other areas of human endeavor) to the specific conditions of each culture and place. Believers can both spread and deepen humanization by *adapting the elicitative approach to their own fields* when they have opportunity to work crossculturally.

This point has a clear corollary. Lederach had to be willing to listen, and open to new understandings, before he could participate in an elicitative process. But his Nicaraguan colleagues also had to be open, vulnerable, and truthful. Had they been reserved, less than frank, or prone to strategic manipulation of information, Lederach could have elicited all day and would have gotten nothing of value. Openness is as crucial as listening in the humanizing process.

Openness is not as easy as it sounds. As the Soviets learned when Gorbachev insisted on glasnost, even a little openness is a

dangerous thing. One cannot become transparent in any meaningful sense without being willing to be changed. It is easy for
us in the West to point out that the citizens of the former Soviet
empire are better off as a result of their leaders' experimentation
with openness. But from many Russians' perspectives, Gorbachev's reforms must have seemed like a reckless leap into a
void—which it may have been, in some sense, given how poorly
Gorbachev seems to have foreseen the revolutionary events that
would follow. But Gorbachev's choice was unavoidable. Ask
the managers and investors in companies recently staggered by
revelations of accounting irregularities whether, in retrospect,
anything was gained by failing to be frank about company finances.

Despite the risks, the benefits of living transparently are
even greater. Refusing to hide embarrassments is an incisive
tool in one's spiritual growth. Honesty before others is connected to honesty before God. Knowing that others will know,
and refusing to hide, will disturb our complacencies and overthrow our self-deceptions. Just as the Soviet Union could not
survive intact the destruction of its comfortable illusions, anyone who takes up transparency runs a severe risk of undergoing
transformation.

But beyond the therapeutic effects of transparency on the
transparent, it also can have a world-changing effect on others.
As an element in a counterterrorism strategy, it is a powerful
tool for stripping away stereotypes and building trust. The
more transparent we are, the less raw material we leave around
from which others can build edifices of conspiracy and mistrust.

Christians can fight terror by *being transparent, not only in
their personal lives, but also in their corporate affairs,* whether in
their churches, their charitable work, or their commercial affairs. Transparency of the type I am talking about does not come
easily or cheaply. It may require a level of honesty that is uncomfortable, a real stretch for people used to thinking in typical
public relations terms. Transparent Christians who put out
press releases when business is up will not go silent when it is
down. They will not cover up scandals when they occur but will
be frank about them, consistent with due regard for the rights of
those people implicated or victimized. They might not flaunt
their dirty laundry, but they will not hide it either.

Let me offer an example of the kinds of dilemmas we will face if we are committed to transparency. I know of a new missionary effort in a North African Moslem country. However, the laws of that country prohibit open evangelism. The relevant missions board has struggled with how to handle the problems this presents. The missions board has tried to find a way to be honest about what it is doing but to be sensitive in how to conceptualize and describe it so as to avoid alarming government officials there.

One way to partly dodge the problem has been "lifestyle evangelism." That is, missionaries enter the target country as businesspeople, to pursue some legal secular trade or profession and look for opportunities to share the gospel that arise in the course of normal life. Besides giving missionaries good and truthful answers for immigration officials, the lifestyle evangelism model has some practical, theological, and perhaps other advantages for the mission. It moves missions even more toward an elicitative model, with influences and ideas running both ways in relationships missionaries form with locals. The gospel only gets shared in this model after both sides in the relationship are humanized enough that spiritual issues arise naturally in their conversation and interaction.

I consider the creative tension of wanting to spread the gospel while telling local officials the truth to be a boon to the mission organization, a spur to new levels of creativity, sensitivity, and in the long run, effectiveness for God. Shifting from traditional missionary models to lifestyle evangelism may be an important improvement in mission methods brought about by this creative tension between desires for success and desires to avoid deception.

However, another aspect of the mission group's strategy is more troubling. Note how I have described the mission field—without naming the country The board has decided to avoid referring in public to the specific country as a way of protecting missionaries there from expulsion and to protect early converts from retribution.

I worry that here the missions board has made a mistake. It has succumbed to the temptation to fudge about its plans for its work to get into the country and be able to have an impact. If it were more open about its new project, its missionaries would probably be turned away at the borders. So it has chosen to be a bit surreptitious, a bit sneaky, in my view a bit dishonest. It is taking active measures to deceive people about the intent of its missionaries as they enter the country. But this dishonesty avoids a resolution on the merits of the question of whether missionaries should be allowed into the country. It simultaneously takes the target country off the hook for what I believe is an unjust law and taints all mission work in that country with a stain of dishonesty.

It may be that in the short run a full commitment to transparency would hinder in some ways the missionaries' work. Some might not be allowed to come into the country and others might be expelled. This would be frustrating and costly, but it might be the best result—forcing the mission board to keep thinking about how it might respond to God's call, and highlighting for locals the costs they are paying with their laws restricting religious freedom. Furthermore, once in the country under false pretenses, missionaries who hide from immigration officials their true intent must operate clandestinely to avoid detection. This slows the process of moving relationships around to spiritual issues.

And what happens when, as it inevitably will, the true nature of these people's work comes to light? The good reputation of Christians for honesty will be smirched. Who knows how many other projects in the future will lose effectiveness, or even become impossible, because word gets around that Christians sometimes practice to deceive? Being careful not to enter the country or to strike up relationships on false pretenses would in the long run reinforce trustworthiness. As in any investment, payoffs could be large in a generation or two if people now could be patient and stick to their word. I hope mission leaders will reconsider and choose to be open about their intentions in all missions targets.

Note here how important is a prior commitment to transparency, to avoiding deception and other means of taking shortcuts in relationships? Note how dependent we are on faith to be able to sustain transparency when its short term results may be frustrating or even traumatic. I can't imagine a commitment to transparency surviving if it is not based on a firm faith that truth is God's tool, and that it always will pay in the long run. There may not be sufficient evidence from our own lives to convince us this is true. But if we believe in a God who is Truth, it is hard to believe that untruth serves divine purposes.

ACTING CONTRARY TO EXPECTATIONS

A benefit of firm commitments to principles is that it can lead directly to humanizing moments. Someone who is developing dehumanizing hatred toward you will have already convinced himself that you are acting out of some form of debased motive—at least out of your own self interest no matter what that may cost others, or perhaps even out of pure spite for his people. Underhandedness, even if well-intentioned, will eventually come to light and reinforce these negative stereotypes. But transparency at direct and clear personal cost, when observed by someone who has begun to hate you, creates a problem for her. Her myths about you do not provide for you to suffer out of faithfulness to a virtue, or out of concern for her people. Her expectations are that you will turn anything you can to your own advantage. When you do not, you create for her cognitive dissonance.

That is, your conspicuous and clear willingness to suffer for him or for a virtue creates in the hating observer a conflict between his myths about you and what he sees you do. Most humans find such cognitive dissonance intolerable. We avoid a lot of it by failing to see things that contradict our theories about the world, sometimes even when they are in plain view. Or we explain what we see as being due to hidden factors that reconcile appearances with our preset notions—conspiracy theories come in handy here. We can count on those who hate us to use these two self-delusory tactics in great volume.

But if the dissonant events persist long enough, at some point they become inescapable. If the facts won't change or easily explain away, then the existing theory has to change. At this point humanization becomes possible. I see it happen all the time in mediations—facts come out that finally force one or both sides to change their theories about one another.

In cases where there has been a long history of distrust and alienation, such as might exist between two hostile cultural groups, theories explaining the nefariousness of each side grow resilient in the face of contrary evidence. Theories about hidden motives and vast conspiracies develop, sometimes approaching incontrovertibility. Some people come to the point where they believe that their enemies have nearly total control over information—so much so that these people believe they themselves are helpless to resist the enemy's smooth talk! The only safe thing to do is to stop up one's ears against the voice of the enemy.

Perhaps Satan has such enchanting power, although the Christian doctrine is that in Christ we have nothing to fear. But as a strategy for dealing with fellow humans, shutting off all input from one's foes helps dehumanization flourish. Progress is difficult under such conditions, but not impossible. Transparency will help, but it doesn't always have the kind of vivid impact that would be needed to change seared and encrusted hearts. We need to apply the power of persistent cognitive dissonance more colorfully, by *looking for authentic yet dramatic ways to act contrary to the expectations of those vulnerable to dehumanizing hatred toward us.*

If budding terrorists expect us to be arrogant, let's be humble. If they expect materialism, let's live simply and generously. If they expect godlessness, let's tend our spiritual lives. If they expect licentiousness or drunkenness, let's live chastely and soberly. In none of these choices would we be hurting ourselves. Some involve giving up what might seem to be a harmless vice or indulgence. But if something gives a terrorist or a tyrant another brick in the wall of his hatred, and it wouldn't really hurt us to give it up, shouldn't we consider abandoning it for the sake of fighting terrorism and tyranny? Or, put it more positively, the more potential haters see of humble, simple, faithful, chaste, and abstinent Americans, the more dissonance he is going to experience in his beliefs about Americans.

But these are general behaviors. We should also look for specific actions we can take, individually or corporately, to act contrary to expectations, the kind that can give a human face to the cognitive dissonance we hope to instill in our observers.

One example of such an act was the visit Egyptian President Anwar Sadat made to Jerusalem in the late 1970s. To an Israeli populace convinced that no Arab would ever recognize the existence of their state, Sadat's visit was a shock. It opened the way for many Israelis to change their minds about the possibility of

166 ❖ Loving Without Giving In

negotiations, at least with some Arabs. I suspect that the heroic performance of fire fighters and police during the attempts to evacuate the Twin Towers at the World Trade Center caught some Al-Qaida sympathizers off-guard, and may have given them pause about whether they really did understand American decadence.

Domestic American terrorists of the Tim McVeigh type expect their government to be hostile to the interests of the ordinary person, perhaps even a tool of the elites to reduce the rest of us to peonage. Christians in government service eager to take momentum away from the expansion of domestic terrorism can be extra careful to do what they aspire to do: treat citizens with respect and kindness. Al-Qaida sympathizers may expect American, or Christian, hostility to Islam. Christians in America can act contrary to this expectation by acting courageously to defend the rights of Moslems residing here, and go out of our way to protect them from threats of violence or injustice. Moral outrage in America over accidental bombings of civilians in Afghanistan or Iraq would help, as would outrage here and in Israel over the deaths of Palestinian children during anti-terrorist operations in Gaza and the West Bank.

I cannot give a comprehensive list of the possibilities for dramatic and even redemptive actions that transform expectations. The more we put ourselves in a position to interact with those suspicious of us, the more opportunities will arise. The best ideas will be those actions that not only would surprise our foes, but that also would be good for us to do anyway. That is, they may be good for *us*, such as living simply or abstaining from alcohol. Or they will be good for us to do because they are good for *others*—such as, again, living simply or generously. Actually, in most cases they will be both.

Take note, it is probably becoming clear that I think we can find ways to act contrary to the expectations of potential terrorists by being better people! There is a germ of truth in many of the terrorists' expectations. We are a gluttonous people, and licentious. We often do behave arrogantly. Our government often does act, through some of its policies, or perhaps through some of its personnel, in a high-handed manner, or in service of the interests of elites at the cost of the poor. I am saying we can learn to be better people by listening to terrorists or their supporters.

I am not saying we can expect to improve by behaving as they would want us to. But we can learn by listening to them and discerning among the possible cacophony of their complaints the parts that ring true. The wise person accepts reproof, says Proverbs.[55] In fact, she accepts it no matter whence it comes—it is not wise to refuse to improve because someone you detest has inspired the insight. In fact, when such an insight comes, we should seize on it with glee, knowing that our discipleship will at this point bear double, no, *triple* fruit: in our own lives, in the lives of those we touch, and in the reduction of dehumanizing hatred among those who are watching us.

Of course, if we are asking our enemies to notice when we act contrary to their expectations, we have to be open to their actions that shatter our preconceptions. In fact, when we see our foes act in constructive ways, we need to be ready to reward those actions no matter how surprising they are. Rewarding constructive action by our enemies is a good way to improve the odds of such behavior becoming routine. (Or it might, in some cases, only be improving the odds that we will recognize the admirable aspects of our enemies' lives more routinely, in those cases where they have been acting this way all along but we didn't notice.) *Rewarding constructive changes in action by our enemies* is an excellent way to promote bilateral humanization.

HELP FROM THIRD PARTIES

In some situations, the barriers between hostile communities are so high that they find it exceedingly difficult to do much about them, acting on their own. If they had the other side's cooperation, maybe something could be done, but they can't get the other side's cooperation because levels of distrust and pain are too high. At this point, third parties become crucial.[56]

Fortunately, there are almost an infinite number of ways for third party peacemakers to impact a dispute. Consider our diagram of a dispute, as modified below[57]:

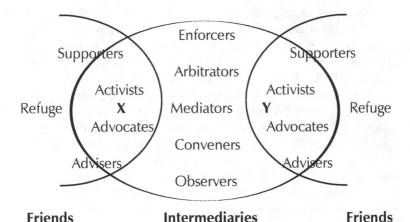

Friends   **Intermediaries**   **Friends**

Here is just a sample of the possible third-party roles in a dispute. Given that X and Y have a gap between their comfort zones, there is room between them for *intermediaries* who have roughly symmetrical relationships with both sides. Intermediaries can help build human connections in a wide variety of ways. They might employ coercion to *enforce* nonviolent processes and create space for resolutions on the merits. Or they might provide those nonviolent processes themselves, encouraging either exchange or affiliation based problem solving in an *arbitration* or *mediation*, or just helping disputants connect by *convening* some kind of joint session. Or they can just provide accurate information to each party about the other, serving as *observers*. These five possibilities only begin the list of potential intermediary roles, which can be extended as far as our creativity will take us. How about *interposers*, physically inserting themselves in scenes of potential violence to help reduce the threat of attack? Or *intercessors*, who pray for both sides? Or *messengers* who take an active role in currying communication among disputants? Or *cheerleaders*, who prod both sides to make greater efforts for peace? Or even *prophets*, who stand between and preach peace and hope and justice and truth? One could argue that the Nobel Prize Committee has been a cheerleader and a prophet for peace for the last century.

There are about as many possible peacemaking roles available to those who have better access to one side than to the other. Being a *friend* for peacemaking (as opposed to a friend who approves of whatever a person does, even warmaking, which is the more frequent connotation) can help each side expand its zone of comfort far enough for both to find areas in common with each other. Remembering that the friend here is working always for peace—either peacebuilding in relationships, peace-making on issues, or peacekeeping for nonviolent processes—she can work from within the arena of conflict, or on its edges, or even entirely outside it.

Advocates help publicize needs and urge merit-based reso-lution of issues, reducing their ally's sense that violence is the only language their opponents understand. *Activists* help orga-nize services and meet needs, to the same end. *Advisers* and *sup-porters* contribute information and material resources toward meeting needs. *Refuges* give people a place to retreat from the conflict and find release from its tension.

And again this list is only partial. One might just be a *lis-tener*, not offering the adviser's input, but just hearing someone out. Or one might serve as a *visitor*, along the lines of what Jesus had in mind in urging us to visit widows, the sick, and those in prison. Or in a more active and longer term role, we might *ac-company* people who are under threat of violence. Or we might go further and assume the risk ourselves rather than sharing it. For example, Jesus is our *surrogate*, having taken on himself the penalty for our sins.

It may seem odd to suggest these as possible roles for Chris-tians concerned about terrorism, tyranny, and other forms of political misery. The friend's options, in particular, seem to strengthen the groups who are doing terrible things, which seems like the last thing one would want to do. But I am think-ing about this from a different angle. Part of my thinking will be clearer in later chapters, when we talk about how critical it is to develop ways other than violence for issues to be addressed. But I also argue that even in conflicts where there are clear good and bad guys, the bad guys need friends. And everyone else needs the bad guys to have friends, too.

People sinking into bitter grievance won't sink so fast or far if they have peacemaking friends to help provide perspective and hope. Friends with an eye toward peace can powerfully speed the humanization of the enemy, building on the invalu-able trust they have earned. Bitter, hateful grievants who feel they are without friends are the most prone to resort to terrorism. Too often we try to run off anyone who shows any inkling of befriending our foes because we focus on the risk that the enemy will thereby become stronger. But an enemy with friends working for peace is less dangerous, not more, because such an enemy has a powerful antidote to dehumanizing hatred. Assuming the peacemaking friends are persistent and courageous, what we risk in strengthening our enemies is more than made up for in what we gain by diminishing corrosive grievance and especially dehumanizing hatred.

So if we see that an enemy is arising, aggrieved and hating, one of our most powerful options is to *help that enemy find and come to rely upon peacemaking friends*, even if we have to recruit the friends for our enemy. *We should at the same time bring to the fore in our own lives trusted friends* whose commitment to justice, hope, truth, and peace we can count on to be stronger than their desire to temporarily please us. We should also *invite intermediaries into the conflict setting*. In cases where we observe others falling into enmity with each other, we should *step forward as opportunity opens to be friends or intermediaries*. Overall, our strategy in any conflict (our own or others') should be to *build a web of intermediaries and friends*, working together from all sides to promote humanization and otherwise advocate for peaceful process, reconciled relationships, and just outcomes.

Working toward reconciliation

Initiating humanizing contacts will help interrupt the process of dehumanization, and may even start its reversal. But as long as the sense of grievance persists, its victims will feel pressure to resume the downward spiral of dehumanizing hatred, as a way of sustaining their account of how they came to suffer in the first place. And it is also possible that everything we have covered so far in this chapter will prove to have been in vain. So it may be that, to reverse permanently trends toward dehumanizing hatred, we may have to go even further—act even farther outside the realm of our foes' expectations—and take the spiritual steps toward full reconciliation.

I am not assuming that every grievance directed against us, or that we might have toward someone else, is grounded in reality. In both interpersonal and international relationships, unrealistic conflict is relatively common. Yet, when someone has something against us, we are supposed to lay aside our gifts at the altar of God and go first to be reconciled before we complete our normal acts of worship.[58]

This does not seem to depend on whether what they have against us is accurate. The problem is secondarily the justice of their claims, and primarily the fact that we are allowing resentment against us to build in the heart of the other. And when we ask God for forgiveness, we are to understand how our forgiveness is tied to our willingness to forgive others.[59] Even if the other is mistaken in his grievance against us, our relationship and even our souls are in some ways bound up against receiving the full measure of God's love until we have cleared the air between us. (And we should remember that a good fraction of the time, even though we can't imagine that we have done anything wrong, we will find out we have once we truly listen to the one resenting us.)

The Bible draws a rich picture of the process of reconciliation in our own relationships with God. We have all offended against God and stand in need of reconciliation, which the Bible describes as having three crucial aspects: accepting suffering, offering forgiveness, and expressing repentance.

ACCEPT SUFFERING

God's central act in the work of reconciling with us was to come to earth and accept for himself the suffering that was due us. This is perhaps the central distinguishing theological pillar of Christianity, separating it from Judaism, Islam, and all other religions. Christianity teaches what we will have to call (to be consistent throughout the book) the myth of redemptive suffering. (Of course, I believe this myth to be true.) That is, the spiritual penalty for our sins was paid by Jesus who, being innocent, took on the guilt of our sins.

I am not ready to believe that humans, as fallen as anyone else, can pay the sin-debt for others. But there are other ways the myth of redemptive suffering works out to be true in our daily lives. If someone sins against me and thereby causes me to suffer, I have a choice. My natural response is to pay them back, to exact vengeance in equal measure. This impulse parallels the Old Testament principle of "an eye for an eye," often called the "lex talionis," which is actually an attempt to put strict and just limits on the impulse for revenge (don't cause more suffering than you have endured).

If I do exact vengeance, it is unlikely that my victims will respond by saying, "Well, yes, we had that coming. No hard feelings." For one thing, they (being the judges of their own case) will likely think they were innocent of hurting me, or that what they did to me was justified by something I previously did to them. (Anyone who has driven two or more kids many miles will remember hearing both of these claims emanating from the back seat, probably argued in the alternative by one child hoping to avoid parental retribution.) For another, the vengeance I wreak, gauged by me in light of my painful experience, is very unlikely to strike them as being justified by their understanding of what they did.

If any of these extremely probable events occur, my foe is likely to believe that there was some excess in my retaliation that now justifies his retaliating in return, to even the score. But since I thought my original response was measured and fit the occasion, any sort of retaliation is going to strike me as overreacting and will open the door for me to strike back again, opening another round in a cycle of violence. This is why it has been so often said that an eye for an eye ends up leaving everyone blind.[60]

So if I break this cycle by *accepting suffering without retaliation*, this is in a very practical sense redemptive. My opponent feels less (or even no) pressure to strike back at me again, and the cycle of suffering ceases. This is the picture Jesus draws for us in the Sermon on the Mount when he contrasts the "eye for an eye" rule with the command to turn the other cheek, go the extra mile, and so forth.[61]

Jesus is, arguably, not entirely clear in the Sermon on the Mount whether turning the other cheek is supposed to be a consistent rule of behavior or a strategy to be adopted only at opportune moments when it can change the dynamics of a relationship. To the extent Jesus was responding to the flawed logic of the *lex talionis*, the new approach would seem to be meant as a rule of thumb to apply over and over as needed. At least in English translations, the language Jesus uses in this passage implies that the new standard is to be universally applied.

As a way of showing love to our enemies, turning the other cheek would apply every time our enemy can recognize what we are doing.

When it comes to terrorism, though, turning the other cheek is extremely hard counsel. It got essentially no consideration in the United States after September 11, 2001. We seldom have acted as if the Sermon on the Mount applied to governments. So we might be tempted, in this case, to read the Sermon as if it only suggests that turning the other cheek should be among the responses in our repertoire as individuals. Of course, even widespread turning of the other cheek by individuals would be dramatically different from what is usually done.

And there is research evidence for this more limited view of Jesus' teaching. Game theorists suggest that the best strategy for dealing with opponents is to pay them back for what they just did to you—the scholars call this "tit for tat" but it's really about the same as "an eye for an eye"—with an occasional break in the pattern where you act cooperatively in response to one of the other side's dirty tricks. But if the opponent does not respond cooperatively, then (according to these studies) you should immediately resume "tit for tat."[62]

At the very least, then, in her private life a Christian should be willing to try one clear response of turning the other cheek, probably as early as possible in a cycle of retribution—preferably at the very first opportunity. If one chooses to go back to "tit for tat" for a while, the Christian will still look for other opportunities from time to time to turn the other cheek and break out of the cycle of violence. Any time a cost is absorbed, it will be painful, and we should not minimize this. Some suggest that we can give God thanks for sufferings because they give us this chance to show God's grace in our own willingness to suffer without retaliation.

Even though opportunistic cheek-turning would be a significant improvement over most current practice, I am uncomfortable with this minimization of the Sermon on the Mount teachings. It seems to me Jesus is going well beyond a mere repeal of the *lex talionis*—we don't just accept the suffering already inflicted by turning the other cheek, we invite the infliction of more suffering. We don't just meet the immediate need of the Roman soldier by carrying his pack one mile, we take it on for him an extra mile as well. We don't just satisfy the demand by delivering a coat, we anticipate future needs by offering the cloak, too. In fact, Jesus concludes this passage by urging us to pray for those who persecute us, which is the same as saying "Stay concerned about this person even after you've gone the extra mile. Pray for him until his need is fully met."

This is not a game of tit for tat that we are trying to win in any traditional sense. Jesus' vision seems to be to call us to a new game. When someone acts out of anger, arrogant power, or vindictiveness toward you, Jesus seems to say, take the opportunity to *enter into a nurturing relationship with your opponent*, meet his immediate needs as you are able, and stay in relationship with him (at least by praying for him) until he has access to means to meet all his needs. That is, meet each attack with love, as fully as possible, not just trying to get away with the minimum, but going all the way. The command is to love our enemies, not get them out of our hair.

OFFER FORGIVENESS

So accepting suffering without retaliation is only the starting point for working toward reconciliation. Accepting suffering will usually not, by itself, meet the other's needs. Christians are asked go beyond merely accepting suffering to taking on additional burdens to meet actual needs.

But this still leaves out a crucial piece. Imagine yourself as the one who has slapped another on his right cheek. She turns to you her left cheek, and you slap it, too. Where does that leave you? At the minimum, it leaves you having hit her twice—and hopefully having the injustice of it dawn on you.

At that moment you need forgiveness. You need an act of grace to help you find your way back into wholeness. Or at least, that's what you need if we can learn your needs by watching the Creator relate to us. From the moment you do the deed, God, who understands your needs better than anyone, offers you forgiveness.

Look at it this way. If your victim turns the other cheek, but does so insolently, with hatred in his eyes, has he lived up to Christ's calling? Hardly. Turning the cheek is to be an act of love toward the enemy. If it is done in any other way, it will not humanize nor will it meet a need to turn the other cheek. Instead, we have to grasp somehow what it would mean to turn the other cheek to someone, forgive the wrong already done, and be openly vulnerable to another attack, out of love for the attacker.

I suppose it is a little easier to visualize this in the case of going an extra mile. The soldier waves you over, invokes the law allowing him to make you carry his pack for one mile, but at the end of the mile you ask him "Is this where you need your pack to go today?" When he says, no, he really needs it taken another mile, you say to him, "Okay, I'll take your pack for you that other mile if it will be a help to you. No point in leaving you stranded, or making someone else carry this in my place. I will see you to your destination with your pack in good order."

You might also invite him to tell you how he is enjoying his stay in your country, and whether he misses his home and family, and end up letting him know that he is welcome to be your guest anytime he needs a home-cooked meal. If your relationship with the soldier lasts long enough, you can help him see that occupying your country is an injustice.

Or the woman who sues you for your coat might inspire you to ask why she needs your coat. Is it to sell for cash? Or because she has nothing to keep warm? Or did you really fail to repay a debt? In any of these cases, you find out that the coat isn't really going to meet her needs. Regardless of the size of your debt, you go further until she has access to what she needs, even if it means going nearly naked yourself. God will provide for you, I suppose the thinking would go. Better that you should be temporarily without, having such faith in a loving God, rather than she, who has too little of such faith to be able to handle the uncertainty. You are happy you could be there when she needs you, equipped as you are with an extra article of clothing—and your faith—that meets her needs.

But the one who has struck you? This is the better analogy to terrorism, even if slapping someone is a vanishingly small act compared to flying planes into crowded towers. How can you, by turning your cheek, show love and serve needs? There are at least four ways.

First, by clearly communicating your refusal to use violence, you remove the threat of retaliation. This serves your enemy's pretty much noncritiquable need for immediate physical security.

Second, by taking retaliation out of the picture, you also change the dynamic in the relationship. Removing threat decreases tension and allows your opponent to perceive more accurately, listen better, and be more creative in his responses. This allows your opponent to hear truth better, from you and from others, and to be more adaptable to his environment.

Third, by not retaliating you act contrary to what your opponent, a believer in violence, has come to expect of his world. Your refusal to respond in kind is subversive in all the most wonderful senses of the word; enough of this new experience will undermine the foundations of his violent worldview—but we will explore this further in the next chapter.

Finally, by forgiving, you lower tension and the noise it creates in your relationship. As a result, you will find it easier to listen deeply to your opponent and discern his underlying needs, the ones that have motivated him, however indistinctly, to slap you. This will allow you to target your service to the real problem, showing love by not only refraining from violence but also by helping to resolve the problems keeping him from meeting his needs.

This last point makes it obvious, I hope, that I am not a passivist. That is, I do not believe in passivity in the face of violence. But I am a pacifist. That is, I believe that responding in love rather than violence, even to a physical attack, is the higher (and perhaps the only) calling for a follower of Christ. Turning the other cheek becomes part of a patient, persistent, and above all *active* response to evil. It starts with accepting suffering without retaliation, and it carries on through offering forgiveness for wrongs done by terrorists.

Perhaps I have made a case for active, nonretaliatory pacifism in personal relationships. How does this translate to relations among nations, or between nations and bands of terrorists? After all, national leaders cannot idly abandon their populations to being victims of ongoing series of terror attacks. One of their chief responsibilities is the maintenance of order, and another is the protection of the nation's chosen ways of life. Active nonretaliation would not deter further attacks through fear of their consequences on the terrorist. Nor would it reliably interrupt attacks in progress by overwhelming attackers with superior force.

To many, the proposal to respond to terror with active non-retaliation seems to amount to a proposal to roll over and let the attackers have their way. This would lead to the deaths of many more innocents and possibly to the destruction of our way of life, neither of which would be tolerable for responsible public leaders.

It is true that active nonretaliation diminishes the role of coercion almost to zero. (Not quite to zero, since it allows for physical restraint where it can be applied without killing terrorists.) Nor does active nonretaliation rely on exchange power, which is the diciest of the three faces of power when it comes to terrorism (as we will see in the next chapter). Instead, it works on the level of affiliation and love. And nation-states have usually found it difficult to operate on this level of influence outside their own borders, which represent the limits of powerful patriotic and nationalistic feelings.

A vision shimmers here; is it out of our reach? The vision is of a nation, transparent in its actions, attentive to the needs of other societies, ready to commit to nonviolence in its foreign relations. This nation is economically, socially, and culturally powerful and prosperous, and it is securely democratic, giving it a form of "strategic depth" which allows it to absorb harsh blows without collapsing or even seriously degrading its strength. It has many friends around the world, other nations which share its deepest values, and which are also strong and democratic.

Would such a community of nations be attractive to others? Would tyrants find it all the harder to ride herd on their own people, when he is all that stands between them and membership in this community of nations? Would terrorists find it hard to sustain the support they need in their communities to attack these countries, especially if these nations had extended themselves to serve the needs of others, and had absorbed blows without retaliation? Would potential terrorists be prevented from falling into the dehumanizing hatred that would transform their grievance into willingness to kill?

The answer is probably "yes." It presumes very high standards—of empathy, hope, humanizing contact, acceptance of suffering, and offers of forgiveness. But each of these standards has precedent in the history of nations. Even forgiveness among nations is possible, if history is any guide to what might happen in the future. And so is the voluntary transfer of resources from one people to another with no guarantee of repayment. The United States is not the only country to have participated in them. But none of these things can happen until Christians are willing to create political space for them by applying Christlikeness to their expectations of their nation's foreign policy.

MAKE RESTITUTION ON THE MERITS

I do not expect patient, active nonretaliation to achieve a revolution in international affairs on its own. Some of the rest of what has to happen is covered in chapters 8 and 9. But one more aspect needs attention here.

If nations are going to shift the foundations of their actions toward loving potential enemies, by listening, serving, accepting suffering, and offering forgiveness, then along the way they are going to encounter information about how they have acted to the detriment of others. No nation is perfect. I suppose we might say that each nation has sinned and fallen short of the glory of God. It should be no surprise to a nation to learn that others have suffered somehow at its hands. The shame citizens feel when they confront their national sins can be partly offset by the realization that their nation is not unique in having done wrong to others.

Recognition of pain caused to another nation or community is a crucial step in international relations, especially where grievance is hardening into hatred. Even a parent regrets having to cause her child pain when punishing him for something. A few minutes alone in a room, or a dessert denied, are painful to a child, even when they are deserved. In the same way, if pain caused was in some sense deserved, it can still be regretted.

More often, however, we (as nations) cause each other pain even when it is undeserved. Sometimes the pain is deliberately caused, or caused with reckless disregard for the consequences to others. Other times it is negligent or accidental. In any of these cases, the nation causing the pain needs to publicly recognize and regret its actions. But recognition and regret are not enough. Without restitution—that is, without some attempt by the wrongdoing nation to make good the harm it has done—expressions of regret are hollow. Words alone without deeds to back them up can be just another way of dehumanizing the other, of discounting their pains and goals as not being worth as much as one's own, and therefore negligible. Whatever good words of regret may do when uttered, the benefit evaporates as the wrongdoer clings to the benefits of his wrong, and leaves the wronged to suffer the consequences.

A nation serious about remedying political misery and preventing terrorism, and thus earnest in combating dehumanizing hatred, will constantly monitor its actions and their effects for signs of having harmed others, whether accidentally or culpably. Many of its victims will not be potential terrorists, either because the wrongs are too minor or infrequent to engender a sense of grievance, or because they come in the context of a rich and varied relationship that includes many positives for the "victim" who can overlook relatively minor offenses. Nevertheless, a conscientious nation will do what it can to right the wrong done. It will offer restitution on the merits, basing the size of its offers on the scope of the injury done.

Do not overlook the phrase "on the merits." When we notice someone feeling wronged, the response is as it always has been: We listen to the ones feeling wronged, and we learn as much as we can about the conditions of their lives. We do our very best to understand how our actions have affected them. We do not base our offers strictly on what they demand. Instead, we base them independently on what they need. If they need more, or other, than what we demand, we do not limit ourselves to their demands. We may meet their demand as a way of expressing love to them, but love for them, and concern that they have means to meet their needs, are our motives, not a desire to appease their demands.

If we suspect we cannot accurately judge their needs, or if they insist that we have not understood them, there may be a need for a third party to help as mediator or even arbitrator. Throughout the process, we focus on the merits of the case, not our desires to protect what is ours, nor their demands. If we can reach consensus with them over what is needed, all the better; if we cannot, we do our best to reliably and accurately measure the needs, and what our contribution should be, either because we caused the need wrongfully, or because we are in a position to help meet the need out of love.

Connection and Reconciliation:
The Heart of the Gospel?

This is the most idealistic chapter in a book many will struggle with as being too idealistic throughout. The vision of reconciliation is hard to apply to terrorists and tyrants. For example, we do not want to give in to terrorism in any sense, as we will explore later, so to respond to an attack with an immediate offer of forgiveness sounds like letting terrorists get away with what they have done, especially when our approach to conflict is to use it as an opportunity to learn another's needs and find ways to meet them. A terrorist or a tyrant might be motivated to launch an attack to stimulate our needs-meeting response, maybe even counting on our forgiveness to get off the hook for the evil done.

If we listen to others well, to find and serve their needs, and if we combat dehumanization effectively, in most cases we are going to be reaching the point of offering and seeking forgiveness long before any terror attacks are launched against us. In other cases, we will prevent the rise of tyrants or the collapse into anarchy or corruption. These steps are are even better as prevention than as response.

But I am suggesting that the same principles apply even after terrorists have attacked or tyrants have oppressed. When wrong has already been done, we face two problems. One is how to treat the culprits, and the other is how to prevent further attacks from the terrorist's community or continuing political misery. I am urging recognition, regret, repentance, and restitution on the merits as central features of our response to the terrorist's community and to those who suffer from tyranny, anarchy, and corruption.

Still, we have some important matters to address in the next chapter. A terrorist having planned or executed an attack has done us enormous evil. Government, as a restrainer of evil, will have to punish him. But governments, and especially the citizens that compose governments in democracies, are not excused from loving even when they are punishing evil.

I am drawing here from the heart of the Christian gospel. What value is it to us if we love only those that do us good? Even the pagans do that, said Jesus.[63] If Christianity is valid in its claim to being the faith God intends for all people, it ought to have something about it that distinguishes itself from other faiths. And here are two ideas which, clearly combined by Jesus' own words, make Christianity a puzzle to others: God died as part of a divine gift to forgive us for our sins, including the injustices we do each other. And Jesus expects us to pursue the same forgiving strategy with those who sin against us, as part of His command to love even our enemies.[64]

Full Christianity includes an unrelenting project of loving even our enemies, the ones that injure us and persecute us. What would that look like in our response to the actual terrorist attackers or the captured tyrant? Might it mean, at least, punishment meted out without vengeance or hatred, but deliberately with full respect for the processes of law? Might it mean taking it upon ourselves to find captured evildoers and befriend them, to learn their personal stories, what drove them to such depths, and what God would still dream for them? Might it mean doing something similar for even evildoers still on the loose?

I don't think we can finish the answer to these questions yet. I raise them because they trouble me, and I hope they will trouble you. In the next two chapters we will explore more about a Christlike response to terrorism and tyranny, and to terrorists and tyrants individually. In Chapter 10 we will return to the problem of how the gospel of love for enemies, and forgiveness God offers all of us, might be put into practice when it comes to these enormous wrongs.

We have added in this chapter twenty more ideas about how to respond to terrorism. As in chapter 6, these are just a beginning of the list of things we might do, only a whiff of what God's omniscient creativity might inspire in us.

22. Avoid labeling or stereotyping others.

23. Avoid assuming other groups to be monolithic, or having only one motive.

24. Avoid the lure of conspiracy theories.

25. Bring members of hostile communities together to get acquainted.

26. Encourage the formation of international voluntary associations of shared interests.

27. Encourage exchanges among youth, possibly in the form of camps or study groups.

28. Organize projects of mutual interest across national and ethnic barriers.

29. Actively corresponding via e-mail and through innovative uses of web pages.

30. Support or participate in international adoption and foreign exchange programs.

31. Expand on missions and development work, through more short-term service opportunities and other exchanges.

32. Adapt the elicitative approach to our own fields of endeavor.

33. Be transparent in our personal lives and corporate affairs.

34. Act authentically yet dramatically contrary to the expectations of those vulnerable to dehumanizing hatred toward us.

35. Watch for and reward constructive action by enemies.

36. Help our enemies find and rely upon peacemaking friends.

37. Bring to the fore in our own lives trusted friends whose commitment to justice, hope, truth, and peace we can count on to be stronger than their desire to temporarily please us.

38. Invite intermediaries to help work through disputes.

39. Step forward as opportunity opens to be friends or intermediaries in conflicts not involving us.

40. Build a web of intermediaries and friends, working together from all sides to promote humanization and otherwise advocate for peaceful process, reconciled relationships, and just outcomes.

41. Accept suffering without retaliation.

42. Enter into a nurturing relationship with communities developing dehumanizing hatred or suffering political misery, meeting immediate needs, and stay in relationship (including active prayer) until they have access to means to meet their needs.

43. Offer forgiveness to those who have hurt us as readily as God offers it to us.

44. Be alert in our international relations to discover where we have injured other nations and communities, and offer restitution based not on our defensive fears nor directly on our victims' demands, but on a careful assessment of the merits of the situation.

Chapter 8

....

The Myth of Effective Violence: The Political Side of Terrorism, Part I

Terrorism and Unconventional Politics

We have explored terrorism's spiritual roots and seen whence comes its awful energy. Along the way we have also been paying attention to the dynamics of political misery. Up to now these two facets of the current international crisis have been loosely connected in our discussion. In the next two chapters we will see more clearly how terrorism is intimately linked to tyranny and other forms of political misery.

We can do this now because we are ready to look at the practical dynamics that lead people to kill others for political purposes. So far we have been paying more attention to the spiritual deformation that stems from corrosive grievance and dehumanization. These maladies exchange desperation for hope, and hardness of heart—even spite—for empathy. Sufferers are likely to end up wishing ill to those they blame for their situation and may even rejoice when those they identify as villains suffer. Anyone who has cheered the death of another has had some such spiritual preparation.

But there is a difference between wishing others ill so that you rejoice in their pain and being ready to cause that pain yourself. Reaching the stage of spite for others may prepare us to take active part in their injury, but it does not propel us to do so. Something else has to happen to make killing look like an attractive option, despite its risks and our general revulsion for killing—especially when that revulsion is reinforced by ethical and religious beliefs widely shared among one's home community. Somehow the desperate one must come to believe that he can accomplish something through lethal violence which cannot be accomplished any other way.

In a way, then, terrorism is an extreme version of unconventional politics. Political scientists classify citizens' political participation into two broad categories: *conventional participation* of the type built into the political system, such as voting or signing petitions in a democracy; and *unconventional participation* in which people stretch or break the accepted norms of political behavior. In a democratic system, unconventional participation might include sit-ins, boycotts, demonstrations involving trespassing, or the like. Some unconventional political activity is legal, but still runs counter to accepted norms in the community. Other unconventional activity would be illegal. The Watergate break-in by some of Richard Nixon's loyalists and the ensuing cover-up qualifies as unconventional political activity.

However, in our system most unconventional political participation is harmless, or even at times good for the polity. When Martin Luther King Jr. led bus boycotts, lunch counter sit-ins, and massive demonstrations such as the one in Washington, D.C. in 1963 when he gave his "I Have a Dream" speech, he was doing his politics unconventionally. Each of these tactics is a little outside the range of things most Americans normally feel comfortable with. King chose these tactics in large part because the "normal" political process generally excluded African-Americans in the 1950s and 1960s. Voting was risky for them in many places, and segregation and discrimination served as nearly impassable barriers to winning elections even in places where voting was possible.

Unconventional politics might look different in other settings. Those who joined the prayer vigils in East German churches in the summer of 1989 practiced unconventional politics in the context of Soviet-style communism, as had Solidarity shipyard workers when they staged a strike some years earlier.

Mass political rallies, unsanctioned by the state or the Communist Party, were unconventional politics in Czechoslovakia in autumn 1989. Strikes are not unconventional in Western democracies, although as strictly political tactics they might be borderline cases. Mass political rallies are a staple of our politics and are hardly to be seen as newsworthy, let alone unconventional.

Students of political behavior have noticed that people who join in unconventional politics share a unique, even inspiring pair of ideas: They do not believe the mainstream political system is responsive to them, yet they believe they can make a difference through their own actions![65] They feel excluded but have not given up. They may be discouraged in ways that would make most of us fatalistic and passive, but they are determined to act against daunting odds.

The vast majority of these people are, in some sense, visionaries. Many of them have joined King among our pantheon of political heroes. The signers of the Declaration of Independence were practicing unconventional politics, as were the conductors and station managers on the Underground Railroad, the bands playing in the temperance movement, the suffragists at their rallies, and the celebrants at Woodstock. Unconventional politics secured Indian independence, ended dictatorships in Korea, Chile, the Philippines, and Haiti, and toppled apartheid in South Africa. European unconventional politics—Polish shipyard workers striking, Germans holding vigils in churches and escaping to the West via Prague, Czechs rallying in Wenceslas Square and on the Letna Plain—brought down the Berlin Wall and shattered the Soviet empire.

But something goes horribly wrong in the political gestation of a terrorist. Under the deforming influence of corrosive grievance and dehumanizing hatred, both of the attitudes that propel heroic unconventional political action twist grotesquely. Terrorists are in the last throes of political despair, convinced that both the conventional and the nonviolent unconventional routes are closed to them. Yet they believe they still have one way to make a difference: by killing civilians. So these are the twin political dynamics of terrorism: *political despair* in the form of a conviction that working through the formal system or its informal nonviolent context is useless, and a belief in the *myth of effective violence* against civilians.

In political systems marked by tyranny, corruption, or anarchy, unconventional politics is the only hope for the people. As long as everyone behaves "normally," according to the usual expectations which prop up these systems, political misery will endure. Hope begins for people in these settings when a critical mass of visionaries begin to believe that, even though the system is against them, they can make a difference. Unconventional politics is the route to their political salvation.

Here we begin to see how closely terrorism is linked to political misery. If one lives in tyranny, corruption, or anarchy, by definition one has essentially no hope of remedying a corrosive grievance through conventional politics. It is possible for citizens of democracy to nurture corrosive grievances—Tim McVeigh is only one of hundreds of thousands like him in this regard within the United States. It is also possible for people to dehumanize their perceived enemies, despite all the advantages open democratic systems have in immunizing us against dehumanizing others. It is possible for residents of democracies to believe there is no nonviolent conventional (or unconventional) means available to address their concerns. But the odds against all three of these happening in any one person are much longer in a democracy than they would be in political misery, where it would be only the exceptional person who is able to avoid all three debilitating attitudes.

And, of course, especially in tyrannies, every day is a lesson in the effectiveness of political violence, and even of terror. Citizens of democracy may believe they have won their freedoms only because their forefathers were willing to kill, or that those freedoms can only be defended through overwhelming defense budgets. But residents of tyranny, who can also see how we go about defending our political systems, have an even more fundamental lessons drilled into them every day: it is fatal to buck the political order. The tyrant wins, he keeps his iron grip on society, because he has so many means of inflicting deadly violence on those who step out of line.

Therefore if we are going to remove the causes of terrorism or tyranny, we have more options than serving needs and humanizing relationships. To address these evils comprehensively, we must provide hope to those in political despair by demonstrating—and in many cases, creating—other, nonviolent means of meeting needs through the political system. We have to work to democratize areas beset by political misery, and extend those democratic processes to the point where they can be used to resolve political conflicts among nations and their peoples. And we must show that progress is also possible—perhaps even more possible—through nonviolence than through violence.

So, we can take one leg out from under terrorism and tyranny by destroying the myth of political effectiveness of violence, making it clear that people cannot win this way. This notion is embedded in the old maxim, "never give in to terrorism." We can take out the other political prop to terror and tyranny by simultaneously removing occasions of political despair. For this we may need a "new" anti-terror maxim, something like *wherever there is despair, sow hope*. This maxim may seem strangely familiar, since I am borrowing it from St. Francis of Assisi, but now we need to use it in a new way as a cornerstone in our struggle against terrorism.

These two maxims have a common thread. They both insist that *we must decide all political issues on their merits*, i.e., under democratic processes hedged about by the rule of law. Never giving in defends the principle of deciding things on their merits. No decision can be accepted that is imposed by anything else, including violence against civilians. In fact, as we will see, the only way to avoid giving in is to avoid a whole range of "lesser evils" which also short-circuit merit-based decision making.

Sowing hope defines the proactive side of the picture. It pushes onto the political agenda questions that might not otherwise get there. Just as we can't circumvent democracy or the law to get things decided, we cannot let the political system build a barrier to keep some people's interests from coming up for consideration. Everyone has the right to hitch her political wagon to the mighty engine of democracy under law.

In other words, George W. Bush is at least partly right to consider terrorism and tyranny as allies in an attack on our ideals of democracy under law. Terrorists and tyrants try to get things done without regard for the opinions of others (such as democratic majorities) or the rights of minorities (including the minority comprising the victims of terrorism). Bush accused Islamic terrorists and tyrants of trying to "hijack Islam"[66] by silencing those who disagree with their views about the faith—that is, by ending the attempt of Moslems everywhere to resolve various issues in Islamic theology and practice on their merits, through dialogue and a mutual search for truth. The accusation sticks and helps us all see why the fight against terrorism and tyranny is so important.

But we need to take President Bush's point another step. We need to make sure that our ideals have meaning for everyone. If, as Bush said in his inaugural address, "no insignificant person was ever born"[67] then nothing can be tolerated that denies any person access to means to meet their political needs. No insignificant dictatorship was ever tolerated, no insignificant corruption has ever festered, no insignificant community ever deserved to be left without a voice.

These two maxims, and their common insistence upon merit-based decisions, open us to a range of activities flowing from our call to love our enemies in our response to terrorism and political misery. In this and the next chapter, we will explore these options, starting with those that address the myth of effective violence.

Is Violence Effective?

I have already described as a myth the belief that violence works. This will strike most people as something of a head-scratcher. One of the most obvious "facts" in the world, it seems to them, is that violence *does* work. Why complicate this self-evident truth by calling it a "myth"?

In chapter 7 I said that the call to accept suffering, offer forgiveness, and make merit-based restitution is at the core of the Christian gospel. These are the basic elements of the central Christian doctrine of salvation, in that God has accepted suffering and offered forgiveness and has explicitly told us our spiritual health depends on doing the same for each other. Making restitution for injuries we cause others flows directly out of the command to love even our enemies, the centerpiece of the Sermon on the Mount. None of these ideas has been prominent in our national debates about how to respond to September 11. Shouldn't the core of the gospel have more impact on most Christians' politics when it comes to terrorism and tyranny?

The explanation for the anomaly lies in the persistent, powerful, and almost entirely unquestioned belief that violence works in the hands of good people to accomplish good things. In calling this belief a "myth" I am not saying it is untrue, only that it is a powerful account we use to explain to ourselves who we are and why we do the things we do. Our belief in the effectiveness of violence is powerful, and we certainly understand ourselves as a people in its light.

Americans believe violence secured our independence; thwarted British attempts to resubjugate us in 1812; won us the desert Southwest in 1845; freed the slaves and preserved the union in the 1860's; collapsed the rotten Spanish empire in 1898; stopped the Kaiser in 1918 and Hitler in the 1940s; and reversed Iraqi aggression in 1991. We also believe it works in domestic matters (such as quelling Native American resistance to European expansion, or as our main line of defense against organized crime); and that it works sometimes against us, such as in Vietnam. People who arm themselves out of fear of intruders in their homes are true believers in the myth of effective violence.

I concede that coercion often works in some sense. I have used it on my own children, and in the attenuated form available to me, even on students. ("I am sorry, but the paper is due Friday; if you turn it in late you will lose points.") I also in general support police work, which is inherently coercive and sometimes even violent.[68]

I also acknowledge, as I think anyone must, that violence has powerful effects. It is true that the birth of the United States came about as a result of a war of independence, slavery ended in the course of the Civil War, and Hitler's regime did not collapse until it had been utterly destroyed in the most massive military conflict in human history. All of these were among the objectives with which the winning side embarked on a path of slaughter as a means of achieving political ends. It is possible to get some things you want through violence.

But be careful about that last sentence. It does not say that you always get what you want through violence. At least half the combatants in warfare do not get what they want—they lose. And sometimes the winners don't win what they were after. Or they win what they sought—but get a lot of things they didn't want, too.

It also does not say that the only way to get what you want is through violence. The United States, I am convinced, could have achieved independence nonviolently and possibly without any delay compared to the bloody six-year war it fought. Had it done so, some of the brightest and most promising of its early leaders would have survived, and lingering animosity with Britain would have been reduced, so that there might have been no need for a War of 1812.

I am also convinced that violence was not the only path to the abolition of slavery. Britain itself, less democratic at the time than the United States, un-equipped with the stirring words of the Declaration of Independence, ended slavery without violence. In fact, no other country on the face of the planet had to have a war to end slavery. Are we so incompetent, so venal as a people, that for us alone it would have been impossible to end such an evil without killing each other?

So we might say that it is possible to get some of what we want through violence, but we should also say that in a surprising number of instances (as a pacifist, I would say in every instance) violence is not the most effective or efficient way to get what we want. If this is ever true, then in those cases at least, violence *isn't as effective as other options.*

There is a third weakness in the myth of effective violence. When we say violence "works" we have to be pretty generous about what we mean by works. Violence "worked" to rid us of Hitler. It is hard to imagine another strategy that would have had a chance to succeed. This is not just a trick of history, in which the past is often treated as if it has been inevitable. During that war, many pacifists the world over despaired. One pacifist, Dietrich Bonhoeffer, despaired to the point of joining a plot to kill Hitler. I am not ready to say there were no options, since the alternatives to violence are probably infinite in number, and the options that were tried were fairly few and often ineptly conceived and executed, Chamberlain's appeasement especially.

But even if we haven't identified what were the alternatives to violence in World War II, when we say it "worked" we are saying this:

- that 35,000,000 deaths[69] is acceptable within a successful strategy;
- that the consignment of a billion Chinese to murderous

Communist rule, along with millions of Eastern Europeans, was part of a successful strategy;
- and that planting the seeds of the Korean and Vietnamese conflicts and the nuclear arms race "worked."

For of all human actions there are few, if any, that have as many unintended and unforeseen consequences as does killing, especially on a massive scale.

Kenneth Boulding points out that we tend to overlook the cost of goods and services we lose because they were never produced.[70] Wartime military production, of course, comes at the cost of producing other good things, from food to health care to education to the latest in consumer technology. But even more devastating is the loss of so many soldiers, and in modern times civilians, who die in war. We'll never know what scientific advances, what business and charitable organizations, what breakthroughs in theology or psychology, or even what entire new fields might have been produced by the people who died in, say, the wars of the twentieth century, the bloodiest century in human history.

To say that war worked in the twentieth century, and is now working in the twenty-first, we have to be ready to include these costs. And also some portion of all the costs of future wars, since one of the major effects of each episode of lethal violence that in some sense "works" is the perpetuation of the myth of effective violence. The more that myth ingrains in us, the less likely we are to take any risks for other means of getting things done, and the sooner we will close off consideration of alternatives. The more the myth looms over our thinking, the more we will pour our resources into weaponry. The more we spend on those resources, the more imperative it will seem to use them when the times seem to demand it. Thus the cycle continues.

And there is another factor which may reinforce the myth more than anything else. When I talk about the possibility that warfare is generally an evil, or even just a mistake, I encounter sharp negative reactions. But these reactions shouldn't be surprising at all. In essence, I am arguing, lethal violence is always, or at least much more often than we realize, the devil's work. It substitutes a crude and wasteful method, one with untold negative side effects, for love of one's enemy. Lethal violence, and our belief in its effectiveness, stands in the way of our commitment to the gospel as articulated by Jesus Christ. When we come to rely on "horses and chariots" we cease to rely on him, that is, we become idolators.

How can this be anything but an outrageous attack against most modern audiences? Our nations are up to their elbows in the blood of our foes. We have been taught since infancy how evil those foes are and how noble our own soldiers are. And many of us have relatives who have given years—perhaps their entire lives, even to the point of dying in battle—in military defense of hearth and home. Some are veterans themselves, proud of their service to their country.

There is, in fact, much for veterans and their kin to be proud of. Soldiers accept suffering on behalf of others, take risks, and are ready to give up their lives for a higher cause. All of these are genuinely heroic—exemplifying the very traits required of Christian peacemakers if they follow the paths laid out in this book. I have no desire to cost my readers their rightful pride in those (including themselves) who have served their countries at the potential or actual cost of their own lives.

Yet I believe the myth of effective violence is as pernicious as any form of evil I can think of—made all the worse by its power to take the awe-inspiring dedication of a nation's best citizens and use them unwittingly in the service of evil. With every fatality it suffers, or inflicts, every nation finds it ever more imperative to believe that the costs of war are worthwhile. How can we even contemplate the possibility that such painful losses were wasted, or worse?

If that is too much for us, at least consider the costs we suffer when terrorists and tyrants believe that *their* form of violence, directed against civilians, is effective. It would be best to undermine the entire myth, but at least we can start with the myth of the effectiveness of terrorist and repressive violence. For everything I have said about the myth applies even more starkly to these forms of violence.

Does terrorism sometimes result in what terrorists were seeking? Yes, but the odds are possibly even worse than other forms of violence. Does terrorism usually (or always) have a better, more efficient, more humane alternative? Yes, and we will explore these more fully in chapter 9. Do tyrants succeed because of violent repression against their subject citizens? Yes, but usually over a short run. Over the long run, their success is always at tremendous costs to the welfare of their citizens and the strength of their nations. Could these nations succeed by moving to more democratic and less violent structures? Yes, although their success may include deposing their tyrants and bringing them to account for their actions.

Does political violence against citizens have unanticipated side-effects? There are multitudes of them, including the problem of what happens if the violence succeeds in some sense. How will the terrorists or tyrants in power manage a society which now has at its root the story of how violence succeeded? Are some of the costs of violence hidden in the productivity lost when people die and institutions are destroyed? Yes, and further hidden by the randomness of terror's victims. Does political violence turn admirable qualities like courage and sacrifice and dedication to evil ends? Of course, although terrorists and tyrants seem to mar their admirable qualities with prominent cowardice and cruelty more than conventional soldiers do, though there are exceptions.

I believe the proper approach to violence for followers of Christ is to witness prophetically against it in all its lethal forms as one of the central deceptions in a fallen world. But for the purposes of this book, we can continue on together if we can agree that belief in the myth of effective terrorist and tyrant violence is an enormous evil that must be combated. If you believe this much about violence, then the rest of the book will still speak to you. As for the violence of democracies, I will quote George Fox's legendary advice to William Penn when Penn asked whether he had to quit wearing his sword: "Wear it as long as thou canst."[71]

Never Give in to Terrorism

We have long been familiar with the rule of not giving in to terrorists by capitulating to their demands. The principle has its roots in love.

Let's consider one of the milder terrorist tactics, hostage-taking for ransom, as an example. This kind of terrorism is a form of coercion that trades on affiliation to induce a sham of exchange. The kidnapper tries to trade on our love for the hostage to force us to come up with the demanded pay-off.

But one should not pay ransom for a hostage, because doing so encourages others to take hostages. We should recognize the game for what it is—coercion, not true exchange—and refuse to go along, in recognition of the side-effects of our action. Paying ransom works in a sense; it gets our loved ones back. But like all decisions based on something other than the merits of the situation, ransoming hostages creates other costs that make the practice a disaster, morally and practically.

Some might be moved by love for the hostage or his family to make an exception to this rule. But they make a tragic mistake. They leave out of their calculations future victims of hostage taking. We cannot rely on the laws against kidnapping to deter future kidnappers. Kidnapping has been illegal for centuries, but these laws have never wiped out the practice. We can stop the practice of kidnapping only by making a firm commitment never to pay ransom—if no kidnapper ever got a ransom, there would be no kidnapping.

Every would-be rescuer who pays a ransom to save a loved one postpones the day when other kidnappers stop. Paying ransom may buy back our loved one's life but just as surely buys future kidnapping and grief for other families and friends. Christ's command to love our neighbors includes those whom we cannot yet identify. We are not permitted to discount our effects on others just because we don't know who they are. Or to put this another way, when the kidnapper states his price for our loved ones' lives, we have to add to that price the eventual cost to other families when their loved ones are kidnapped, because we encouraged the practice of kidnapping by paying up. Thus, if we assume our loved ones are equal in God's eyes to future victims, the price of the ransom becomes a huge loss—especially if, as seems likely, paying ransoms would lead to an increase in kidnapping rather than just keeping it constant.

Of course, in many cases people who take hostages aren't seeking a ransom in money. They may be pushing for something else, some political objective. That, too, should be denied them. Nothing should ever be achievable by terrorism or tyranny. Any more lenient practice is selling out people in the future, unnamed, faceless to us now. But it won't be long before their names and faces become clear—when they become the next victims.

This is not to say there is nothing we can do about a kidnapping. In particular we can work to change the game the kidnappers play to give them reasons to release the hostages that do not include winning what they seek. Offers to substitute oneself for the hostage fit this strategy, although they only change the game modestly. Hostages might refuse to go free when the ransom has been paid, as a way of turning another cheek.

Or, perhaps those who care about the hostages could redefine the game by seeking ways to meet the true needs of the community kidnappers represent, being careful to start with needs that most discomfit the kidnappers. For one thing, support for the establishment of the rule of law, which will also require some sort of democratic legitimacy from the government, will include insisting that the kidnappers' own people capture, try, and (if convicted) punish the kidnappers vigorously.

Addressing terrorism and tyranny broadly, if we are going to deny them the objectives they seek, here are things we can do:

1. Act in defiance of fear.

The predator, be he terrorist or tyrant, wants us to be afraid, to cower, to be intimidated. This is why he chooses an attack on civilians.

We must refuse to be cowed. The more we stand up to fear, the less coercive power the predator has at his disposal. This reduces the pay-offs he can expect from violence and makes it less likely that he or his cohorts will try something in the future.

This requires courage from all of us, not just those to whom we normally delegate the task of courage. Police officers, fire fighters, and soldiers are all expected to be brave. But if they are brave while the rest of us cower, the predator will have won one of his objectives.

We should *flock to our public monuments and commercial nerve centers*. The September 11 terrorist attack was aimed at the symbolic and actual heart of the American government and economy. We should show we are not afraid to be in places predators attack. We can't sit-in at some of these places without disrupting them ourselves. But we should visit in steady streams.

We should *take to the air in record numbers*. One goal of the terrorist is to disrupt our life as much as possible. If we reduce our liberty in travel by being afraid, the terrorist succeeds.

We should *carry on with public events*. Concerts, sporting events, public gatherings—all these should go on normally. The Expos should draw 30,000, not 3,000, the next time they play; and the next time the Marlins are the hottest team in baseball, their fans should fill the stadium, or shame on them.

Some of us will be called to go a giant step further. If not giving in is going to have any effect, it has to be a worldwide phenomenon. Even if we root out all political violence from North America, but it continues to "work" everywhere else, the myth of effectiveness will not be broken. It wasn't broken before terrorism came here, and the myth won't be broken if somehow we push terrorism back offshore, as long as there are vast areas where the myth continues to gather evidence in its support. This means we have to carry our bravery into every corner of the earth.

Is there a country beset by terrorist attacks? *Some of us should go there*. We should ride the Jerusalem buses, we should live in the Palestinian camps and towns, and we should station ourselves in every mall in Tel Aviv. We should picnic along Derry parade routes, minister in Bujumbura and Kigali, teach in Pakistani schools, work to reconstruct Baghdad and Kabul.

Is there a tyranny running roughshod over its people? Or a nation mired in debilitating corruption? *We should visit them, too*, and live with their people, attend their public rallies, accompany the leaders of their democratic opposition. Teheran could use some development workers. Damascus may need help with public health. People in Havana and Pyongyang need English teachers.

Is our country threatening what would amount to a terrorist attack somewhere else? Well, then we should send people there, too.

If our government wants to apprehend and arrest terrorists or overthrow tyrants, our presence will not be a hindrance to them. We may even be able to help—in fact, we should make it clear that we will help if we can do so nonviolently. But if someone wants to bomb populations in the hopes of hitting a few perpetrators, we should deny the bombers a free ride in American public opinion, regardless of which Christian doctrine of war we follow. If we don't, our government will be more likely to respond to terrorism by unjustified military action, which is itself strongly resembles terrorism when done systematically, and which will lend strength to the myth of effective violence.

If at first our presence in these hot spots leads to casualties among us, we must absorb them without retaliation. In fact we have to insist on this: *our deaths or injuries cannot be the occasion for causing the same to others, or for leaving others to their fate.* The U.N. has undermined much of its effectiveness by scampering out of tough spots when its workers are potential targets. Haiti suffered an extra year of tyranny under the Cedras regime in 1993-94 as a result of U.N. cowardice. The potential for the U.N. to play a crucial internationalizing role in Iraq has been repeatedly undermined by the U.N.'s inability to keep workers on the scene when staff have been casualties of terrorist bombings there. Of course, this means that at least some of the U.N.'s workers need to be hired on a different basis, as nonviolent combatants rather than safe civilians. Until this is done, the U.N.'s usefulness in fighting terror and tyranny will continue to be very limited.

We also have to insist that no one make even the slightest concession to those who would injure us lest they deprive our sacrifice of all its meaning. Our goal instead is to deprive coercive acts against us of their power by refusing to be coerced, even at the risk of our lives. Our refusal has to be steadfast in the face of risk and loss, or it will not be a refusal and won't have the effect we need.

2. Deny terrorists the means to act again.

The most dramatic immediate response America made to the World Trade Center bombing was to shut down all air traffic. This is a good example of the kinds of *sacrificial measures* we all need to be willing to take to deny opportunity to terrorists. By submitting cheerfully to increased airport security and resulting travel delays, every world citizen makes a crucial contribution to stamping out terrorism.

Any step we can take to stifle the opportunity for terror, or shrink its profits, is potentially a good thing. Some of these steps are *defensive*. While some proposals go too far—such as the idea floated in 2002 to turn delivery workers into organized government informants—we play good defense against terrorists when we volunteer on our own to cooperate with law enforcement efforts, take responsibility to watch our neighborhoods for suspicious activity, and refuse to ask our neighbors to accept unnecessary risks so we can act as we please without inconvenience. For example, if reducing our carry-on baggage on our next flight reduces the risk of terrorism, we should cheerfully go along.

We must also be vigilant against terrorism by our own government. Our nation's strategy in the war on terror and tyranny is still being put into effect. Some Christians are trying to channel our nation's response by *turning public opinion against at least the more irresponsible military actions*. This good work needs to continue, but we need to do it responsibly. It won't do to fire off criticisms of national policy without offering alternatives. Getting our government to stop the worst aspects of its current anti-terrorist campaigns without being ready with an equally effective substitute would be a way of giving in to terrorists. We cannot stand by doing nothing nor make political arguments that amount to appeals to do less than we are already doing. Our objective needs to be better anti-terrorism, more effective overthrows of dictators—different tactics, not lesser ones.

If our country kills civilians to punish others for killing civilians, we need to be ready to *starve our leadership* of the public support it would need to continue these actions. Letters to the editors, sit-ins, demonstrations, cheerful and civil discussion with fellow citizens, symbolic actions: all these and more should be in the works.

Some steps are more proactive. *Can we use the power of exchange?* We could outbid drug lords for the productive effort of Colombian farmers. We could help willing but weak countries root out terrorists in their midst by suspending or canceling their international debts in exchange for their domestic vigor against killers.

Can we use affiliation? I suspect that all the images of the planes flying into the World Trade Center, and all the stories of victims and survivors getting such attention around the world, dried up some support for terrorists. These stories and pictures engage our affiliative senses, because we can empathize with the people involved. Their stories humanize them and help us to see them as worthy of our compassion and help—they give these people power over us. They certainly help all of us steel ourselves to prevent further attacks. They may also help stave off the kind of dehumanization necessary to the development of more political killers.

Perhaps we should publish a book of all the posters created in 2001 in New York by victims' families searching for news of their lost loved ones. Someone might translate the book into as many languages as possible and distribute it widely. Sooner or later movies will come out depicting events that day. One can hope that the producers of the movies will do well at humanizing the victims, without overreaching or manipulation.

But September 11 is not the last word, nor the only image being created of those of us from Western, Christianized cultures. In order for victims' stories to have a humanizing effect, they cannot become hidden in others' eyes behind newer, more immediate dehumanizing images. Every accidental bombing or shooting by American and coalition troops in Afghanistan and Iraq creates a counter-image to the one of victims falling from the World Trade Center. Even though one of these incidents causes only a small number of casualties, to someone living in the affected countries their proximity to home magnifies their impact. Since these incidents seem to be inescapable when military units under stress interact with civilian populations, they are going to continue to pile up. Indeed, one suspects that resisters in Iraq and Afghanistan know this, and may be trying to stir up trouble partly to help generate negative images of westerners in the world's eyes. Sometime soon, the world is going to remember how American soldiers killed innocents in the Middle East better than they are going to remember how radical Middle Easterners killed Americans in New York, Washington, and Pennsylvania.

To make any use of affiliation, we will have to work hard to create clear, well-grounded human connections, as mentioned in the last chapter, so that people living in troubled places can remember us as worthy of humane treatment. Travel, service, and other forms of human connection are crucial to creating the conditions of human affiliation that will dry up the sources of recruits for future terrorism.

I recognize the tensions here. If we are to go readily to places that are likely targets, as I earlier suggested, does this conflict with the advice to act prudently in public, or my praise for the rapid temporary closure of American airspace? And if we are to deny terrorists room to maneuver, should we go places where many of them lurk?

The answer lies in being wise as to timing and context. In the extreme uncertainty after four nearly simultaneous attacks (only one of which was thwarted, but still cost the lives of every passenger on the plane), it was prudent to ensure that no others could be immediately carried out by getting every airplane down to the ground. Once the immediate threat was past, the task shifted to deterring future attacks. At that point the usefulness of sending a clear message of unbowed courage began to outweigh the risk that an attack would be resumed.

A similar need to be wise governs the idea of inserting Christians into probable targets for Western military reprisal. *Our intent is to frustrate indiscriminate killing, not to slow the apprehension of the perpetrators.* This is why Christians going somewhere to forestall a military attack need to make it clear that they will help whenever they can in the apprehension and arrest of terrorists and conspirators, and the undermining of dictators. Assuming we go in sufficient numbers and with training to be of some help to international law enforcement agencies, the terrorists may vacate that locale, making it one less place they can hide (or the Western military can usefully attack). Terrorists who remain in town would do so at the risk of capture, either at the hands of the peacemakers and their local allies, or at the hands of international law enforcement officers who get our tips as to terrorist whereabouts.

It is, of course, possible that local authorities will not let us into tyrant-ruled or terrorist-infested areas with such a public intent. I do not think we should take their "no" for an answer. Even if our repeated attempts to enter the country are rebuffed, we can make our point, both to the terrorists and the tyrants, that no place will be a haven for their ilk. And it may be that some will conclude that God and justice require them to enter an area without the local government's approval. The American military does not always wait for passports to get stamped when military strategy calls for it. Why should we?

These notions will sound unrealistic to some. Some of the people doing such work will lose their lives, as do soldiers. And I admit I do not know for sure that the specific ideas I have offered in this section will work. I offer them anyway as examples of the kind of creative initiatives God might have in mind to ensure that our message is consistent: No terrorism from any source can be effective, ever. And no tyrant will ever rest easy on the throne. Other ideas could be developed from the catalog of historical examples Gene Sharp assembles in *The Politics of Nonviolence*[72], from the dramatic examples of the about twenty nonviolent regime changes we have witnessed in the last generation, or from the experiments in nonviolent peacemaking conducted by the Christian Peacemaker Teams and others.

Not all of our options for denying terrorists room to maneuver are so controversial or cutting edge. Americans are noted for their individualism. A corollary is our inattention to our neighbors. As we are reminded after every major tragedy when strangers take heroic measures to help and support each other, this kind of civic isolationism is not the only way we could live. We could *invest ourselves in our communities* with lots of positive returns.

One positive return would be making it harder for terrorists to slip through our communities unnoticed as they spend months training in flight schools or otherwise plotting their attacks. The more healthy involvement we have with our neighbors, the fewer places terrorists can hide in plain view, as several of the suicide hijackers did. While the anti-terrorism benefits of increased civic connection would admittedly be minor when it came to foreigners in our country temporarily, the effects on domestic terror could be quite significant. What if neighbors had taken more interest in Timothy McVeigh?

I am not suggesting it would be good for neighbors to become informants on one another. The short-lived scheme to recruit plumbers and delivery people as spies for the FBI earned its early demise. Nor can we turn a civic connection defense into an occasion for singling out any one nationality for suspicion and hostility. The point of civic connection is to *get to know our neighbors and find ways to be of value in their lives*. The project will fail if we focus on one nationality for special suspicion, since the world is full of people who have grievances against us.

This civic connection defense can extend beyond our borders. If nothing else, the more Americans are positively involved in communities around the world, the fewer foreigners there will be who get their entire picture of America from TV and hatemongers.

So far my suggestions in this section have emphasized ways we can play defense against terrorists by denying them access to turf to do their dirty work. *We can also play offense, and take away assets they already have.* Osama bin Laden, for example, spends a lot of money. Terrorists and tyrants should wake up some morning and find their assets have been identified and frozen, hopefully to be used by victims and survivors (if they can win their lawsuits against them) to heal as much as possible. So should indicted or convicted co-conspirators. To completely freeze a terrorist's assets, his safe harbors need to be called to responsibility, too, an action I will discuss in the next section.

But money isn't the only currency terrorists and tyrants spend. They also distribute counterfeit religion, spinning monstrous perversions of Islam, Christianity, and other faiths in which to straitjacket followers.[73] So we should *give platforms to the majority of religious leaders of various faiths who denounce both murder and suicide*, to help their message spread to believers everywhere.

3. Deny terrorists and tyrants their safe harbors.

President Bush was right when he said there should be no distinction between terrorism and those who harbor it.[74] For reflective believers, Bush's lesson makes us tender to how we harbor some of the elements of terrorism in our own hearts: corrosive grievance, hatred, despair. Convicted, we turn to God for forgiveness and help in repentance and restitution.

President Bush was mostly talking about the violent terrorism behind attacks on civilian targets. When we lift our eyes back to the world scene, we see that he is also right about the scope of the effort necessary to end terrorism writ large. As long as perpetrators can hide in various places around the globe, stash resources there, and recruit supporters and new killers, the myth of effective violence will never pass away.

Those who shelter terrorists and their co-conspirators should be challenged to give them up for trial. Anyone who knowingly has any financial dealing with any indicted or convicted terrorist is a conspirator in his terrorism. This is true whether they are the Saudis or Swiss. Anyone who refuses legitimate cooperation with the worldwide project to strip indicted terrorists of access to their assets should be charged with the crime of abetting terrorism and have their own assets frozen. They should find it impossible to trade or conduct commerce until they either answer to their indictments or begin proper cooperation.

Tony Blair and George Bush have both argued that terrorist attacks like September 11 are aimed at our entire civilization. We are learning which nations are on the side of civilization and which are on the side of terror. *Any nation should be a pariah for refusing to help with investigating terrorism, or to capture indicted terrorists and hold them for trial, or for persisting in tyranny.* All traffic into and out of pariah nations should be monitored at the point of entry in a cooperating country. Nothing should be allowed into a pariah nation except humanitarian supplies. No one should be permitted to enter such a country except aid workers and anyone carrying on a mission that tends to subvert the resisting government or terrorism in general. (Visitors pursuing an objective mentioned in this book would, of course, qualify for entry since they would be undertaking projects terrorists abhor, such as resolving disputes on their merits and undermining the myth of effective violence.)

Nothing should be allowed out of the country at all except payments for the humanitarian goods, and no one except the people allowed in. Any air carrier, shipping company, or individual refusing to comply with this directive should be refused entry into any cooperating country. We should freeze all the available assets of any such noncooperative person or entity until they do comply, with an expedited court hearing afforded to anyone unjustly accused. Any ship or plane in a cooperating country that belongs to a noncompliant organization should be impounded until there is compliance.

I want to stress that when I describe a nation as "cooperating" I mean with the struggle to eradicate terrorism, not necessarily with the United States. If we are going to insist that other nations abandon terrorism, we are going to have to submit to the same standard. The threat to isolate terrorist-harboring nations applies to us as well.

But I also want to suggest that nations are not the only ones who should be targets of these kinds of sanctions, nor are they the only ones who should be applying them. Nongovernmental

204 ❖ Loving Without Giving In

organizations and individuals can coddle terrorists or climb into bed with tyrants, too. And we can act in our private and personal capacities to deny these accomplices the means to act.

Here is an example. In 2003, Robert Mugabe's regime in Zimbabwe took steps toward tyranny by attacking the rule of law in that country, stifling democracy and free speech through threats and violence by his thugs. The cricket world cup was scheduled to play some of its matches in Zimbabwe, but the English team refused to travel there to play. Their motive was partly concern for their own safety in the lawless Zimbabwean environment but also partly players' unwillingness to do anything that might help prop up Mugabe's rule. The English team took this decision even though it meant forfeiting the match, risking the chance to advance to the final playoffs.

Later in the year, Mennonites were scheduled to host their world conference in Zimbabwe. Many Mennonites felt uneasy about any scent of complicity with the Mugabe government, so the church considered moving its conference elsewhere. In the end, the group felt it should continue with its plans in Zimbabwe as a way of showing support for Zimbabwean Mennonites beset by both economic and political hardship.

I consider both these incidents significant victories in the struggle against tyranny and thus indirectly against the terrorism. The first helped bring the injustice in Zimbabwe to the eyes of cricket fans the world over, some of whom (if cricket fans are like other sports fans) do not normally take much interest in world politics. Expanding awareness of political repression creates political space in other countries for leaders to spend more energy applying pressure to Mugabe and his followers. It brings to light what is going on there and makes it harder for Mugabe to get away with moves toward tyranny which might otherwise go unnoticed by the world community.

On the other hand, the Mennonites' decision to go ahead with their plans, even though it seems to run counter to the cricketeers' strategy, also cut down on Mugabe's options. It put his enforcers on notice that his Zimbabwean victims have people from around the world who know about, care about, and will support them if they are made targets of repression.

The world should make clear that it will no longer excuse or tolerate terrorism or tyranny on any grounds. An international *congress should convene to negotiate a uniform worldwide anti-ter-rorism and anti-tyranny code* along these lines. Congress should legislate forthwith accordingly, and our diplomats should encourage other countries to do likewise.

We need a consistent record of not letting violence pay. The code should thus cover all uses of violence or other means to short-circuit resolution of decisions on their merits or in defiance of the rule of law. The United States led as the international community rightly spoke out against the Iraqi invasion of Kuwait. In 2002, the U.S. led again to try to hold Iraq accountable for living up to its agreements and U.N. Security Council resolutions. This was also a good thing, although the U.S. readiness to resort to violence to achieve it may turn out in the long run to have been a way of substituting new wrongs for old.

Applying these standards just to Iraq would be hypocritical and ineffective. *The message has to be consistently applied*, to friend and foe alike. For example, the anti-terror and tyranny code should be written to insist that Israel abandon its illegal settlements, and turn them over to Palestinian residents as it promptly retreats to its internationally recognized borders. The settlements will make a nice down payment on a compensation package for land expropriated from Arabs in the aftermath of the war in 1948.

Another provision of that code should be a *prohibition of assassination*, even of known tyrants or terrorists. The justification for assassination is prevention—by taking out leaders, the thinking goes, other lives will be saved. Or perhaps other leaders will shy away from tyranny and terror out of concern for their own safety.

But these calculations do not account for where terrorists come from. The myth of violence's effectiveness expands—now to include the supposed effectiveness of assassination. And the sense of grievance without redress is in no way diminished. In fact, it is at least as likely to grow as to diminish. Some will be bitter that their families or loved ones were targets with no chance to defend themselves against allegations against them. Others will be outraged because innocents die in the cross-fire. Even where the target was a terrorist or a tyrant, friends and kinsfolk will still resent their deaths. Since almost everyone has many relatives, and since it is a natural reaction to want revenge when one of your family is killed, assassinations are likely to hasten the terrorist-making process of spiritual deformation among the target's circle of friends and family. The more outrageous the killing in the eyes of the survivors, the more readily it will serve as a recruiting poster for replacement terrorist.

Consider the attempts during the invasion of Iraq in 2003 to find Saddam Hussein and kill him with bombs. None of those attacks succeeded in killing Saddam, nor even his sons. Confirmed deaths of any key Iraqi leaders were almost totally absent. However, we know that people died—small fry in the Baathist regime, perhaps, or people who happened to be neighbors to restaurants. How much did these deaths do to create new resentment against the U.S., without doing anything to rid the world of Saddam and his thuggish followers?

Claims that targeted assassinations of terrorists are legal under the norms of warfare do not assuage the bitterness of victims' families. The "war" on terror is in a legal gray area anyway, since laws of war deal with conflicts among states. And the upshot of targeted assassinations is always that a person is executed on suspicion, with no chance to defend himself. Furthermore, in most targeted assassinations, others are killed as well, often those with no connection to terrorism. In many cases, these other casualties have been children. If we want to spatter terrorism all over the globe, I can think of no better way than to pursue a policy that kills the children of families whose members are ripe to become terrorists already.

Targeted assassination would never be tolerated in any other law enforcement setting. Imagine if your governor began targeted assassinations against various suspected criminals in your neighborhood. Imagine if your state's police carried out these attacks with missiles and bombs, routinely resulting in the deaths of obviously innocent bystanders. Would you tolerate this situation? If not, then why should we expect the families and friends of terrorists, and of the innocents killed in such attacks, to accept them passively?

An assassination bears all the hallmarks of terrorism. It is violent, it despairs of deciding things on the merits about the target's actions, it relies on an erroneous myth of effectiveness, and it is outside the processes of democracy and definitely beyond the constraint of law.

The result of a policy of assassination will be, then, increased political desperation mixed with increased conviction that violence can work. We might see fewer attacks in the short run, but over time we will see more desperate attacks with ever more ferocious weapons and tactics coming from an ever-growing horde of terrorists.

Avoid Becoming Terrorists or Tyrants Ourselves

1. Resist the terrorist within

Not giving in to terrorism or tyranny is crucial to dissolve the myth of effectiveness that holds people to their destructive projects. If we give in, new terrorists will spring up as fast as we can thwart or capture the old ones, and tyrants will sit more firmly in their seats of power. But a victory over terrorists or tyrants will be hollow if in the process we become indistinguishable from those we oppose.

Slipping into terrorism ourselves is much easier than we would like to admit. Quakers like to remind us there is that of God in every person. But there is also that of the terrorist in each of us. Do you disagree? Think back to your first reaction when you saw one of the twin towers coming down on September 11, 2001. Did you think about revenge? Did you jump to conclusions about who did this, or what America or others should do in response? Did you say to yourself, "Nuke them all"? I did all of these things.

Deception, fraud, manipulation of the evidence, intimidation, nepotism, bribery—all have at their core our unwillingness to *let matters be decided on their merits*, a stonehearted refusal to *let the legitimate interests of others affect the outcome of disputes*, a cowardly failure to *face up to the possibility of being wrong*; an act of despair about the love or power of God. And not only do we nourish the tendency in our own hearts to ignore our victims in pursuit of our ends, we foster in our victims the despair and the myth of effective violence that fertilize their own inner terrorist.

Any attempt to resolve a matter on something other than its merits has a terrorist seed planted at its heart. Anything less than democracy under the rule of law is, in effect, a form of proto-terrorism. Osama bin Laden working out his hatred by orchestrating suicide bombings is a terrorist. Palestinians bombing Israeli citizens to force Israel into concessions are terrorists. Israeli settlers building and expanding their settlements (and knocking down Palestinian homes in defiance of law and right) are hard to distinguish from terrorists. Anti-WTO demonstrators trying to shut down meetings are, in their milder nonlethal way, proto-terrorists. All these people are marked by their unwillingness to let democratic processes decide or to be subject to the rule of law. They want a short cut to results, one that does not let others' views delay them.

These are not the only cases. Bill Clinton lying to the American public was listening too closely to that of the terrorist in him, evading having his actions judged on their merits. During the days of the Reagan administration, Oliver North made the same mistake, unwilling to be accountable to Congress or the people and thus ready to subvert the U.S. Constitution in his haste to achieve his ends. Corporations feed their internal terrorism when they insulate themselves from being judged on their merits in the market, by pursuing monopolies, conducting insider trading, altering or concealing material information, or bribing officials. Labor unions terrorize when they threaten violence against their members or against replacement workers.

The student who cheats on an exam or plagiarizes a paper may be coddling the terrorist within. The professor who stifles student questions might be, too. And the taxpayer lying on his return, the dog owner sending her pooch out at night to do its business on someone else's property under cover of darkness, the parent berating the Little League umpire, the writer who hides his computer game under his word processor when his overworked wife wanders by. . . . All of us give in sometimes to the terrorist's rationalizations for taking ethical shortcuts toward our goals. We feed destructive myths when we think we've gotten away with it, or others see it and think so, too. And our victims lose a little hope that issues can be resolved on their merits, which means our actions feed their despair.

If we are to join our nation's worldwide crusade against terrorism, we have to fight on the internal personal front all the while we are taking the struggle onto the streets and around the world. We must never give into terrorism—not even our own little bits of terror from within.

Now that we have looked around us and seen how infectious the terrorists' spiritual bugs can be, maybe it would help to consider examples of people who had a serious grievance, a political system that didn't work for them, and a sense that they could still find nonviolent, unconventional ways to make a difference. Martin Luther King, Jr., was not a terrorist. Civil disobedience was his tool to move the issue of race to where it *could* be decided on its merits. Nonviolence was his safeguard to ensure that love, not coercion, would be the means of getting things done. King wanted to be sure that the process of deciding on the merits what to do about discrimination would not be short-circuited by violence that prevented people from hearing each other.

Mohandas Gandhi was not a terrorist. Like King, he chose as his targets policies that were imposed on his people without a chance for their democratic participation. He used nonviolent methods specifically so there could be a dialogue, so the British could still hear him and he them.

Lech Walesa and Vaclav Havel were not terrorists. They operated outside communist law, but they did so without violence. They focused not just on an immediate end to despotic regimes, but rather on building a civic process that allowed their people a vehicle for choosing their futures on the merits, democratically. Havel's movement in Czechoslovakia was even called "Civic Forum."

Police operating under a rule of law are not terrorists. Their job is to prevent crimes in commission, if possible—even to stop the terrorist in action. Or if the crime is already committed, their job is to capture suspected criminals and bring them to trial. These are the methods of getting such cases resolved on their merits.

The apostle Paul worried about Christians giving in to the terrorist within. Already by the time he wrote Romans, about a generation after Jesus' death and resurrection, some believers tended to think of themselves as not bound by the secular law around them. In their pride and justified joy in being free in Christ, disciples were arrogating to themselves the sole authority to decide what was right and wrong. This was a dangerous course, eroding the idea of respect for law and inviting a lawless state of nature in which it would be almost impossible to resolve disputes on their merits. So Paul wrote to Christians in Rome, urging their submission to the civil authorities.[75]

Judging by Paul's own history, we know he did not consider the legal norms of whatever locality he visited to be the highest standard for his behavior. When God called him to do something that might get him in trouble with the local authorities, Paul followed the call rather than the law. But Paul also submitted to the authorities when they enforced their laws, or even when they acted outside the law, based on just their sense of what was needed for social order. In Philippi, he even stayed in jail when his bonds were miraculously broken and his prison door swung open. The result? The jailer converted to Christianity, which turned out to be the opening Paul needed to reach the entire Philippian community with the gospel.

If it was good enough for Paul and Silas, it is good enough for us: Christian resistance to the terrorist within includes *submission to governing authorities*, even when they punish the believer for following her sense of God's calling. Such submission is necessary if the Christian is to live out a consistent witness in favor of deciding public and political questions on their merits, rather than on the whims or quirks of individuals following their conscience (or some less exalted motivation).

Gandhi, King, Walesa, Havel, Paul, and the professional police officer offer us good models for dealing with terrorists. All find ways to answer violence with persistent resistance, and restrain themselves from imposing the final resolution of a matter until arrangements can be made to submit it for resolution on the merits of the case. In doing so, all struck a blow to the myth of effective violence and the growth of terrorism everywhere.

2. Resist the tyrant within

We fight terror and tyranny so people can live their lives freely and without fear, and so as much of the world as possible lives under economic, political, and legal systems that resolve disputes on their merits. Nothing will be gained if, after all our efforts, our own societies descend into tyranny. And we can undermine our work if we succumb to the temptations of tyranny even just in our personal lives.

It's probably not too hard to imagine what I mean by warning against letting our nation begin to resemble the tyranny we are fighting. Frightened by terror, we can easily be tempted to go too far in efforts to track down terrorists before they can attack us again. I am not against all measures to provide investigators and security people extra powers—such as more thorough searches at airports, as I mentioned earlier. But we can only go so far without imposing on ourselves the defeat terrorists and tyrants would foist on us.

The great strength of modern Western society is openness. Freedom to think and to design our lives as we see fit, plus an economy that rewards cleverness and wisdom in serving each other's needs and wants, are the engines of our prosperity. Order is necessary, too, but we have learned it can be overdone. In particular, we have done well to hedge our security forces with legal restraints to preserve the integrity of our system—to make sure questions of guilt are decided on the merits rather than by the power of the state and its guardians; and to ensure that those who regulate our lives are transparent, and thus accountable, to our democratic representatives.

Certainly those who track terrorists could catch them better if they had all the tools tyrants have. At least this would be true if all of us didn't turn secretive and sullen, as people do in tyrannies. But the costs would be staggering. Our prosperity, our ability to design our own lives, the open debate we need in order to have meaningful elections—all these are vulnerable. Even the financial costs of increased security are a drain on the productive areas of our economy and would sink us all toward poverty.

It is hard to know where to draw the line between prudent precaution and security that sabotages our society's central strengths. It is easy to see the costs when security fails, as we all experienced on September 11. It is easy to imagine even greater costs if the next big attack is, say, nuclear—and we all hope imagination is the only place we have to see such a security breach. But we have to be careful in knowing how much weight to give to these images.

What are the images of a successful open society? How can we get a visceral feel for what excess security might cost us, on the order of the sensation we had in the pits of our stomachs watching the World Trade Center towers fall?

This is not easy. Stacks of emaciated bodies found at Nazi concentration camps are a warning, but they come from such an extreme state of political misery it's hard to imagine us ever going that far. So these far-fetched images, like those of extreme poverty in Haiti, or mass graves in Bosnia or Iraq, don't really seem to apply to us—even though each of these cases is a logical conclusion of what could happen, at least to some of us, if we trade our open society for a promise of security.

Perhaps we should regularly revisit photos and accounts of Japanese-American relocation camps in World War II, as a way of bringing closer to home what overreacting to security threats can do to us. It's a tribute to the Japanese-American community that their experience during that war did not translate into any significant terrorist activity. Anyone forcibly relocated to a camp, stripped of his prior life, and often forced to abandon property or sell it at a steep discount, then kept prisoner for years in primitive conditions in remote locations is a spectacular candidate for corrosive grievance.

Our current security situation is in many ways even graver than it was in 1941 and 1942. Has our society learned enough since then to avoid our earlier errors? If not, we could wind up repeating them, costing our victims their place in society and costing us their contributions to our common lives. And with terrorism amok in the world, we probably won't be as lucky next time we alienate an entire ethnic group.

Even though the dangers of a societal turn toward tyranny are staggering, they aren't my main focus. For tyrannic impulses are not confined to societies. Individuals also struggle with the temptation of power.

If our goal is to love our neighbors (and our enemies) then we want the best for them. The temptation of power, at its very best, is the temptation to take control of how needs get met. Masquerading as responsibility, the desire to control outcomes can easily lead us across important moral fault lines.

For example, taking too much control of another's welfare deprives him of his opportunity to take charge of his own life, to make of it what he will, and to take responsibility on his own part. If I determine the conditions of your life, even if my intent is benign, I leach away an essential part of your humanity. In fact, it might be the central part that makes you human, the part that is in the likeness of God—the part which allows you to be a co-creator with God. Overdoing my own responsibility to the extent that it decides for you how to co-create your own life is a theft only a little short of murder. You were put here, created by God, as a human rather than an automaton for a reason. You only get one chance to be steward of your own life and of your own duties to your neighbors and enemies. If I take that one chance away from you, I might not rob you of your existence, but I do rob it of its full humanity.

Even if there is some good to be gotten by taking in my own hands the duty and the power to make your life decisions for you, what makes me qualified to do the job? Am I omniscient? Do I know the long-range impacts of my actions on you and everyone else? Do I know your deepest desires? In every respect I am woefully finite and fallible. But even if I weren't, would this justify my taking over your life? God is perfect, we believe, in all these respects: all-knowing, all-loving without fail, infinite, wise. Who better to be our tyrant?

Yet God turns down the role. We are created from the outset with free will, and God does not overrule us even when our choices are monstrous for ourselves, and even for others. God certainly offers to be our monarch, but even if we accept the offer, the relationship is less one of command and coerced obedience than one of counsel and willing adherence. If God, infinitely better qualified than any human, refuses to be our dictator, who among us would be wise to take on such a role?

The temptation to control others' lives is thus demonic at its best. But of course power corrupts. Our good intentions cannot survive the exercise of power in their pursuit. Political tyrants, even if once well-motivated, have an apparently universal tendency to decay over time until their central motivation is self-perpetuation rather then service. As we have already seen, tyrants lose touch because they insulate themselves from the free flow of information.

Part of this is inevitable any time decision-making is centralized. If you know best what you need and want, then delegating the power to decide how to provide for you to someone else substitutes ignorance for expertise. But as the tyrant progressively impoverishes her information supply, the illusion grows that she, and she alone, knows what it takes to get things done right. Her tyranny, originally a tool for the betterment of her people, becomes an end in itself as it becomes harder for the tyrant to imagine anyone but herself doing the job.

So benign intent can wed itself to more venal motives. Tyranny begets fawning, fibbing, and flattery, as the unscrupulous (or those in a hurry) learn the shortcuts to the tyrant's favor that can bring them sweet rewards. Tyrants are like anyone else, prone to become addicted to praise, to wealth, to being the center of attention. So most tyrants from the outset, and all tyrants before long, seek tyranny for their own selfish ends.

Similar things happen in the petty tyrannies we find outside the world of national politics. Tyranny can be found in families, workplaces, neighborhoods, churches—in any human group. Coercion and control of our fellows even in small things infringes on gifts only God can give. Any petty manipulation, deception, or other attempt to steer things our way regardless of the wills of others is a minor form of tyranny, a usurpation of their God-given role as co-creators in the divine plan.

It may be that some people are not yet ready to assume their full role as co-creators—children and the mentally disordered come to mind. It may also be that some abandon their right to be co-creators because they have shown their eagerness to deny others of their autonomous rights—criminals are examples of such outlaws. But among normal adults any attempt to usurp another's right to exercise their own will is a theft of life and a form of tyranny.

Perhaps there would be times when we might argue that we all need to give up a major portion of our free will for the good of all. But here we encounter another demonic dimension to tyranny: its main promise is a lie. Tyranny cannot work for the benefit of everyone, not nearly as well as openness and freedom. Tyranny starves the system of information and starves its subjects of incentive. The result is tragic misapplication of resources, usually exacerbated by corruption that siphons wealth into private ratholes.

Private tyranny is also a lie. Abraham Lincoln understood this when he argued in slave-ridden America that slavery was impoverishing the country. Slaves had less incentive to work than did free laborers, so that productivity in slave-owning states always lagged behind others. At the same time, slavery impoverished free laborers by driving down the price of labor. No one benefitted. Individual slave owners might live easier lives than they would have to if they helped work their own plantations, but to define this as being "better off" would require discounting to zero the value of work, of serving your neighbors, and of being an agent in one's own life. So only by assuming the only value in life is monetary could one even come close to arguing that some people benefitted from slavery. But ignoring moral value in calculating benefits is the same as lying.

So the modern enterprise owner who treats her labor only as a means of production, to be deployed as instrumentally as machines, has made an exceptionally foolish purchase, buying her moral supplies from the parent of lies. So too the parent who reduces maturing children to spiritual peonage by trying to control their lives and cancel their age-appropriate choices. So too the salesman who defrauds, even in small ways; or the public relations worker who hides blemishes and exaggerates the beauty marks on his clients; or the pastor who pretends that all is well at home . . . each has bought a parcel of misery from the purveyor of the lie: that keeping control, even when it costs others the option to choose, is potentially profitable.

The profits of even private tyranny are illusory to begin with. They pale even worse when compared to the benefits of recognizing that of God in all we encounter, and of working with God in partnerships wherever we find him, including in the persons of other people. Would we lie to God? Try to foreshorten his choices for our convenience or profit? Order him about? Then why would we do so with our fellow humans, each of whom is carrying with her a bit of God's work in this world?

Instead of giving in to the tyrant within, believers should practice listening to all those they deal with, seeking to work with them in discerning the right in any situation, *respecting them as equal partners in the vast divine project of redeeming the world.* This form of putting love into practice will create more space in our culture for larger scale loving between nations, and increase the odds that political despair will not take root in our global neighbors. It will also directly lead to better information on how to serve others in the ways we discussed in previous chapters.

3. Act in defiance of rage.

The terrorist works from anger. Terrorists win when we become like them. Our outbursts will be observed by and make it easier for others to justify putting legs under their own rage.

This, of course, requires that we monitor ourselves. When anger understandably overwhelms us, as it will in the face of outrages, we must *delay our immediate response until our anger can be channeled into something constructive*. On the day of the World Trade center bombing, a colleague of mine claimed that Christian just war theory would permit retaliation against the hijackers' supporters. Up to that point I had been calm, focused on learning as much as I could about the developing events and comforting my wife and my students, some of whom were distraught. But I found myself reacting strongly to my colleague's comment, and my response was rather more heated than I expected. In that situation I had to do what all of us will have to do sometimes: I had to step back from the conversation for a while and recognize my own emotional distress.

Sometimes our self-monitoring will not be enough. We all lose perspective when we feel threatened or under pressure. We need outriggers to keep us from toppling over in the surge of our anger. We need to *make ourselves accountable to others* who, hopefully, are more objective or removed from our emotional vortex. We sometimes need to check with these mentors before acting or reacting, so we do not spread anger with our actions.

One of the benefits of America's decision to try to build a worldwide coalition against terrorism is that it put us in a position of dependence on others for the success of our joint enterprise. Because so many countries responded to the World Trade Center bombings with spontaneous outpourings of empathy and solidarity, Americans felt they had friends on their side. They were not alone in their misery. But by the same token, Europeans and Asians, Latin Americans and Africans were one step (or more) removed from the full impact of the bombings. Many of them lost citizens in the attack, too, but most suffered much less than America did. Thus they had the ability to provide a sense of perspective and to urge a more measured response. And because America needed others' cooperation to succeed in its goals, our allies carried a big stick. We in essence gave them the power to restrain our more destructive impulses.

This laid the groundwork for others to try to rein America in for a while when President Bush was determined in mid-2002 to attack Iraq. Even though the United States went forward with only Britain as a frontline ally, involving others in the international decision-making leading up to the invasion of Iraq laid important groundwork for post-war cooperation and mutual discernment of the path forward from there.

Christians can play the same perspective-maintaining, rage-deflecting role for those around them. Some have invited Islamic neighbors for picnics. Others have attended mosques. When enraged Americans attacked mosques, in some cities neighboring churches offered to send people to serve as informal night watchmen to guard against further attacks. The next time an American sought to punish all Moslems at that mosque, he would find people who looked like himself, and who were obviously not Moslem, occupying his target, giving him the grace of one more reason to reconsider his actions. These believers were fighting terrorism by *acting as a check on others who were ready to give in to the terrorist within*. Accompanying possible targets of violence is one way to suppress outraged action as a friend to those who might be victims, but this is only one of countless examples. Peacemaking can be something as simple as being a non-anxious presence, listening empathetically while staying out of the vortex of another's emotions. Even giving a soft answer so as to turn away wrath is a peacemaking ministry.

One can also work to counter rage by being a friend to the enraged. When a group is calling for vengeance, Christians in the group may need to show courage to stand up against the prevailing mood and *urge forbearance and submission to a merit-based process*. Christians can provide an outlet for the expression of anger, a compassionate ear to listen to outrage until it can at least partly spend itself on something other than revenge. To be most effective in this role, we believers will have to earn trust to such a degree that those who are angry will recognize our trustworthiness despite the shock of having us stand in their way and oppose their choices.

Never Give in to Terrorism

In this chapter we have examined another stack of ideas for what believers can do about terrorism:

45. Offer to substitute oneself for hostages.

46. If taken hostage, refuse to leave when ransomed.

47. Flock to public monuments and commercial centers.

48. Take to the air in record numbers.

49. Carry on with public events.

50. Ride the Jerusalem busses and station observers in Israeli malls.

51. Live in the Palestinian camps and towns.

52. Picnic along Derry parade routes.

53. Minister in Bujumbura and Kigali.

54. Teach in missions schools in Pakistan.

55. Submit cheerfully to increased airport security and resulting travel delays.

56. Insist that our deaths or injuries while serving in terrorist-infested areas must not be the occasion for causing the same to others.

57. Cooperate with law enforcement to identify and capture terrorists.

58. Take responsibility to watch our neighborhoods for suspicious activity.

59. Refuse to ask our neighbors to accept unnecessary risks resulting from our own insistence upon full personal freedom to act as we please without inconvenience.

60. Work to turn public opinion against irresponsible military actions.

61. Create letters to the editors, sit-ins, demonstrations, and other symbolic actions designed to stimulate cheerful and civil discussion with fellow citizens.

62. Outbid drug lords for the productive effort of Colombian farmers.

63. Suspend or cancel international debts in exchange for debtors' domestic vigor against killers.

64. Share the stories of victims and survivors.

65. Invest ourselves in our communities.

66. Know neighbors and seek to be of value in their lives.

67. Identify and freeze terrorists' and tyrants' assets, hopefully for use by victims and survivors.

68. Give platforms to the majority of Islamic and other religious leaders who denounce both murder and suicide, along with other forms of terrorism.

69. Challenge those who shelter terrorists or tyrants, and their co-conspirators, to give them up for trial.

70. Prosecute those who refuse to legitimately cooperate with the worldwide project to strip tyrants and indicted terrorists of access to their assets.

71. Make pariahs of any nations that sponsor tyranny, refuse to help with investigating terrorism, or resist capturing indicted terrorists and holding them for trial.

72. Convene an international congress to negotiate a uniform worldwide anti-terrorism/anti-tyranny code.

73. Condemn expansion by conquest in all cases, including both Iraq's invasion of Kuwait and Israel's illegal settlement policy in the West Bank and Gaza.

74. Work to prohibit assassination, even of known terrorists.

75. Always let matters be decided on their merits.

76. Let the legitimate interests of others affect the outcome of disputes.

77. Face up to the possibility of being wrong.

78. Submit to governing authorities.

79. Work to improve our habits of listening to others, and work as equal partners with them in God's project of redeeming the world, rather than succumbing to the temptation of petty tyranny in our relations with others.

80. Recognize our own emotional distress, and delay immediate responses to affronts until distress can be channeled into something constructive.

81. Make ourselves accountable to others who are more objective or removed from our emotional vortex.

82. Act as a check on others who may be ready to give in to the terrorist within, urging forbearance.

This is a partial list, of course. I will recite yet again my refrains about the infinite inventiveness of a loving, omnipotent God as compared to our human myopia. Not only have we likely missed entire regions of possibility for acting in defiance of terrorism, but even in the ideas we have considered, the number of options for putting them into effect is greater than we could ever have time to carry out.

Think of it—God's good ideas flow by us like a surging river. We Christians often give up on the existence of good ideas without even opening our eyes to God's abundant supply, or we dip in with our teaspoons and declare we have plumbed the depths of the possible. The reality is that, even if we did our very best to drink from the river of God's creativity, our cups over-flowing, we cannot make a dent in what God can think up. Most of it flows on past, untouched and only seen on its surface, well beyond our capacity to comprehend its richness let alone make use of it—unless we dive in and explore the flood in depth and at length.

Some of the hope we might derive from this image of God's profligate love is undermined by a tension which, with this chapter, becomes unmistakable. We spoke in earlier chapters of how loving our enemies is a central theme of Jesus' gospel and applies even in our relationships with terrorists. Because we love them, we are motivated to meet their needs and reconcile our relationships with them, if they will allow it. But in this chapter we have stressed the absolute necessity of not giving in to terrorists. If we serve the needs we find in terrorist communities, how will we avoid the appearance, or even the reality, of re-warding terrorism with our help? Or if we forgive and seek reconciliation, doesn't the terrorist get off without the justice due him for what he has done?

This is the central issue in our approach to terrorism. It has been lurking behind all the discussion so far. We are almost ready to face it head-on.

..

Chapter 9

Sowing Practical Hope: The Political Side of Terrorism, Part II

If all we do is try to break the myth of effective violence, we will not stop terrorism. Three-legged terrorism might be slowed somewhat in recruiting and carrying out its plans. But we have learned how exceptionally vulnerable we are, so even a limping terrorist movement can wreak unacceptable destruction.

For there is a danger in cutting off people's perceived options. If we make it clear that terrorism as we have so far seen it cannot bring about the terrorist's goals, the terrorist is going to look for some other means of being heard and having an impact. If we aren't careful to open new, nonviolent options that were not apparent before, she will be tempted to think her only option is to hit us harder, using even more destructive methods.

We have not seen the worst that could happen. Planes are still flying without foolproof security—there is and will always be an ample supply of these manned guided missiles, since the only foolproof security for airplanes is to forbid anyone or anything from being loaded upon them. And there are even worse specters on the horizon. So far no terrorist has used nuclear weapons, nor have they tapped any significant part of the potential for pain from biological, chemical, or cyber-terrorism. Worldwide terrorism could be significantly wounded and still be capable of hitting back much harder than we have been hit so far.

Herein lies the danger in trying to convince, by violent means, that violence does not pay. The lesson may be misunderstood as follows: The way to be effective is to be even more violent than your opponent. Current levels of violence may not work, but higher levels will. Imagine two warring groups both adopting this view, that they can persuade the other to give up on violence by overwhelming the other with even greater violence. What a recipe for disaster! What a tragic, if imperfect, description of the Israeli-Palestinian conflict and some of the U.S.-Iraq dynamics.

Here is where the Christian peace worker needs to be ready to step into the role of process advocate. If we work to build and improve processes for translating needs into solutions based on the merits of the situation, we fill two needs at once. Merit-based problem resolving processes provide an effective alternative to violence for getting things done, and they at the same time strengthen our ability to suppress, apprehend, and punish appropriately those that purvey violence.

The Power of Merit-Based Processes

I have spent many words in this book urging my fellow Christians to get more involved in meeting human needs all over the planet, especially in those areas susceptible to corrosive grievance. Such efforts are crucial, both to erode grievance and to build the kind of human connections that best inoculate people from choosing to destroy those they disagree with.

But I can imagine many believers sighing with exasperation. Some followers of Jesus have already been putting all they have into meeting needs and struggle with discouragement. The needs are so vast, and our impact so small! Part of the problem, of course, is that most Christians, even many who also heave sighs, are not really doing much, certainly only a small fraction of what they might do to meet needs. We slackers, we who think of sponsoring a Compassion child as if our sacrifice of $28 a month were somehow heroic, are preventing God from meeting the true needs of many of our fellow humans. We are doing so simply because we see so many luxuries as unquestionable "needs" of our own.

Perhaps the world terrorist problem would be solved if Christians all *understood their "personal" wealth as being on loan from God* and treated it as good stewards should—as the assets of Another entrusted to their care, to be managed for the Other's good purposes. Multiplying world relief, missions, and peace work several times over—a pretty good summary of many of the recommendations already made—is probably within the reach of the Christian community, if it understood its priorities better and had a more accurate self-image.

But it is more likely that, no matter how much we can do as Christians coming to the situation from the outside, meeting all needs is not within our human power. While we should be constantly reviewing our management of God's resources in our personal care, cutting back on waste and selfishness and expanding the share put to the service of human need, there are at least four significant barriers to our ability to match our resources perfectly with needs.

The first is our imperfect knowledge of each other. I am not a Burundian recovering from the effects of recurring genocide in my country. I can listen to a Burundian like David Niyonzima, and he can tell me much of what he and his people need. I can then try to target my resources toward meeting those needs. But when David tells me of his people's needs, he can only describe them in general terms. Neither of us has time to go over every Burundian's case and accurately describe the details of what each needs. David's information will provide a one-size-fits-all picture of the needs. And my attempts to meet them will be plagued by the inevitable points of misunderstanding between David and I, my laziness or haste to cut corners, or even by my culturally inappropriate ideas about how to get the work done. The resulting help will be one-size-fits all—and poorly tailored to boot. People living in planned economies will recognize the imperfections in this approach.

A second problem lurks, too. If I act to meet your needs, it will be hard for us to avoid falling into a situation where you come to depend on me permanently for your own welfare. Providing food aid to a society sometimes drives local food producers out of business, unable to compete with the price of free food aid. With local producers losing local buyers, either they shift to producing for export, or they go out of business. Either way, ability to meet needs locally is undermined. Debilitating economic dependence is always a danger lurking behind aid programs. This is not to say that we should suspend aid programs, only that we cannot infinitely expand them.

The third problem is with how decisions get made. A donor-dependent economy concentrates decision-making power in the hands of the donors. Even donors that are careful to listen to locals and to work toward meeting felt needs still end up holding the purse strings. Communication tends to become centripetal—members of the target community making their most important attempts to communicate bilaterally with donors (figure A), instead of communally in negotiation or discussion with neighbors (figure B).

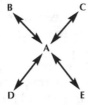 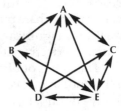

Figure A: Centripetal Communication   Figure B: Communal Negotiation

Where a healthy community will find cooperative relationships among its members, working together to get things done, a community dependent on one or a few outside sources of donations can become competitive internally, as different sectors compete for largesse. Furthermore, a centralized source of resource flows and information will end up stratifying the community, as those closer to the source of goodies gain power over those further away. Veterans of colonization will recognize this pattern.

The fourth problem stems from how charitable distributions can interrupt the flow of key information about human needs. One of the principle organizing agents in any human community is the market. Markets exist in some form in every modern community, as people match their abilities to others' needs and wants. In adequately functioning markets, prices reflect the relative intensity of people's unmet demands for a good or service. Those looking for ways to make a living can take cues from price levels relative to costs of production to find areas where their efforts are going to make the biggest difference in the lives of their potential customers. Markets thus can be powerful tools for encouraging people to abandon useless pursuits and switch to ones where needs (or at least wants) are greatest.

Communities dependent on relief lose much of their access to this market information. In goods and services related to those being provided by outside donors, prices get skewed compared to where they would be in times when the community is closer to being self-sufficient. For example, where food distribution is widespread, land may be taken out of farm production and even converted to industrial or other uses of relatively low value. If food donations are cut off, land that could have been used to meet the suddenly surging demand will now be unavailable. Since food donations are likely to be cut off someday, this dislocation is almost inevitable.

One alternative is destitution among farmers as they wait for the return of normal market conditions and, in the meantime, can't sell their produce against competition from free food. Certainly someone looking for a way to make an income for her family will not give agriculture much thought under these circumstances. Even prices for other goods and services, only tangentially related to food production, will be skewed. For example, unskilled labor costs may be depressed somewhat by the loss of agricultural work, while those qualified to be managers may be in short supply, soaked up in the administration of aid programs.

Compounding the loss of market information, long-term relief dependency can also distort the local political system. For the goods and services offered by the local public sector, democracy paired with the rule of law forms a powerful information system analogous to the market in commercial affairs. Having equipped each voter with an equal unit of political power—a vote—democracy (with freedom of expression, protections of the vote, and competitive elections) aggregates the political views of the population and encourages decision-makers to heed these results in making decisions. Pluralist democracy, with a variety of power centers and levels of decision-making, allows for flexibility in responding to some minorities as well as the majority. Where markets and democracy operate together, over time government policies and practices tend to maximize the welfare of the majority and respond to the most significant needs of even relatively small minorities.

Democracies and markets require reliable rule of law to achieve these goals. Corruption—including bribery, voting irregularities, and opaqueness and falsehood in public affairs and financial statements—introduces distortions in the flow of information. Contracts that should go to the bidder offering the best value at the best price go instead to cronies, bribers, or family members. The result is either extra cost, diverting resources from other valuable projects, or shoddy work, to the detriment of customers. If the product is a building or a bridge, the detriment may appear when the structure collapses. People die of corruption. This is an iron law of human systems, and comes true everywhere, sooner or later.

The need for honesty and independence in the judiciary is clear to anyone who has suffered from a corrupt or politically captive judge or police officer. The same thing applies to legislators, bureaucrats, or even corporate executives—as investors the world over rediscovered in the early 2000s with the Enron-class cases of corporate corruption.

In each case, the breakdown of democracy or a market means a move away from deciding matters on their merits to deciding them based on something else. The briber wants to decide based on his superior ability to "get to" a key decision-maker, who is willing to decide based on what is best for himself, rather than what is best for the community he is supposed to serve. In essence, the bribed official or executive has begun to treat his enterprise's assets as if they were intended primarily to benefit himself, almost as if his position were part of his personal estate. (The parallels with my position when I think of "my" property as being for my benefit, rather than belonging to God, are staggering in their implications.)

The pattern repeats itself for other forms of corrupt (ie, non-merit-based) activity. The nepotist puts his family's welfare ahead of the merits for the community. The liar puts her political or business career ahead of the welfare of the voters or investors she is trying to manipulate. They are very like the terrorist, who puts her own political views above others' and is willing to impose her will on those around her rather than find a way to submit her claim to the testing of a political process. Each is stealing something from the public to advance her own agenda, and each is eluding a decision on the merits in favor of a decision based on something else.

A healthy community has access to means to meet its needs which do not depend on the charity of others. Communities overdependent on charity lose their chance to benefit from a properly functioning market, or (more subtly) from a healthy democracy. Again, Christians need to be more proactive in helping find ways to meet needs around the globe, especially in communities vulnerable to corrosive grievance. The alternatives to helping meet needs are too stark—suffering, death, terrorism's pernicious growth. But care must be taken. Immediate responses to crises, development projects, education to build human capital—all these and more are very good, even critical in keeping people's lives together until crises pass. But something else is needed, too. For a community to successfully provide for itself, functioning markets and democracies under the rule of law are crucial. Anything less consigns the community to poverty and dependence and quite likely to the eventual outbreak of corrosive grievance.

Ultimately, permanent and stable remedies for injustice depend on political capacity, moral strength including its expression in a functioning legal system, and market-based prosperity of the people who live in vulnerable areas. But most of the governments in terror-prone areas do not meet these demanding standards. They are not transparent enough with their own people. They are too suspicious of freedom and too willing to succumb to the temptation to shortchange the rule of law. Under these conditions, it becomes hard for anyone to know what the most pressing needs are or how they might be met.

Apart from misdirecting resources due to lack of good information about needs, autocratic or corrupt governments cannot allocate development resources to maximum impact. Too much siphons into personal accounts or is directed toward the interests of family and friends of those in power. Locals don't get the education required to perform some of the technical services needed, such as public health, civil engineering, and so forth. And when they do, they often find they have irresistible opportunities to make a better life abroad. As prospects weaken for making a difference at home, those who can—usually the most wealthy, best connected, or most energetic and entrepreneurial—find ways to leave their homelands and start over somewhere else. So just when they need their best people most, undemocratic societies under stress are most likely to lose them.

Installing Merit-Based Political Processes

Ultimately all the undemocratic governments and all the corrupted markets will have to be replaced as a part of the war on terror, since they are seedbeds for terrorism. They create conditions under which people's needs go unmet, and in which there are poor or nonexistent political means for people to express their needs and improve the conditions of their lives. Given the poor track record of monarchies and dictatorships in reforming for the best interests of their people, I don't think there should be much care taken to act at their direction or convenience.

Christians ought to *stand firmly against policies that prop up undemocratic regimes or perpetuate corrupted markets.* In the long run, those who help such governments are, in every case, joining the wrong side of history. Their error will at least show up in the persistence of unnecessary human suffering. In most cases, backing such regimes will, in a relatively short time, leave us in the position we have already been in places like Iran in the late 1970s: caught in bed with fallen villains.

We also ought to do what we can to promote the spread of democracy and the rule of law. I am tempted to propose that believers instigate or join open, transparent, nonviolent campaigns to topple the worst regimes. However, I worry about the precedent that would be set if private citizens take upon themselves the right to determine the fate of other people's governments. *Perhaps our government should create a special operations unit designed to destabilize and overthrow undemocratic regimes wherever they are found, using the methods of active nonviolence* most conducive to creating conditions conducive to democracy in the aftermath of a revolution. We have twenty years of recent history in Eastern Europe and around the world to guide us in the formation of such a unit.

If we don't feel comfortable actively overthrowing dictatorships and kleptocracies, what can we do to promote their
demise or reform? One of the ways we can be of best service in
such a case is to *help in the creation of local and national political
structures that are responsive and democratically accountable to the
needs of the citizens.* We should urge our own leaders to stead-
fastly promote democracy in the Middle East, for example, as
well as every other region of the world.[76] Iran has been creeping
in this direction over the last fifteen years. Israel has a decent
record—at least for its non-Arab citizens—and in particular
should be proud of its promotion of free speech and governmental transparency throughout the worst of the second inte-
fadah, at least up to the time when this was written. Turkey and
Jordan are partly on track, as are some of the North African nations. Pakistan's record is mixed and currently not in its best
form under military rule. Other governments nearby have better records—India comes to mind, especially—but Hindu-
Moslem conflicts make India unlikely to be accepted as a role
model in the Islamic world.

On occasion we have experimented with *making democracy
and human rights the touchstones of our foreign policy.* There is good
evidence that Jimmy Carter's brief four-year term in office had
impressive effects in advancing the cause of democracy. At least
in the Philippines and Haiti, his pressure on two of our "client
dictatorships" set events in motion that eventually led to their
downfall.[77] President Carter didn't get much public credit for
his work, because its benefits were mostly delayed until well
after he left office, and because in each case democracy also got
a subsequent, crucial, and more conspicuous boost from Pope
John Paul II.

And maybe the work Carter did was even more important
than we can document. How do we know what would have
happened had Haiti and the Philippines been missing from the
domino trail of falling dictatorships that brought dramatic
change to Poland, East Germany, and the entire Soviet bloc?
Nonviolent demonstrators in the latter countries drew inspiration from the concept of "people power" which got huge worldwide play in January and February 1986.

Now the struggle against terrorism demands that all the democratic governments in the world redouble their efforts to

*make democracy and the rule of law a minimum requirement for accep-
tance in the community of civilized nations.* When we tolerate less,
we leave tyrants in power and safe harbors for terror. Everyone
has the right to a voice in her own self-government. Only when
people feel they have lost a voice can terrorists recruit.

Perhaps it is time for the democracies of the world to form
their own international organization to coordinate their efforts
to rid the rest of the world of tyranny. NATO countries sometimes seem to think of themselves as guarantors of democracy
in Europe and perhaps nearby areas. But NATO is colored in the
rest of the world by its reliance on the United States to provide
the decisive majority of its military and political power. It thus
lacks the aura of an independent, dispassionate advocate of democratic process, suspected instead to be a tool of American (or
perhaps American and European) self-interest.

Furthermore, NATO's roots are as a collective military defensive alliance. I am not advocating for an old-fashioned collective security arrangement; such an organization would miss
the target in at least two ways. First, its dominant tool of influence would be military, especially in NATO's specific case. We
need to shift our focus away from military responses to the
broader exchange and affiliation-oriented options.

Second, a traditional collective security organization would
not be nearly aggressive enough. Instead of collective defense of
a perimeter, designed to keep an enemy from advancing, what
we need is a collective offense to preemptively (but nonviolently) intervene in tyrannies, helping indigenous agents of
democracy to rid themselves of the dead weight of dictators.

Maybe the democracies should create a formal caucus in the UN,
an inner circle to create and enforce UN policies that would rel-
egate dictatorships to marginal roles and reward transitions to
democracy. For example, the Security Council might be limited
to democratic governments. China's permanent membership
could be suspended until its political and human rights reforms
catch up to its economic liberalization.[78] India and Pakistan
could be guaranteed a permanent seat on the Security Council
when they work out their dispute over Kashmir, both establish
stable democracies, and both rid themselves of nuclear
weapons—with the proviso that neither gets in until both qualify. Japan should get such a seat too, and the remaining seats

should rotate only among democracies. Once it transforms itself, the Security Council should redefine its function as being the central coordinating council for the democratization of the planet.

These reforms would be exceptionally difficult given the current structure of the UN. China's veto alone is likely to thwart any attempt to even temporarily remove it from the Security Council. But the payoff would be enormous. Democratizing the UN would give democracies more confidence in international structures. Tying international courts to a solidly democratized UN would give more nations confidence to allow such courts to exercise jurisdiction. The International Criminal Court, currently hobbled by the refusal of the US to fully cooperate, might be able to do effective and important anti-terror and anti-tyranny work if the U.S. Government had better assurance that the court would be constrained by democratically created law .

But if the UN can't be turned into a tool for collective offense against tyranny, *democracies need to form their own global club,* somewhere between a NATO and a UN, complete with its own international judiciary, law enforcement, and development agencies.

I am not saying that every country has to adopt a Western model of democracy. The key isn't whether there is a directly elected president or a parliamentary government with a prime minister. The keys are these:

- freedom of expression and political organization;
- freedom to form private associations to provide alternative means to meet human needs;
- freedom of religion and conscience, to prevent terrorists or tyrants from monopolizing the spiritual terrain and spreading lies unchecked;
- political leaders accountable to citizens via frequent, fair, contested elections;
- civil rights protecting minorities against majorities, and citizens against the temptation of governments to operate outside the law;
- due process for those accused of crimes.

Political theorists might add to this list some other protections—property rights, for instance, to allow private citizens to carve out a sanctuary for themselves from dependence on government; political parties to aggregate interests into effective political blocs; interest groups to help articulate those interests; and so forth. I am willing to let that debate burble along its healthy way. But the core is clear: every country must assure its citizens a reliable way to voice their concerns, a guarantee of effectiveness when their concerns are widely shared, and protection from annihilation when they find themselves in small minorities.

Any country that does not meet these standards is, in effect, harboring terrorism. Even if international terrorist gangs are not operating on a particular despotic state's soil, the charge still sticks: The government itself is feeding corrosive grievance. It is doing so by starving its people of information, and thus contributing to dehumanization, as well as by its unwillingness to let issues be decided on their merits, which contributes to the myth of the political effectiveness of violence.

Some will point out that even in the world's oldest democracies, terrorism persists. Britain is embroiled in a lingering battle with the Irish Republican "Army." The worst terrorist bombing in the U.S. before the World Trade Center was at the hands of U.S. citizen Timothy McVeigh. Both of these cases match our terrorist profile—people who believe they have no voice in the political system while also believing in the myth of terrorism's political effectiveness.

These cases shine a spotlight on the critical need to avoid any compromise with terrorism. McVeigh blew up the federal building in Oklahoma City on the anniversary of the government assault at Waco, Texas. McVeigh's actions were a monstrously twisted response to our government's failure in the Waco case to *discipline itself to acting within the confines of the law.* I do not accuse the agents at Waco of acting in bad faith, but it is clear that the attack on the Koresh compound endangered innocent people—children, at least—and resulted in their deaths. If such a relatively defensible attack with relatively small collateral damage can sow the seeds for future terrorism, how much more will any massive military operation do?

Or consider the Northern Irish situation. The roots of this conflict go back into history well before the English kings were constrained by democratic checks and balances. Ironically, the

IRA and its Protestant counterparts among loyalists are the last major avatars in the British Isles of the undemocratic policies of British imperialism. The IRA is still fighting a war against British imperialism that ended everywhere else two generations ago. Perhaps this IRA persistence in fighting an outdated war is explained by the fact they are fighting it in the wrong place—maybe the only place left in the Commonwealth with both a significant independence movement and a large majority opposed to independence. Democracy does not offer the IRA a means to their chosen ends. Were the IRA to win its objectives, it would be over the objections of most of the people who live there.

The facts on the ground now in Northern Ireland demand democratic solutions with full respect for all the residents of the land, but the extremists do not get it. They lack the courage to submit the question for resolution on its merits. Should the worldwide myth of terrorism's effectiveness be undermined, the IRA and its mirror-images on the Protestant side will pass from the scene.

Perhaps it is time for the world community to begin treating terrorist and other violent solutions of border conflicts the way it treats slavery—as behavior well beyond the pale of what is accepted among civilized nations. *Christians should be leading the way.* Kenneth Boulding advocated, a generation ago, that border conflicts should just be taken off the table, making discussion of border changes taboo.[79] This strikes me as an uncharacteristic slip on the great Quaker's part. People will inevitably discuss their borders, both in terms of independence and in relation to where the borders will be. Making these discussions taboo will just force them into backrooms and underground, where none of the benefits of transparency and democracy are available. This is a recipe for terrorism. Rather than hiding from the issue of borders, Christians might *support the creation of an internationally monitored electoral mechanism* in which populations in areas near national boundaries are given the right once each generation to vote on which of the neighboring nations they wish to join, or possibly to become independent.

I see this as one way to implement in our day some of the spirit of the Old Testament Year of Jubilee, in which debts were

234 ❖ Loving Without Giving In

to be forgiven, property returned to its original owners, and the social structure in general reset with the goal of renewing justice and refreshing spiritual health in the citizenry. To have once each generation a chance to rethink with one's community the region's political status would be a powerful force for reflection and possibly even renewal. Of course, any citizens involved in terrorist violence, or even belonging to an organization that did not forswear such violence, would be barred from voting, no matter which side of the issue they were supporting.

And perhaps we can add spark to this proposal by *requiring any nation hoping to benefit from such an election to first promulgate and meaningfully implement a democratic constitution*, guaranteeing the political rights referred to above, and including the rule of law through an independent judiciary and police force. To qualify as a democracy, the *national constitution would also have to be abandon claims on other territory*—so the Palestinian constitution would, for example, have to describe Palestine within its internationally recognized borders, as would Israel's, and India's and Pakistan's (after the residents of Kashmir had finalized their first election as to whether to affiliate with Pakistan or India or be independent).

We can add a series of incentives to this requirement: Governments which comply would be eligible not only to gain territory by election but also to have terrorism suspects tried on their soil if the attack occurred there or their citizens are victims; and be eligible to have its citizens tried by its own courts if accused of crimes under the jurisdiction of the International War Crimes Tribunal. Of course this implies that democratic nations should ratify and be subject to this tribunal, a recommendation I make, with qualifications, in the next section.

Democracy in the form of elections and political rights is not enough. After all, Israel and perhaps Iran are almost the only two democracies in the Middle East, and both engage in widespread suppression of people's human rights (the Palestinians in Israel's case, and the Iranians who dissent against Islamic rule in Iran's case). But both have spotty records when it comes to supporting terrorism or responding to it. This is because neither democracy is fully constrained by respect for overarching principles of law or justice. They are democracies, but in at least some of their policy areas, they are not democracies governed by law. The Iranians compromise their democracy with the un-elected and unaccountable power of the ayatollah and other religious leaders. The Israelis do not have a good record of extending the full measure of their political rights to their Arab citizens, let alone the Palestinians under their occupation. Israel's democracy, as vibrant and admirable as it is, confines its main protections and benefits to its Jewish citizens. *Every country aspiring to the status of democracy has to extend its full political rights to all its citizens,* regardless of ethnic or religious background or profession.

Similarly sweeping goals call us when it comes to the rule of law. If we don't insist on the rule of law in every case, we cannot expect anyone else to submit to it. *This means we must examine our own practices and history for cases where the rule of law was ignored.* If we punished Iraq for invading Kuwait because expansion by conquest is an evil on the scale of terrorism, we have to apply the same standard to Israel. If we expect the Israelis to abandon their post-1967 conquests, and to compensate Arabs for expulsions in 1948, we must apply the same standard to ourselves. We expanded across an entire continent at the ultimate expense of the Native Americans who were here first and at the immediate expense of our neighbor Mexico in the southwest. Have we settled our accounts with these people justly? Christians should lead the way in pushing our society to do so.

What about slavery? While it was hedged about with legal protections once the slaves arrived in America, were the original slaves ever afforded protection of law when they became slaves? And are we content to cite the laws of the slave states as justifications for the maintenance of slavery after American independence?

If I can claim to be above the law, so can you. Then there is no law. That is just another form of lawlessness—if not terrorist itself, certainly its breeding ground. Nor can we have a system where any one of us can declare all by himself what the law is. We know that road is a short one and leads right back to lawlessness, because without accountability we all end up succumbing to self-interest. To be law, the rules must be made with equal regard for all who are to be governed by them.

Part of our worldwide anti-terrorism policy, then, is a much more rigorous self-examination and a readiness on everyone's part to be bound by the principles of law. To be an effective world leader in the struggle to replace terrorism with democracy and the rule of law, the United States must itself abide by the highest standards of lawfulness. This brings us back to an "International Golden Rule": *Any action a nation initiates must be defensible under the same standards it would want applied to actions against that nation.* Do unto others as you would be done by.

Can we justify acting alone, without being accountable to an objective authority empowered to keep us under the restraint of justice? Can we be judges in our own case? Can we ignore cases in our own history where we expanded by conquest at the expense of people who were already there? Not if we really want to replace the terrorist's political despair with democracy and the rule of law.

Because corruption threatens merit-based decision processes wherever it is found, it also needs to be part of this new international standard for nations. *Christians should never engage in corruption.* Bribery, even when part of the local culture, still has its pernicious merit-destroying effects. Morally it is no different than administering stab wounds or a whipping to random citizens unlucky enough not to be in a position of public or corporate trust or a member of the family or crony-set of a powerful person. Would a Christian missionary or businessman fire into a crowd at random if a local magistrate required this in exchange for approval to bring in a vehicle or open a church? Some bribes would be even more damaging than firing a random bullet. But because we cannot see our victims, we might be tempted to give in to the bribe demand to get a visible and known "good" accomplished.

We should also support legislation such as the Foreign Corrupt Practices Act that require our businesses to live by the same standards abroad as they adhere to at home. If international versions of such legislation prove to be impossible, then we should encourage our national authorities to impose sanctions on countries who do not enforce such rules on their citizens, to make the playing field in international business as level as possible.

Nepotism is a tougher issue. Palestine suffered a long, difficult period following the breakdown of the second Camp David talks in 2000. It was a time marked by travel restrictions, closures, curfews, and many people losing their jobs or access to customers and suppliers. For many, all that stood between them and starvation was their connection to extended families. As long as someone among the cousins had assets or income, no one starved. Were it not for extended families, the humanitarian catastrophe which beset Palestinians would have been far worse.

But there is another side to this commitment to family. In business, the obligation to provide for one's family means that jobs in the firm must go first to kin. This cuts a manager off from sources of more qualified and capable employees. Human resources are not optimally allocated in such a system, and performance (and service to customers) suffers. This may be tolerable in business, but in government it is pernicious. Even in the charitable sector, recipients of grants and relief contracts feel bound to hire from the family and may even make sure that the first fruits of the program go to benefit family or the extended kin among the target population. And in the Palestinian Authority as well as other areas around the world, some of the conduits through which public money disappears without accomplishing public good are family connections.

Nepotism is not alien to North American culture, but strong norms have developed in many sectors against it. Should these expectations be exported to other societies, despite our admiration for how strong families are in many of them? Perhaps, *in our commercial and non-profit enterprises in such cultures, we can create a sector in their societies that is not nepotistic*, where the employment of relatives is forbidden or permitted only when objective criteria tied to job descriptions warrant. This might introduce an element of flexibility into the culture which would allow public and private managers some freedom to make personnel decisions based on merits other than kinship.

This principle of firm commitment to the rule of law extends, of course, to other laws. Since the days of Peter and John before the Sanhedrin, Christians have recognized that some laws requiring them to disobey God cannot claim their obedience. But in every other case, *Christians should scrupulously adhere to the local laws.* Even in cases where civil disobedience is necessary to remain faithful to the will of God, Christians should submit without resistance to local authorities enforcing such laws and accept punishments meted out to them if in accord with the law.

Existing political mechanisms may not be enough to provide people with corrosive grievances an alternative to violence. This is true especially in countries without democratic traditions or a rich civil society offering privately initiated institutions to get things done. *Believers should work to help create these mechanisms.* We should also work to help people devise their own forms of informal conflict resolution, such as mediation and arbitration, to allow for merit-based resolution of conflicts in situations where resorting to the more formal (and expensive) judicial processes is not the best option.

John Paul Lederach's elicitative model was developed for just such a purpose. Eastern Europeans have experimented in this direction, with help from the West, as have communities in parts of the former Soviet Union and in Burundi. The Afghani *loya jirga* is an example of an apparently successful use of a local cultural tradition in this general direction. The traditional Palestinian *sulha* offers another promising start for that troubled region.[80]

In Haiti, during the turbulent years after the fall of the Duvalier regime and before the election of President Aristide, I had the privilege of meeting with a local organizer of a community development group in a regional center in the north-central part of the country. In addition to the many practically oriented development projects his organization sponsored—marketing programs for local farmers, a local credit association, infrastructure improvements like irrigation and roads—this organization was consciously pursuing a political goal: the development of local political institutions, such as interest groups, literacy projects, and trade organizations.

Money was available through his organization, and people came to it because it was a source of needed funds. But cash wasn't just handed out. It was distributed largely according to the directives of local citizen committees. They had to organize their committees to have an institutional structure to receive and administer the funds. Money was used as a catalyst for political and spiritual organization. The local churches provided some of the logistical support for this project, and some of the groups included a devotional dimension, encouraging citizens to consider the spiritual dimensions of their community's development.

Haiti is still a poor and troubled country. But this project is one of many I know of in Haiti, Palestine, Central America, and elsewhere—some with an even clearer spiritual focus—which combine development projects with local institution-building, working on the short- and middle-term economic issues in the community as well as the long-term social and political structures necessary to ensure that they will benefit fully from their labors. This is anti-terrorism at its very best.

Using Merit-Based Processes to Neutralize Terrorists

Creating political structures is a good anti-terrorism strategy, because it gives people with grievances alternatives to violence and undermines thereby the myth that only violence can be effective. But it also gives alternatives to violence in our battle against terrorism. This undermines even further the myth of effective violence and allows us to take direct measures against terrorists without risking making them into martyrs or splattering the sense of corrosive grievance to sympathizers.

Take fact finding, one of the simplest proposals made in Chapter 5, for a start. If more nations had democratic institutions in place, we might with some confidence turn to their own authorities for guidance on what a community's needs are and how they relate to their sense of grievance. *Relying on the vast interest aggregating mechanisms of democracy and markets to highlight a people's most urgent needs,* we could refer to prices on key items as indicators of felt needs, or of a community's lack of capacity to translate their needs into economic or even political demands.

Food might be an obvious example. If the price of food in an urban area exceeds a certain fraction of disposable household income, this could be viewed as signalling impending hunger. Corrosive grievances would be expected to increase in frequency in such a community, especially if there were marked contrasts between conditions there and conditions in a more privileged section of the city or if destitution was plaguing only one ethnic or religious group.

If the country was a democracy, where people were free to express their grievance, and if there was little complaint about

the situation, observers could be fairly confident that grievances were not getting more serious or at least not turning corrosive. What would appear in public discussion would match
the private opinions of the affected citizens.

Where democracy had been strangled, it would be harder to
estimate the grievance in the hungry community. Silence might
mean the community has found a way to cope, as it would in a
democracy. Or it might mean the community was simmering
but afraid to speak out. The latter would be bad news on two
fronts. Corrosive grievance would be expected to be rampant,
and members of the community would have little reason for
confidence that they could be heard or could secure changes
through the political process. Such a community is already
halfway toward producing a crop of terrorists.

The non-democratic scenario is worrisome both because
terrorism is more likely to sprout without democracy and because it offers such unreliable means of detecting spreading
grievance and frustrated expression. This suggests that one response we can make to terrorist threats is to call their bluff. Terrorists claim to represent people who are suffering injustice, but
they resort to violence in a form incompatible with democracy
and merit-based decisions. We have a legitimate concern that
the terrorist may not represent the prevailing views in his own
home community.

So, what if we responded by insisting on conducting an
election, perhaps for a local version of a loya jirga, and *submitting the question of what is needed to a democratic process*? The terrorist's supporters would be required to agree in advance to
submit to the results of the process and foreswear violence as a
tactic thenceforth. We would agree to support the accomplish-
ment of goals selected through an internationally supervised
democratic process, with the proviso that if those goals con-
flicted with the goals of other communities, the two communities would have to negotiate a mutually agreeable outcome
before it received our support. The inspiration here is akin to
what Fisher and Ury term "negotiation ju-jitsu."[81] We would
take their claim and turn its momentum to the service of our
goal of democratizing politics everywhere. Their grievance
would thus be dealt with on its political merits via the democratic process.

Where there is no rule of law, we lose access to the benefits of an independent lawful judiciary, and with it one of the most powerful anti-terrorist tools we could imagine: the careful, meticulous, legally restrained public trial of a terrorism suspect. We do not have the luxury of taking any old route to what we define as justice. We can only take one path and make headway—we must bring our enemies to justice, and we must do it while conspicuously confining ourselves to the restraints imposed by the rule of law.

Certainly we should *indict anyone about whom we have sufficient evidence that could lead to a conviction*. We can then insist that any nation harboring an indicted terrorist suspect capture him and hand him over for trial, or the harboring nation will be treated as a pariah, as outlined earlier. And we can also conduct our own manhunts, looking for the criminals and apprehending them. We can even do this without permission in the territory of noncooperating nations, disregarding as illegitimate any government that refuses to treat terrorism as the evil it is.

But we cannot do anything until we have evidence of guilt. Once we have it, have submitted it to an independent judiciary—our own or the world's—and have gotten the indictments we seek, we must still operate within the law. Suspects who resist arrest, by flight or fight, may be apprehended against their will. We will spend a lot of time outside besieged compounds, or staking out whole districts where terrorists cower, thwarting breakouts and rescue attempts alike, but also doing everything possible—including waiting—to save the lives of innocents inside and to catch as many suspects as possible alive.

We will lose some lives in the process, but we will earn them back with interest when we starve hatemongers of their fodder by being so conspicuously bound by the rule of law, thus reducing the supply of new terrorist recruits.

If we transform our antiterrorism policy, moving away from Israel's failed "eye-for-an-eye" strategy with its disrepect for legal restraints, a huge payoff awaits.

The Trials of Osama bin Laden and Saddam Hussein

What will ultimately happen to Osama bin Laden or Saddam Hussein during the shelf life of this book I can't fully know. But consider these pictures, which may at points bear little re-

242 ❖ Loving Without Giving In

semblance to what has happened or will happen in the real world but may teach us as much by how they deviate from reality as by how they end up matching it.

Osama bin Laden and a few dozen of his co-conspirators go on trial in America. They get the best defense attorneys their money can buy, who face off against the best prosecutors in the country (who would line up for the chance at this trial). For weeks testimony comes in. Bin Laden and some of the others are on trial for the embassy bombings; another group including some of the same defendants is on trial for the September 11 hijack attack.

Bin Laden sympathizers the world over tune in to watch the trial. The United States has distributed televisions in key Al-Qaida sympathizing areas to make sure everyone gets to watch the trial. The hype makes the O.J. Simpson trial look like a fixed parking ticket. There are about 3000 counts of conspiracy to murder at issue. Prosecutors carefully lay out their evidence that each defendant was involved in planning or executing the attacks. Defense attorneys try to poke holes in the prosecution case. Perhaps some of the defendants are shown not to be involved, but others clearly are.

Then the prosecutors have to show that the defendants' actions caused the deaths of each victim. So each victim's picture goes up on television screens all over the world. Witnesses have to link each victim to the crime scene. They tell about kissing loved ones goodbye at the airport, about phone calls from victims received from the top floors of the World Trade Center while the building burned out from under them. Stories of heroism come out, one by one—firefighters climbing the burning building in a vain attempt to put out the fire or save people who have been delayed in their attempt to escape the building; the chaplain killed when he took off his helmet to pray for another victim.

One of the most contested areas of the trial concerns the victims in the airplane that came down in Pennsylvania. Some defendants are arguing that their actions did not cause that crash, because passengers took over the plane and couldn't fly it. Prosecutors have to demonstrate why the passengers felt they had to act once they knew the World Trade center had already been attacked by another hijacked plane. They have to show that the passengers were acting reasonably and that their deaths were not caused by their own negligence.

The prosecutors provide evidence that the plane was headed for Washington, D.C., perhaps to hit the White House in an attempt to kill the President and his cabinet. Cell phone calls from passengers to wives and family are entered as evidence. The whole world hears a 911 transcript from a passenger on the plane. They hear testimony of widows whose husbands explained to them why they were taking action against the hijackers. Pictures of victims again go up on screens the world over, again superimposed on live images of loved ones still grieving.

Except for a few soldiers killed while in the line of peacetime duty at the Pentagon, all of the victims are civilians—as everyone the world over can see. Many are from other countries—Europeans, Indians, Asians, even Arabs are among the dead.

On the counts of attempted murder, which number in the tens of thousands, prosecutors bring forward witness after witness who tell of harrowing escapes from the World Trade Center or the Pentagon. These witnesses also tell what they saw of those left behind, whose bodies were never found, as prosecutors attempt to prove those missing are actually among the dead.

Day after day the human story pours out over the world. The American judicial system grinds slow, as one of our famous jurists said, but it grinds "exceeding fine". No one anywhere can misunderstand what happened. Palestinians who once celebrated, not thinking of what they were doing, think again. Young Arabs who were on the point of succumbing to some coward's siren song—"You will go to eternal paradise if you die while killing others"—stop and reflect for a crucial extra day. The human stories, the ponderous majesty of the law and its obvious advantages over endless cycles of retaliation shine forth. Democracy and the rule of law gain converts in every corner of the globe. Israelis eager for aggressive retaliation in Gaza or Jenin stop to consider the benefits of restraint under the rule of law. World terrorism finds at least some of the soil in which it recruits suddenly poisonous to its deadly nightshade.

When Osama bin Laden hears his fate read to him—thousands of life sentences to be served consecutively without possi-

bility of parole—his last hopes are dashed. Not for him martyr-
dom. His head and beard shaved, he goes off to spend the rest of
his days in a nondescript maximum security cell somewhere,
preferably in solitary confinement. So do dozens of his cohorts.

Years pass. These people, especially the wealthy bin Laden,
find themselves defendants again, this time in civil lawsuits.
Their wealth, long ago frozen in anticipation of this day, is
stripped from them to compensate victims and survivors.
Again the stories are told, those heart-wrenching photos go up,
reminding people around the globe what terrorism truly
wreaks.

Pictures of the shaved, pathetic bin Laden in Western garb
sitting at the defendant's table undermine any charismatic appeal that may linger.

I do not insist on this trial being held in America, although
there are good reasons to defend the principle that these cases
be tried in courts where the attack happened. But it may work as
well if it's a World Court case. The effects will be satisfactory as
long as the proceedings are televised, there is a jury, and the defendants get the benefit of a presumption of innocence until
proven guilty by a very high standard—something like "beyond a reasonable doubt"—so that the world sees a legal
process responsive to democracy but constrained by law.

We will not forget what he did—no, never, those victims
will be remembered forever. And if Osama is no longer with us,
the trial will lose a bit of its luster. But other, smaller fish will still
fry, so to speak. And in our lifetimes, as bin Laden or his minions
molder away in a jail cell somewhere, we will think of him as a
sort of super-inflated Charles Manson. He will be an odd relic of
another day, when terror could flourish in various corners of the
world and then strike out of the air on a bright late-summer day.
Bin Laden's greatest achievement will be the beginning of the
end of terrorism, because no one who watches his trial will ever
again believe the big lie that ends justify terrorist means.

Then to Saddam Hussein. And if by this reading his trial is
history, let this scenario be compared and contrasted with what
actually happened, so that we learn both from what actually
happens as well as what could have been.

Let Saddam Hussein also go on televised trial, with strong
procedural protections for the defendant set in place to force the

prosecution to make a compelling case and to assure conspicuous fairness. But let one big difference be this: Let Hussein be tried in Baghdad as one of the first acts of the new Iraqi government. Let Western detectives help build the case and provide other logistical support, but let the prosecutors be Iraqi-born, the law Iraqi-adopted, and the processes Iraqi-designed based on the highest democratic standards.

Hussein's trial will expose the brutalities of the Ba'athist regime, making it harder for his remaining loyalists to tell themselves sunny lies about life under Saddam. It will also send a message to other despots and tyrant wannabes about the short and inglorious future that awaits them. And once more let it show the contrast between just and reliable rule of law versus the capricious tyranny of terror.

Such trials, whether current or future, hold potential to be among the larger events in our campaign to spread democracy and the rule of law as an antidote to political despair and the myth of effective violence. They can mark the beginning of the end of the era, spanning all of human history so far, when humans tolerate anything less than democratization and the rule of law anywhere. Let there be no more sympathy with terrorism or tyranny than with rape or murder.

The Right Thing to Do is the Right Thing to Do

The trials of Osama bin Laden and Saddam Hussein or future leaders like them, as I have envisioned them here, are the conceptual centerpieces of this chapter. They embody many of the most important benefits we might expect from emphasizing the promotion of the rule of law and uncorrupted democracy. There are other ideas in this chapter, to be sure, including the following:

83. Treat personal wealth as being on loan from God, and transform our sense of ownership to one of stewardship.

84. Stand firmly against policies that prop up undemocratic regimes or perpetuate corrupted markets.

85. Consider whether the U.S. should create special operations unit designed to destabilize and overthrow undemocratic regimes wherever they are found, using the methods of active nonviolence.

86. Help in the creation of local and national political structures that are responsive to the needs of the citizens and democratically accountable to them.

87. Make democracy and human rights the touchstones of foreign policy.

88. Make democracy and the rule of law a minimum requirement for acceptance in the community of civilized nations.

89. Change the UN into an international enforcer of democracy, with non-democracies relegated to marginal membership, or create a new international organization of democracies for aggressive collective nonviolent offense against totalitarians.

90. Insist on our own governments disciplining themselves to act within the confines of the law.

91. Encourage the development of a worldwide ethic that views terrorism as unthinkable, like slavery.

92. Create an internationally monitored electoral mechanism allowing populations living near national boundaries to vote once each generation, choosing which of the neighbors they wish to join (or possibly whether to become independent).

93. Tie various national privileges (such as to annex territory after a boundary vote) to a requirement to promulgate and meaningfully implement a democratic constitution.

94. Require countries seeking the label "democratic" to abandon claims on other territory.

95. Require countries seeking the label "democratic" to treat all citizens equally.

96. Examine our own histories for cases where the rule of law was ignored and offer restitution to our victims.

97. Live by the International Golden Rule: Any action by one nation must be defensible under the same standards that nation would want applied to actions against it.

98. Never engage in corruption.

99. Create a non-nepotistic sector in every culture.

100. Scrupulously adhere to local law, unless it requires a violation of a command of God.

101. Create opportunities for people in non-democratic countries to develop mechanisms to practice democracy and organize for it.

102. Encourage creation of locally appropriate forms of informal conflict resolution, parallel to mediation and arbitration.

103. Where democracy and markets thrive, rely on them rather than terrorists to provide information about basic needs.

104. Pressure terrorists to submit their claims to democratic processes. Exchange their agreement to foreswear violence for our agreement to support the democratically generated outcome.

105. Indict suspected terrorists about whom we have sufficient evidence which could lead to a conviction.

106. Put Osama bin Laden and Saddam Hussein on trial. Adhere scrupulously to standards of law, including protections of defendant's rights. Televise the trial as widely as possible.

Underlying all these suggestions is a fundamental assumption: the right thing to do is the right thing to do. We humans are prone to see life as being full of terrible, tragic choices between doing the right thing and getting good things done. America's strategy during the first years of its war on terror has been dominated by the war metaphor. The advantage is clear. Thinking in terms of warfare allows us to unleash our vast array of military forces and gives us permission to move quickly and spectacularly against our foes. Not having to quibble too much about whether we get them dead or alive saves us time and trouble and reduces our soldiers' short-term exposure to danger.

But these shortcuts, in the long run, disserve us. If we kill our enemies, if terrorist leaders simply end up dead in bunkers, we at best win short-term victories by removing current ringleaders and masterminds. But genius and grievance are in plentiful supply. Others will always be ready to step forward as long as the conditions for terror and tyranny exist. Instead of fighting these scourges with their own tools, we need to create the conditions that keep them from taking root in a community. Democracy, markets, and the rule of law provide the means to get things done, as well as the cultural commitment to decisions on the merits, which make the resort to violence unnecessary and even counterproductive to a community's needs.

We can't wait until after the war on terror to commit ourselves to combating terrorism only on its merits. The war on terror will never end and the supply of new terrorists will never run out as long as we use the methods of violence to fight terrorist violence.

Chapter 10

Loving Without Giving In: Christians, Terror, and Tyranny

A New Christian Mission

Since September 11, Americans have come to grips with some important facts about the world. The immediate lesson was that we in North America could no longer ignore terrorism. It can now reach us where we live.

This may in part be due to an overall increase in the conditions that give rise to terrorism. Corrosive grievance, dehumanizing hatred, political despair, and the myth of effective violence have always been with us. But it is easy to see how contemporary life could multiply the numbers of people who succumb to terror's siren song. Population increase naturally ties to resource scarcity and more pressure on human communities. Scarcity can be an ingredient of corrosive grievance. Mass society and its attendant depersonalization abets dehumanization as well as a sense of hopelessness about one's ability to influence public policy. Continuous media coverage in modern warfare preaches the myth of effective violence—as does much of the supposedly peace-time fare television offers.

The conditions that cradle terrorists are becoming more plentiful. But modern life offers some antidotes to terrorism,

too. Technological advances and improvements in social organization may be keeping pace so far with the population, so the
proportion of people in misery may not be increasing (and may
even be decreasing) taking the broadest view of human history.
It is hard for us to know, since we tend to discount historical suffering, and since modern media bring a greater percentage of
suffering to us in vivid, simultaneous images.

But whether the incidence of corrosive grievance and so
forth is increasing as fast as the population or not, the global
reach of terrorists certainly is. September 11 was our notice that
thousands of miles of oceans, and only two land borders—with
large, friendly nations—were no longer enough to keep us safe
from terror. Even if there were fewer people now inclined to terror, which I doubt, the same global networks that show us more
of the misery some people suffer also make it easier for the mis-
erably homicidal to reach us and do us harm.

Once we understood that we were in for a long hard battle
against terror, it wasn't long before we understood that terror
and tyranny are correlated. Tyranny is one of the most efficient
means of increasing global terror rates. It will be exceptionally
hard to rid the free world of terror if it is always incubating in
the despotic hellholes of the planet, and is always leaking out of
them to infect healthier societies. To clean up terrorism, we need
to clean up tyranny, too.

As I write this, we are also learning a third lesson. Cleaning
up tyranny is not a mission accomplished just because the
tyrant is no longer in power. Something better than tyranny has
to take its place. Anarchy won't do, nor will corrupt kleptocracy.
Terrorism flourishes under these maladjusted political systems
roughly as well as it does under dictatorship.

One can hardly overstate the urgency of the task before us,
the twin-barreled offensive against both terror and tyranny.
Civilization may depend on it. At minimum, heading off suffering for thousands or millions should be adequate motivation.

But this book argues that urgency should not equal readiness to use lethal force. More of the same—more military might,
more risks on the frontlines, more ultimate sacrifices in violent
defense of our way of life—will not achieve our goals.

For one thing, if terrorism breeds in corrosive grievance, dehumanization, and a conviction that violence is ultimately the

only effective way to achieve one's goal, then using violence is more likely to spread terrorism than to eliminate it. Our urgent need is for a nonviolent, broadly targeted, intensive, committed campaign to correct the conditions that create terrorists, including tyrannical government and political misery in general.

Governments can play crucial roles in nonviolent overthrow of dictators, and supplying law enforcement mechanisms to capture, try, and punish criminal terrorists and tyrants. But a large part, perhaps even the central part of loving our enemies is the work of private parties—churches, individuals, and nongovernmental organizations. This will be a massive private effort, costing millions or maybe a few billion dollars each year, engaging the very best efforts of tens or even hundreds of thousands of volunteers. Anything less will not be robust enough. The social inertia behind tyranny, corruption, and terror is massive. It runs deeply through dozens of societies spread all over the world. The momentum of misery can't be changed with a token effort.

Anyone considering this vision has good reason to wonder if it is possible. And even if it is, what difference can one person make? Is it worth spending any effort on loving our worst enemies if token efforts won't change anything noticeably? How could Christians possibly overcome all their doctrinal and political differences, and their comfortable homeside inertia to cooperate in such massive ways on international peacemaking? It would sure help if there was some hopeful precedent, some indication that believers can accomplish so much starting from scratch to address big problems in new ways.

And there is.

Today there are over 400,000 Christians serving outside their native lands in some form of evangelistic missions work.[82] This work is a model for the peacemaking vision I am trying to articulate for a number of reasons, which we will examine now.

1. Peacemaking, like missions, is our response to specific instructions from God.

Evangelistic missionary work draws its most basic inspiration from the great commission, Jesus' final exhortation to the disciples before ascending to heaven to "go and make disciples of all nations."[83] Christian peacemakers also have a commission from the Messiah. Consider these passages, all of them from Matthew 5:

v. 9: "Blessed are the peacemakers, for they shall be called the sons of God."

vv. 23-24: "Therefore, if you are offering your gift at the altar and there remember that your brother has something against you, leave your gift there in front of the altar. First go and be reconciled to your brother; then come and offer your gift."

vv. 43-44: "You have heard that it was said, 'Love your neighbor and hate your enemy.' But I tell you: Love your enemies and pray for those who persecute you.... "

In these three passages, Jesus rings forth a theme that echoes throughout Matthew 5 and the rest of the New Testament: Christians are called to be peacemakers, reconcilers, Good Samaritans ready to lay down their lives as an act of love to their neighbors—including those "neighbors" they might meet while passing through alien territory.

I have tried to outline in this book some of the many ways that Christians can answer this call to become peacemakers who labor to bring about nonviolence, marked by justice and right relationships, amid which all work together to ensure everyone has means to meet her or his needs.

2. Peacemaking and missions are planet-sized works that depend on sacrificial commitment by individuals and a supportive culture in churches.

No insignificant person was ever born. No person is unworthy of the gospel, in the sense either of the good news of salvation or of the peace Christ offers. No nation is beyond the scope of God's love or outside the boundaries of Christian mission.

To change the spiritual direction of entire nations, missionaries have always known that casual efforts would be insufficient. Their work has to be as deep and as broad, as ambitious and committed as anything we have suggested in this book. And since evangelism has eternal implications, Christians in every age have not taken it lightly. They have understood that it demands of some their entire careers, their comfort, their fortunes, sometimes their lives. And from the rest of us it demands much of our wealth, our prayers, and the kind of unwavering reliable support that those in the field need.

Churches that take missions seriously consciously develop a culture of missions awareness and support within their congregations. They have missions weeks, special guest missions preachers, missions bulletin boards, missions societies, and missions offerings. Missionaries on furlough are featured, even honored. Missions heroes get books written about them and are even featured in Sunday schools. Promising young people are encouraged repeatedly to consider whether God is calling them to the field. Some go on short-term missions trips to explore their sense of vocation and to support the long-term missionaries in their work.

It is now time for Christians everywhere to recognize peace work, including terror-prevention and tyrant-subversion, as a part of the overall Christian mission field, and to apply the well-honed techniques of missions recruiting to the task of recruiting peacemakers. We will know we are making progress when churches begin recognizing the hope-bringers, the development workers, the grievance-healers, the humanizers that will form the next great missions movement of peacemakers, treating them with as much honor and respect as we now treat more traditional missionaries. The first pioneers in this work who come home from tours of duty will be sought out to speak about their experiences. Donors will underwrite peacemaking missionaries and create college scholarships to help prepare young people for the task. Missions bulletin boards will display photos of the peacemakers who have been sent by the local congregation. A culture of excitement and a spiritual atmosphere of devotion and challenge will accompany discussions of peacemaking as a possible vocation.

When all these things are happening, when our congregations think of themselves as being, in part, recruiting grounds for a global effort to bring peace, justice, and reconciliation to troubled lands, the world will have the thousands of peace workers it needs.

3. Like evangelism, peacemaking can be supported at the grass roots.

Evangelistic missions manage to support a worldwide effort involving hundreds of thousands of staff members without much in the way of central organization. The largest missions organizations are denominational, no one of which dominates the missions of any major host country. Others are interdenominational, but none of these also are large enough to meet more than a small fraction of the need. Much missionary work is officially supported at the level of individual congregations—and most of the work organized by larger units is still dependent on congregational giving.

In other words, missions work today depends on a vast network of supporters, one that overlaps and tangles in ways no one person has ever understood. The movement enjoys all the advantages that come from having grown organically, in response to leadings at the local level. It is not locked into one way of doing things as dictated by some central authority—different missions groups are free to experiment. It generates its own recruits without having to compete for them at market rates. It can survive declines among some supporting denominations by fostering growth among other groups.

The missionary movement is responsive to new opportunities without having to be centrally planned. Missionaries on the field who spot needs and opportunities are the most influential agents in change. They elicit more resources where they are needed, initiate cutbacks where local churches become self-supporting, and suggest opening new fields as they encounter peoples who are not hearing the gospel. An economist would love this form of organization—the people most influential in deciding the allocation of resources are those with the best information, the ones on the scenes who see for themselves what the needs are.

At the other end of the system, the home churches providing the resources and the people to support missions come to think of various missionaries as "theirs." They take responsibility for making sure the missionaries have sufficient resources to stay on the field and accomplish their work. Missionary work is not a vast faceless enterprise to members of local churches—they know exactly who their resources support and (if they attend the missionary services at church) they know what their contributions are accomplishing. This is a crucial advantage over governmental programs of similar scope, where taxpayers cannot see what their taxes are accomplishing and have little concrete grasp of many of the problems being addressed.

254 ❖ Loving Without Giving In

Shalomic peacemaking needs all these advantages. Peacemakers need to be motivated by a vision for the ministry more than by the chance to make a living. The enterprise should be geared to respond to the insights and inspirations of those on the scene, rather than the presumptions of home-based leaders. Support should come from diverse groups, ranging widely in size, locale, and even cultural assumptions, as another aid to flexibility and agility in responding to needs that arise. A vibrant peacemaking ministry could grow alongside the current evangelistic missions organizations, borrowing their organizing principles—or maybe sometimes even being directly part of some churches' mission organizations.

4. Shalomic peacemakers need to come from as many places as evangelistic missionaries do.

Another advantage of a missions-oriented organic organizational model is that its roots are deep in many very different places. Although the U.S. sends out more missionaries than any other single nation, this only totals a little more than one-fourth of all missionaries. Europe sends even more than North America. In the last generation, countries that were early targets for missionaries have started sending out tens of thousands of their own. If all Christian missionaries were gathered in one place, they would not perfectly mirror the world's population, but they would represent every continent and most major ethnic groups.

Christian peacemaking needs the same kind of diversity. Americans are poorly positioned to be peacemakers in many areas, where locals' memories are seared with bad experiences at American hands. Other regions, open to Americans, might prove resistant to members of other nationalities. Christian peacemaking will succeed best if it can draw on a wide range of nationalities.

The same can be said for some of the other divisions represented in the broader church. Various denominations may be better suited for working in some places rather than others. Perhaps their histories are conducive here, or their contacts better there, or their internal cultures resonate better in yet another locale. Anglicans, for example, have opportunities in Israel and Palestine that other denominations may not, due to their history there in recent generations. Quakers also have opened doors for themselves with both nations, through development work and schools.

Shalomic peacemaking should be organized so some peacemaking units are identifiable by their nationalities, others by their denominational homes, and others on other grounds—by profession, perhaps, or maybe even by stylistic differences in how they accomplish various peacemaking tasks. Someday you may find yourself in Burma working with locals to replace dictatorship with democracy. Your Texas Baptist Accompaniment Team will find itself working with another group of Catholic accompaniers from the Philippines, a Brazilian Pentecostal Symbolic Action team, some language experts from Belgium, and a high-tech satellite video support team composed of alumni from George Fox University's video communications and computer science programs.

Actually a start in this direction is already under way. Probably the leading experiment in this kind of peacemaking right now is under the aegis of Christian Peacemaker Teams (CPT), an interdenominational group whose core of support comes from the historic peace churches: Quaker, Brethren, and especially Mennonite. CPT recognizes that these three groups only represent a relatively small niche in the overall range of North American Christianity. While CPT is growing, it is still a very small organization, with permanent delegations in only two or three places at a time, comprising perhaps fifteen or twenty full-time volunteers.

To get much done, CPT has to be ready to work with other groups—and has done so. For example, in Colombia, CPT has worked with Mennonite Central Committee, Fellowship of Reconciliation, and others, including (of course) local groups of pastors. No one of these groups is large enough to work in more than a small area at a time, but by coordinating their efforts, peacemakers can extend their influence across a wider area.

Shalomic peacemakers may actually find themselves working with groups from outside the Christian faith, in some areas. As I write this, a secular international Nonviolent Peace Force has begun its first project in Sri Lanka. Inspired in part by the example set by CPT, the NPF has opened an entry into what amounts to shalomic peacemaking for non-believers.[84] Eventually, if secular peacemaking groups proliferate, coordinating committees representing Christians and non-Christians will find themselves working together to remedy injustices, help meet needs, overthrow political misery, and rehumanize enemies. To the extent such cooperation proves possible in other cases, Christians may find their work abetted somewhat by the efforts of secular groups—much like the current experiences of Christian development workers in areas of poverty or post-war devastation.[85] This is an advantage not often shared by evangelistic missionaries, since I suppose by definition secular groups aren't going to help us lead others to Christ.

What Would Shalomic Peacemakers Do?

One could summarize the argument of this book as follows: *Christians should respond to terrorism by loving their enemies.*

Loving enemies has not had a prominent place in public discussion about anti-terror strategy, at least not in the U.S. This is not surprising. Despite centuries of Christian influence on European thought, the idea that nations should respond with love toward their enemies has not had much of an effect on the foreign policies of supposedly Christian nations. It will continue to have no influence until Christians have the courage to bring love of enemies to the fore, despite the misunderstanding and opposition it will arouse.

Perhaps Christian reticence to highlight the option to love our enemies is not just a reluctance to be ridiculed. Perhaps we are hesitant to ask our secular society to adopt a foreign policy based on a radical religious teaching. Why should non-Christians be willing to risk all they hold dear based on the faith of a few believers that a loving God knows how to meet everyone's needs? Christians who can't articulate good secular reasons for loving enemies find it better to hold their tongues than to ask their neighbors to act on someone else's faith.

I have tried to offer solid secular reasons for loving our enemies. I have suggested more than 100 steps (a paltry starting point for the flood of ideas God can show us) believers can take to combat terrorism and political misery and have just sketched the broad outlines of a vision for making shalomic peacemaking a priority similar to missions in the work of the church. These are among the core affirmations:

- Empathetic listening and hope-generating service are our best medicines for corrosive grievance.
- Humanizing contact and working toward reconciliation are crucial to stem the growth of dehumanizing hatred.
- Democracy and the rule of law are the universal antidotes to political despair.
- Never giving in to terrorists or tyrants is critical to undoing the power of the myth of effective violence.

Consider this list. Clearly, a large part of our response to terror and tyranny is to work to meet needs in the communities where these evils arise. God tells us to love our neighbors and our enemies, and one or both of those categories covers those who live in terrorists' and tyrants' communities.

But the last item on the list is a stark warning: We can never let ourselves give in to terror or unwittingly prop up tyrants. There is a clear tension here. We must act to meet needs and open opportunities to people, but if we are careless, our well-meaning efforts could reward terrorists for their terror, or help dictators stay in power. All our other counter-terrorism and anti-tyranny efforts, whether violent or nonviolent, could be worthless or worse.

If we try to meet needs to detoxify corrosive grievance, or offer forgiveness and restitution to build a human connection, or even work to build democratic structures governed by law, but in the process give terrorists what they want, we will surely draw new terrorists into the business, having proven its value in circumventing the slow and often frustrating routes toward resolving issues on their merits. We might not even get rid of the terrorists we have now. Why quit, the terrorist will say, when it has just become so clear that he has found how to get attention and override objections to getting one's way? Giving in to terrorism, even for the best of motives, is effectively a pro-terrorism strategy, since it will inevitably lead to more and more of it.

And if we meet human needs for those under tyranny without at the same time introducing influences that will help undermine the tyrant, we may be helping to distract or mollify potential opponents. The result could be to extend the tyrant's tenure for an unknown time.

So the final question for this book is this: How should we go about loving our enemies, which I have presented here as being at the heart of the gospel and the soul of our counter-terrorist and liberationist work, without in the process giving in to the evils we oppose? Do we face an unresolvable paradox? Must we either give up opposing terror or give up loving terrorists?

In a world with an omnipotent loving God meddling, there are never only two options—or at least this is a useful working assumption. In relation to something this important, the believer makes her contribution in part by being the last person to give up the search for the options that meet all needs. But if we are going to urge such policies on our secular governments, or at least convince them to let us follow our callings, we need to go beyond faith-based hope. We must be able to describe how one can love one's terrorist enemy without giving in to her.

Some leaders respond to the tension between loving terrorists and not giving in to them by ignoring the first half of the dilemma. Israel's leadership, often supported by American presidents, has frequently taken the line that no concessions toward Palestinian interests can be made in the context of Palestinian violence. So Palestinians have been forced into unlivable situations. They have chafed under heavy restrictions on movement, Israeli attacks on homes and infrastructure, and steadily expanding Israeli settlements pressing in on all sides—all leading to impoverishment and even occasions of food shortage and destitution of a once-thriving population. Israelis recognize much of the suffering imposed on the entire Palestinian population but have not taken many measures to relieve it because they worry that it will seem to terrorists a reward for suicide bombings. Peace talks to find permanent solutions to pressing problems stall on the same basis.

I empathize with the Israelis. Worldwide, we cannot afford to have a significant terrorist campaign end in victory for the terrorists, even in their own eyes. Obstinance in the face of terrorists' demands may seem a relatively humane policy, since it would in the long run reduce the suffering caused by terrorism.

But before we consign entire communities to ruin because a few of their members embrace terrorism, I wish we would renew our attention to the call to love our enemies and give it equal weight to the principle of not giving in to terrorists. For I believe the dilemma can be resolved, allowing us to love the terrorist and his neighbors without giving in to him.

There are three keys to unlocking this problem. The first is to target our work to *meeting needs to prevent terrorism and undermine tyranny*, rather than meeting them in response to terrorists or tyrants. Christians are called to love their neighbors, including their enemies, even when these people are not causing us any particular trouble. This point should be obvious. Only a monstrous kind of love doesn't act until the loved one threatens violence. Terrorism and tyranny are not confined to a few star-crossed ethnic groups or nationalities. Every culture creates terrorists, and all may be subject to tyranny someday. This makes our job dauntingly huge but just as urgent. We should publicly define our mission as meeting needs anywhere that conditions might foster, or have already fostered, corrosive grievance.

In other words, we cannot do anything about terrorism or tyranny in the long run by setting up a cut-rate, targeted needs-meeting program that serves only those in communities that have already produced terrorist attacks and tyrants threats against their neighbors. To do that would convey, unintentionally but nonetheless powerfully, the message that terrorism and tyranny pay since they produce aid programs and other offers of help. On the other hand, if Christians begin now a worldwide effort to scan for unmet needs generating corrosive grievance, and meet those needs, terrorists (who will be active in only some of those communities) will not be able to claim that their tactics worked to get us to meet needs, and some states will never fall under a tyrant's sway.

Or, to put this another way, if we are wanting to meet needs and humanize relationships out of love, we will do so wherever suffering is greatest, not wherever our fear is greatest.

Along with making sure our purpose and focus is genuinely loving, we need to *draw a clear distinction between meeting needs and satisfying demands*. If we are trying to love and serve, we will look behind terrorist or tyrant demands to the needs the community is actually experiencing. This will be difficult to do from a distance, so if possible we will encourage people to live in the communities who can listen for the needs behind the grievances. These can be tentmaker missionaries, development workers, business people, teachers, indigenous church leaders, democratically elected representatives, or even (in part) individuals expressing their needs in the form of economic demand in a market. Since one need we can assume every community has is to be free of terrorists and tyrants, defining our mission this way will lead us to include catching and imprisoning these criminals as part of what we are there to do.

Consider Al-Qaida's demand that we stop "polluting" Islamic countries with Western culture. There is no future in acceding to this demand. It would trap millions of Moslems, especially women, in a stultifying version of Islam, for example, and extend their misery. It would condemn Islamic societies to an extended imprisonment in radical Islam's dead-end vision of static societies, maladapted to the modern world. It would also encourage further attacks from radicals within Islam, emboldened by this success. And it would send a message to others that terrorists can win what they want that way. All of these consequences would, ironically, have the effect of accelerating the spread of corrosive grievance, dehumanizing prejudice, and political despair by trapping hundreds of millions of Moslems in a social and political system that can't meet their needs.

Instead, as we consider our work in Islamic countries, we will want to analyze for ourselves the extent to which Western influences have been detrimental to Islamic cultures. Christians might join forces with responsible Islamic leaders to fight pornography and some of the excesses in sexually suggestive fashions. We might also make common cause with Moslems on building more safeguards for the family, or encouraging reductions in the consumption of alcohol, or the worst of materialism. In all these areas both our cultures and theirs are suffering decay due to licentiousness.

On the other hand, we may conclude that we must stand in witness against aspects of Moslem culture that are clearly out of line with justice and God's truth. We may decide to work in Moslem society for political rights for women, for example, and to expand educational opportunities for both boys and girls. And we certainly will want to work for democracy as a replacement for the autocratic dictatorships that have played such a big role in keeping many Islamic nations falling behind the rest of the world in providing for their citizens.

Most radically, from an Islamic point of view, we will want to insist on religious freedom as part of the democratization of Moslem nations. This is not just a ploy to make life easier for

Christian evangelistic missions, although it would have that effect. There are strong secular reasons for religious freedom, as well, particularly in the effect it has of creating space in a society for all its members to feel at home, as if they belong there. People who are constantly reminded of being aliens or second-class citizens are a source of friction, even rebellion. The host nation loses the benefit of their skill and enterprise. Valuable human resources from the religiously favored communities are wasted on enforcing religious discrimination. Lack of religious freedom enhances the odds of leaving pockets of the population out of a nation's progress, subjecting the society to an epidemic of corrosive grievance.

The third key is to *emphasize process advocacy*. Shalomic peacemakers will use all three of the major approaches to peace outlined earlier. We advocate for persons when we take the side of an oppressed people—a population subject to tyranny, for example, or a community suffering deprivation that might stir corrosive grievances. We advocate for outcomes when we insist on justice, including that all have means to meet their needs, or when we insist on the downfall of dictators. It is possible, if we are careful, to advocate for persons and/or outcomes without giving in to terrorism, as shown in the example of how we can respond to charges of polluting Islamic culture I just described.

However, where it seems impossible to advocate for persons or outcomes without in some way giving in to terror or tyranny, we can choose to respond by working to build merit-based processes into a troubled community's life. Terrorists and tyrants thrive in part because they are able to intimidate or imprison those who disagree with them. Replacing systems of domination with democracy, law, and free markets will strike at the heart of both the terrorist's and the tyrant's enterprise.

If everyone in the community has a voice in political decisions—including women and religious or ethnic minorities— space for nourishing corrosive grievance will shrink. Those who benefit from dehumanizing opponents will find themselves competing on the market with other news sources more committed to accuracy. Good information will help drive out bad information, as market forces eventually reward accurate information with increased patronage. Few will pay for long to get erroneous news, not when their investments, careers, or

even vacation plans are disrupted by realities kept from them
by censored news sources. This is true even in the Middle East,
where the relatively accurate Al Jazira news network has com-
peted so well against other "news" organizations managed by
the various governments.

Furthermore, once a community has tasted democracy and
come to appreciate the benefits of the rule of law, it will take the
lead in the struggle against terror and tyranny in its own behalf.
A potential terrorist's neighbors will be less likely to tolerate the
terrorist enterprise, seeing its incompatibility with the democratic processes and legal rights that give them a voice in their
own lives. And, of course, the tyrant will find no hospitality in a
democratized community.

The most secular good we can do for any community is help
it find its own path to democracy, free markets, and the rule of
law. No terrorist will thrive in such an environment, because his
terrorism is incompatible with it. To achieve democratization,
the community will have to bring the terrorist to account and
rid itself of the myth that terror is a way to get things done.
Other callings should be pursued with vigor, of course, because
meeting physical, educational, and especially spiritual needs
are also crucial. But when we get stuck, our general strategy
should be to focus on the ways we can help build and sustain
democratic institutions and practices.

Finally, I want to comment on why this book, with so many
public policy recommendations, is written to a Christian audi-
ence. I do not assume that Christians control governments, or
even that this would be a good thing. But I do assume that
Christians are responsible for the state of the world's communities. Justice is the church's job just as salvation is. Or rather, justice is the church's job because it is part of salvation.

Consider again the story of the Good Samaritan. He understands that his life as a follower of God requires that he love his
neighbors, including those "neighbors" who are of other nationalities, and whom he chances upon during his travels. Their
welfare is his concern. As a steward of God's resources, put in
his care so he can serve as God's delivery system, the Samaritan
does not assume he can turn his back on suffering.

Whether the villain is terror or tryanny, or both, victims suffer. Since terrorism involves hurting someone other than the tar-

get of one's actions, and since terrorists seek maximum visceral impact in their attacks, terrorists will work to find the most innocent targets they can. And since tyrants feed off the weakness of their subjects, tyranny will root itself where people are most vulnerable. These victims deserve their suffering as little as did the man beset by robbers on the road to Jericho.

Terrorists and tyrants build their lives on the suffering of their home communities. That suffering is at the core of the terrorist's corrosive grievance. That suffering created the opportunity for tyranny to take root and keeps people in its thrall. It may be that some of these communities bring some of their suffering upon themselves, but that does not reduce the injustice in the situation; it just redistributes some of it. Would the Samaritan have been excused if he had found two victims by the road, each of whom had victimized the other? No, he would still have been called to meet their needs.

The churches, and the Christians in them, do not have the luxury of passing by on the other side when we encounter these evils. In a world of global terrorism and nuclear-armed tyrants, we all encounter them. We do not encounter them alone; unlike the Samaritan, we are traveling in a group through this life. This means that the entire burden will fall on no one of us. Some of us will do a little, maybe by resisting dehumanization or rewarding political leaders who act constructively. Others of us will do more—perhaps travel to an aggrieved community, stand up to a mob demanding vengeance, risk talking in public about what it would mean to accept suffering and offer forgiveness or restitution. But each of us will do our part.

Peggy Noonan says we are living in "a time of lore" invoking heroism and fateful decisions that will resonate for generations.[86] I agree. Terrorism is not God's will for us. But God is a resilient, resourceful Person. Just as He used the Assyrians and Babylonians to teach ancient Israel about what was required of it, God is ready to use these frightening times to lead us to a new understanding of our discipleship and what it means for the world around us.

Notes

1. Among the many examples are Caleb Carr, *The Lessons of Terror* (New York: Random House, 2002), 6: "warfare against civilians with the purpose of destroying their will to support . . . leaders or policies. . . ."; Paul Pillar, *Terrorism and U.S. Foreign Policy* (Washington, D.C.: Brooking Institution, 2001), 13: "premeditated, politically motivated violence against noncombatant targets by subnational groups or clandestine agents"; Mark Juergensmeyer, *Terror in the Mind of God* (Berkeley: University of California, 2000), 4-10: unwarranted public acts of violence or destruction committed without a clear military objective by groups attempting to gain power or influence by arousing a widespread sense of fear.

2. Peter Sederberg, "Defining Terrorism" in *Annual Editions: Violence and Terrorism 99/00* (Guilford, Conn.: McGraw-Hill/Dushkin, 1999), 9.

3. Thomas Hobbes, *Leviathan* in *Great Books of the Western World*, vol. 23 (Chicago: Encyclopedia Britannica, 1952), 85.

4. Some eco-terrorists would deny the charge, saying that their acts against mink farmers and cosmetic manufacturers are justified because the farmers and manufacturers have chosen to play the game of oppressing and killing victims. The eco-terrorist's argument is that being violent toward an animal is approximately the moral equivalent of being violent toward a human being. I am listening to animal rights activists, and looking for the strengths in their arguments, but so far I cannot say that I find them persuasive. So, for the purposes of this book, I will assume that my consumption of meat and fish does not mean I have joined a game that includes the killing of humans, or risking their deaths in the course of destroying property.

5. John Keegan, *The Face of Battle* (New York: Viking Press, 1976), 331-343 .

6. Of course, the issue of civilian casualties still besets us. Assuming for now that the U.S. didn't *target* civilians, but many still died, at what level does the incidental killing of civilians cease to be regrettable "collat-

eral damage" and become instead another form of terrorism? We get to this question in Chapter 2.

7. Many in the UN and among peace groups claimed at the time that the U.S. and Britain had no legitimate basis for invading Iraq. I do not plan to address this question in this book—it is not germane to our point, nor can we devote the chapter(s) it would require to sort this out. But even if the invasion was illegitimate, Iraqi troops and security personnel could not call it terrorism, since illegitimate warfare was a staple in the Iraqi military diet. At worst, then, the U.S. was playing the same game the Iraqis had played for years, even against their own people.

8. This principle is embodied in the second version of Kant's categorical imperative: treat every person as an end, never as a means only. See Immanuel Kant, *Fundamental Principles of the Metaphysics of Morals, Section Two* (1785), in Thomas Kingmill Abbott, tran., *Great Books of the Western World*, vol. 42 (Chicago: Encyclopedia Britannica, 1952), 272

9. Thomas Hobbes, *Leviathan* in *Great Books of the Western World*, vol. 23 (Chicago: Encyclopedia Britannica: 1952), 99-101.

10. Perhaps if the books of the Maccabees had made the canon, we would have more biblical text in favor of regime change as a mission of the faithful.

11. George W. Bush, "President's Remarks at the National Day of Prayer and Remembrance at the National Cathedral" (White House Office of the Press Secretary, September 14, 2001), found at http://www.whitehouse.gov/news/releases/2001/09/20010914-2.html.

12. Even in his joint appearance with President Bush at the White House on September 18, 2001, by which time Bush and the American press had already decided that the American response would be a war, Chirac's first sentence in response to a reporter's question was "I don't know whether we should use the word *war*, but what I can say is that now we are faced with a conflict of a completely new nature." "President Chirac Pledges Support: Remarks by President Bush and President Chirac of France in Photo Opportunity The Oval Office" (White House Office of the Press Secretary, September 14, 2001), found at http://www.whitehouse.gov/news/releases/2001/09/20010918-8.html.

13. John Keegan, *The Face of Battle* (New York: Viking Press, 1976), 302.

14. William Wilmot and Joyce Hocker, *Interpersonal Conflict*, 6th. ed. (Boston: McGraw-Hill, 2001), 48-58.

15. Judges 7.

16. 1 Samuel 17.

17. 1 Samuel 13, 15.

18. 1 Samuel 8.

19. Psalm 20:7.

20. Jonah 3, 4.

21. Matthew 5:39

22. Matthew 6:9-15.

23. Matthew 5:23-26.

24. Matthew 5:43-48.

25. Charles Colson, "Just War in Iraq: Sometimes Going to War Is the Charitable Thing to Do," *Christianity Today* (December 9, 2002), 72.

26. Beebe cites several examples in Ralph Beebe and John Lamoreau, *Waging Peace* (Newberg, Ore.: Barclay Press, 1980), 24-25. An interesting analysis of whether it is possible for both sides to be fighting justly under classic and Aquinian versions of just war is found in Colm McKeogh, *Innocent Civilians: The Morality of Killing in War* (New York: Palgrave, 2002), 40-41, 56-57.

27. It is possible that democracy, with its transparency in decision-making and free debate over national policies, may move nations in just this direction. There has been no clear-cut case of war between democracies since at least the American Civil War, for reasons that are not entirely clear. However, it may be that when societies engage on both sides in debating the merits of war, they tend to learn about each other's needs and goals, and develop empathy that creates more political space for negotiation and nonviolent conflict resolution. Thus, it is possible that democracy on both sides of an international conflict creates conditions that echo or parallel the kind of pre-war reflection just war theory requires.

28. Tacitus, *Agricola*, Ch. 30.

29. Martin Luther King Jr., described his nonviolent ethic as being the path toward "the beloved community", which is another good way of describing the shalomic ideal. King understood nonviolence as being the process by which one might achieve both justice and reconciliation. We are following in those footsteps.

30. Smith, *An Inquiry Into the Nature and Causes of the Wealth of Nations (1776)*, in *Great Books of the Western World*, vol. 39 (Chicago: Encyclopedia Britannica, 1952), 196.

31. Madison, *Federalist*, Nos. 10, 47.

32. For a good introduction to game theory, featuring its assumptions about human rationality, see Roxanne Luloffs, *Conflict: From Theory to Action* (Scottsdale, Ariz.: Gorsuch Scarisbrick, 1994), 78-81.

33. See, for example, Roger Fisher and William Ury, *Getting to Yes* (New York: Penguin, 1983).

34. C. Douglass Lewis, *Resolving Church Conflicts: A Case Study Approach for Local Congregations* (San Francisco: Harper & Row, 1981), 4-19.

35. John 10:10.

36. Kenneth Boulding, *The Three Faces of Power* (Newbury Park, Calif.: Sage, 1990).

37. I would be willing to settle for just one hymn a week, sung in parts, as an exchange-driven compromise.

38. Lewis Coser, *The Functions of Social Conflict* (Glencoe, Ill.: Free Press, 1956), 49-55.

39. For example, see Elias Chacour, *Blood Brothers* (Grand Rapids: Zondervan, 1984); Ralph Beebe and Audeh Rantisi, *Blessed Are the Peacemakers* (Grand Rapids: Zondervan, 1990); Naim Ateek, *Justice and Only*

Justice: A Palestinian Liberation Theology (Maryknoll, N.Y.: Orbis, 1998); Hanan Ashrawi, *This Side of Peace: A Personal Account* (New York: Simon & Schuster, 1996).

40. Philip Gourevitch, *We Wish to Inform You That Tomorrow We Will be Killed With Our Families: Stories from Rwanda* (New York : Farrar, Straus, and Giroux, 1998); David Niyonzima and Lon Fendall, *Unlocking Horns: Forgiveness and Reconciliation in Burundi* (Newberg, Ore.: Barclay Press, 2001); Zalata Filipovic, *Zlata's Diary: A Child's Life in Sarajevo* (New York: Viking Press, 1998); Mary McAleese, *Love in Chaos: Spiritual Growth and the Search for Peace in Northern Ireland* (New York: Continuum Publishing, 1999). These are just a few of the available examples.

41. You can contact CPT at www.cpt.org. CPT delegations are open primarily to those who are actively considering taking the CPT training and serving as a reservist or a full-time member of the CPT program.

42. And, by way of taking my own advice, I would like to publicly praise the creators of the West Wing television series for an excellent episode on this topic aired on Wednesday, October 3, 2001. Several thoughtful theories of why some Arabic or Islamic groups would have a grievance against America were shared, as well as a subplot dealing sympathetically with American suspicions about Arab-Americans and the plight of those who are erroneously suspected.

43. We will explore further why we cannot give in to terrorists and tyrants in Chapter 8.

44. Beebe and Rantisi, *Blood Brothers*; Fendall and Niyonzima, *Unlocking Horns*.

45. Anthony Bing, *Israeli Pacifist: The Life of Joseph Abileah* (Syracuse, N.Y.: Syracuse University Press, 1990).

46. See Roxanne Luloffs, *Conflict: From Theory to Action* (Scottsdale, Ariz.: Gorsuch Scarisbrick, 1994), 72-75 for a good introduction to attribution theory.

47. Matthew 6:14-15; 18: 21-35.

48. Lewis Coser, *The Functions of Social Conflict* (Glencoe, Ill.: Free Press, 1956), 87-104.

49. Dave Grossman, *On Killing: The Psychological Cost of Learning to Kill in War and Society* (Boston: Little, Brown and Company, 1996), 299-332.

50. One is tempted to describe disputants who make a greater than 90-degree turn in their attitude toward the other as being "acute", and those whose attitudes are barely deflected as being "obtuse." (This is a geometry joke, for those who may be mystified.)

51. Philip Smith, *The Virtue of Civility in the Practice of Politics* (Lanham, Md.: University Press, 2002), esp. 30-34.

52. Elise Boulding, *Building a Global Civic Culture: Education for an Interdependent World* (Syracus, N.Y.: Syracuse University Press, 1990).

53. E-mail can even lead to marriage—it happened to me!

54. John Paul Lederach, *Preparing for Peace: Conflict Transformation Across Cultures* (Syracuse, N. Y.: Syracuse University Press, 1995).

55. Proverbs repeats this theme many times—see, for example, 9:7-9;

10:8; 15 passim; 17:10; 19:25; 21:11.

56. Jesus made this point clear in His description of how a believer should handle a dispute—if one-on-one interaction doesn't work, involve one or two others. Matthew 18:15-19.

57. The diagram as displayed here owes much of its inspiration to a similar model developed for another purpose by the late James Laue, Laue, "Ethical Considerations in Choosing Intervention Roles," *Peace & Change* 8.2/3 (1982): 34.

58. Matthew 5:23-24.

59. Matthew 6:14-15; 18:20 ff.

60. This quote has been variously attributed, including to Martin Luther King Jr. and Mohandas Gandhi.

61. Matthew 5: 38-48.

62. This modified *lex talionis* strategy is known as Graduated Reduction in Tension, or GRIT. For more on GRIT, see C. D. Osgood, *An Alternative to War or Surrender* (Urbana, Ill.: University of Illinois Press, 1962).

63. Matthew 5:48.

64. Matthew 6:9-15.

65. A good introduction to the concepts of conventional and unconventional participation can be found in any good introductory political science text, including Kenneth Janda, Jeffrey Berry, and Jerry Goldman, *The Challenge of Democracy: Government in America*, 5th. ed. (Boston: Houghton Mifflin, 1997), 212-219.

66. George W. Bush, "Address to a Joint Session of Congress and the American People" September 20, 2001, found at www.whitehouse.gov/news/releases/2001/09/20010920-8.html

67. George W. Bush, "President George W. Bush's Inaugural Address" January 20, 2001, found at www.whitehouse.gov/news/inaugural-address.html

68. As a pacifist, I favor non-lethal police methods. But I recognize there are complex and troubling issues here, which I have not entirely resolved. At least I am in keeping with long-standing Quaker tradition. Alone of the peace churches, Quakers have traditionally been pacifist and simultaneously generally supportive of police work. How we manage the obvious tensions in these positions is not entirely clear to me, and is also beyond the scope of this book.

69. According to the *Encyclopedia Britannica*, this is roughly the number of total deaths, military and civilian, in World War II. Found at www.britannica.com/eb/article?eu=126559 (accessed November 26, 2003).

70. Kenneth Boulding, *Stable Peace* (Austin: University of Texas Press, 1978), 28-30.

71. Samuel M. Janney, *The Life of William Penn; With Selections from His Correspondence and Auto-Biography* (Philadelphia: Hogan, Perkins, & Co., 1852), 42-43. This citation is from the Quaker Writing Home Page maintained by Peter Sippel at www.qhpress.org/quakerpages/qwhp/-pennswor.htm. He is skeptical of the story's historical accuracy.

72. Gene Sharp, *The Politics of Nonviolence* (Boston: Porter Sargent,

1973), especially volume two, *The Methods of Nonviolent Action*.

73. See Mark Juergensmeyer, *Terror in the Mind of God* (Berkeley, Calif.: University of California Press, 2000) for an intriguing examination of terrorism in several religious traditions.

74. George W. Bush, "Address to a Joint Session of Congress and the American People" September 20, 2003, found at www.whitehouse.gov/news/releases/2001/09/20010920-8.html

75. Romans 13:1-7.

76. George W. Bush made a strong argument on just these grounds on November 6, 2003. George W. Bush, "President Bush Discusses Freedom in Iraq and the Middle East" found at www.whitehouse.gov/news/releases/2003/11/20031106-2.html. He reiterated the theme in London a few days later. George W. Bush, "President Bush Discusses Iraqi Policy at Whitehall Palace in London," November 19, 2003, found at www.whitehouse.gov/news/releases/2003/11/20031119-1.html.

77. Lon Fendall and Ron Mock, *Nonviolent Revolution in The Philippines and Haiti* (Unpublished manuscript funded by the United States Institute of Peace, 1989).

78. While we are at it, France's permanent seat on the Security Council should be transformed into a European Union seat; and maybe Britain's should be converted into a British Commonwealth seat.

79. Kenneth Boulding, *Stable Peace* (Austin: University of Texas Press, 1978), 109-112.

80. See Elias Jabbour, *Sulha: Palestinian Traditional Peacemaking Process* (Montreat, N.C.: House of Hope Publications, 1996).

81. Roger Fisher & William Ury, *Getting to Yes* (New York: Viking, 1981), 114-118.

82. Michael Jaffarian, "The Statistical State of the Missionary Enterprise," *Missiology* 30.15 (January, 2002): 27.

83. Matthew 28:19.

84. Similar cooperation goes on in Hebron between CPT and other groups active in the area, including international secular peace groups and local Islamic, Jewish, and Christian groups. In some cases, to be sure, CPT has found itself in some tension with the goals or methods of other groups. However, cooperation has been possible on some parts of these groups' work.

85. In fact, international development work provides, in many ways, another model for the kind of organic organization we are talking about here.

86. Peggy Noonan, "A Time of Lore," *Opinion Journal;* from the *Wall Street Journal*, July 26, 2005, found at www.opinionjournal.com/forms/prinThis.html?id=11000203802

The Index

The Author

Ron Mock is Associate Professor of Political Science and
Peace Studies at George Fox
University in Newberg, Oregon. After finishing his law degree
at the University of Michigan in 1982 and practicing law for a
year, he was founding director of the Christian Conciliation Service of Southeastern Michigan. His experiences in interpersonal
peacemaking led him to his undergraduate alma mater, George
Fox University, where he joined the Center for Peace Learning
in 1985.

Mock has done research, taught, and worked on nonviolent
resolution of conflict across the broad range of human interaction, from interpersonal disputes to international warfare. At
the interpersonal level, he has been a mediator for over twenty
years and currently serves as a board member of Your Community Mediators of Yamhill County, Oregon. As a resource for
training in interpersonal conflict transformation, he edited *The
Role Play Book for the Mennonite Conciliation Service*, the second
edition of which was published in 1997. At the group level, he
has worked with churches and other organizations to find ways
to deal with difficult conflicts. At the level of conflict among nations and ethnic groups, he has done studies in Haiti, Central
America, and Eastern Europe, and most recently has been a
member of the International Quaker Working Party on Israel
and Palestine.

Although he is a pacifist, Mock has been an outspoken critic of opponents to war, impatient with what he calls their antiwar "jingoism." He has urged pacifists and others interested in nonviolent alternatives to war to take more seriously the challenges facing policy-makers charged with doing justice and protecting social order. Before public leaders are going to reject "tried and true" military means for achieving these goals, they will need to see that alternative nonviolent means are feasible, reliable, and more effective than armed violence. Thus, opponents of war need to commit much more of their lives and financial resources to experiments in practical nonviolence, and be willing to make the kinds of sacrifices, personally and as communities, that secular society invests in armed national defense.

In *Loving Without Giving In*, Mock articulates a vision for the kind of cultural change needed among Christians committed to peaceful means of resolving conflict. He applies this vision to the problems of international terrorism and tyranny. Grounding his approach firmly in both Scripture and the best thinking of peace scholars around the world, Mock suggests more than a hundred practical steps believers could take to respond to terrorism and, at the same time, begin to transform their own assumptions and commitments in ways that can lead to a global rejection of the "myth of effective violence."

Mock lives now in Dundee, Oregan with his wife Melanie and their son Benjamin Quan. He has a grown daughter in Ithaca, New York, and a son in Canberra, Australia. He is a member of Newberg Friends Church.

CPSIA information can be obtained
at www.ICGtesting.com
Printed in the USA
FSHW010505220121
77897FS